The Carlisle Ship Canal

David Ramshaw

This book is dedicated to my granddaughter *'Summer'*

Publishing Information

British Library Cataloguing in Publication Data

A catalogue record for this book is available from the British Library

ISBN 978-0-9572412-4-4

First published in Great Britain in 1997 by:- P3 Publications,13 Beaver Road, Carlisle, Cumbria, CA2 7PS

This edition published in October 2013.

Printed in Wales by:- Gomer Press, Llandysul Enterprise Park, Ceredigion SA44 4JL

Cover illustration - *Carlisle and Canal,* W H Nutter 1842 (Tullie House Museum & Art Gallery).

Acknowledgements

I would like to gratefully acknowledge the help given by many individuals and organisations in the preparation of this book. Special mention must go to Denis Perriam, who has freely provided me with a wealth of references and other information from his own extensive researches into the canal and its history. His advice and help has been indispensable. I am also very grateful to Gordon Hunt for letting me have free access to his research material on the canal. This has greatly helped my own research. My thanks also to the staff of Tullie House Museum and Art Gallery Trust, as well as the staff of Cumbria Archive Centre, Carlisle, and at Carlisle Library, for their patience and help and for permission to reproduce various documents and pictures, together with Michael Finlay and Peter Neil Innes, authors of previous dissertations on the canal, who have deposited their work in Carlisle Library.

I am grateful to Lord Lonsdale for giving permission to reproduce various items from the Lowther Family Trusts, with whom copyright resides, relating to the docks at Port Carlisle and the Ravenbank Jetty; to Guthrie Hutton for his picture of the Forth and Clyde pattern bridge; to Michael Towill for Sam Bough's painting, *Burgh by Sands Church - Winter Morning*; to the late Teddy Robinson for Osborne family history; to George Tinkler for the Nutter family painting of the *Canal and Coal Staithes*; to the late Jim Templeton for the use of several photographs from his collection and to Cumbrian Newspapers Ltd, for use of their records in Carlisle Library and Cumbria Archive Centre, Carlisle.

I must also thank the local farmers at Knockupworth farm, Sandsfield farm, Reservoir farm, Ratlingate farm, and Wormanby farm for their help with local infomation and access to the line of the canal. Thanks also to Roger Brough of Port Carlisle for information on the Victoria Baths. Finally may I thank everyone else who has helped me in the preparation of this book whose names I have failed to record above.

Introduction

The Carlisle Canal had a very short life compared to most canals. Construction work began in 1819 and the canal was closed in 1853. As a result there is probably less known about it than many other canals which still exist today.

In spite of its short existence there is much local interest even now in the project which brought seagoing ships to the centre of Carlisle. I first published the book *The Carlisle Navigation Canal* in 1997 in monochrome and A5 landscape format. During the 15 years since then I have given many presentations on the subject and a lot more information has come my way in the course of my other research into local history.

This fully revised edition includes that new material and, as it is in A4 format with full colour illlustrations, will, I hope, provide the reader with a more visual appreciation of the importance of the canal to the industrial development of Carlisle in the early 19th century.

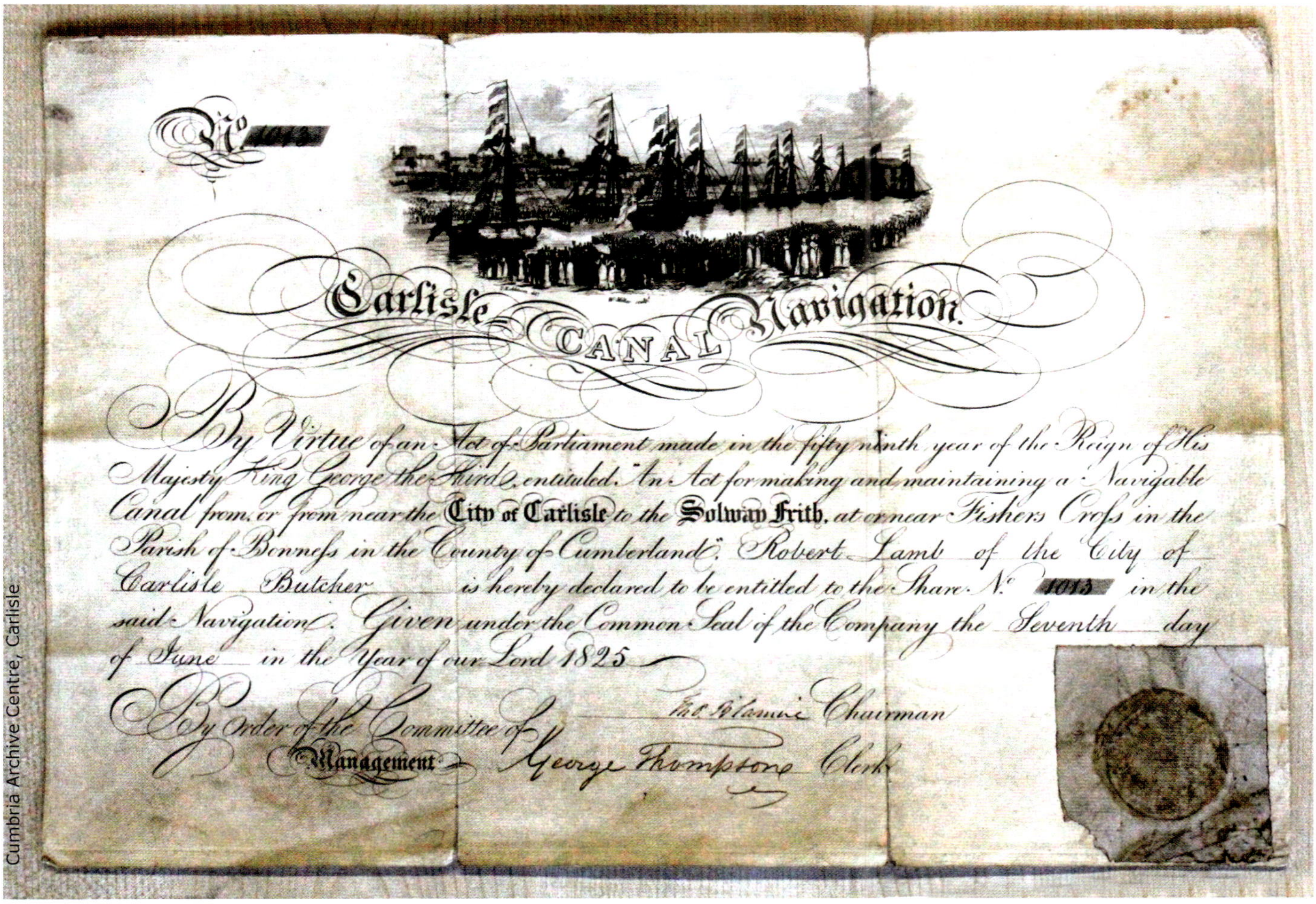

No 1013

Carlisle CANAL Navigation.

By Virtue of an Act of Parliament made in the fifty ninth year of the Reign of His Majesty King George the Third, entituled "An Act for making and maintaining a Navigable Canal from, or from near the City of Carlisle to the Solway Frith, at or near Fishers Cross in the Parish of Bowness in the County of Cumberland". Robert Lamb of the City of Carlisle Butcher is hereby declared to be entitled to the Share No 1013 in the said Navigation. Given under the Common Seal of the Company the Seventh day of June in the Year of our Lord 1825

By Order of the Committee of Management — Chairman

George Thompson Clerk

Cumbria Archive Centre, Carlisle

Carlisle Canal share certificate No.1013

The life of the Carlisle Ship Canal

Part	Contents	Page
Part 1	**Conception** of a canal from Newcastle to Maryport.	5
	The disadvantages of Sandsfield as a port and the potential benefits to Carlisle of a canal.	6
	Proposals for a canal between Carlisle and Fisher's Cross.	9
Part 2	**The Beginning of Labour** An Act for making a navigable canal from Carlisle to the Solway Firth	14
	The beginnings of construction, the influx of labour and the social problems resulting. Keeping the canal filled with water.	14
	Construction of the canal basin, working conditions, accidents.	18
	Increase of public interest. First reports of sailings along the completed sections. Canal bridges.	22
Part 3	**The Birth and the Early Years** The opening, the speeches, the celebrations, the euphoria and the congratulations.	22
	Teething troubles, problems with water supply. Proposal for a railway from Newcastle to Carlisle. Shipbuilding in Carlisle.	35
Part 4	**The Formative Years and Middle Age**	41
	The *Solway* steamship commences services between Liverpool and Port Carlisle.	46
	Steam Barges in use at the Canal Basin.	51
	Emigration by canal	61
	Development of Fishers' Cross (later Port Carlisle), opening of the Solway Hotel.	69
	Introduction of the *Arrow* passage boat.	71
	Plans for new dock facilities at Port Carlisle and for buoying and lighting the Firth.	75
Part 5	**The Final Years leading to Death and Resurrection as a Railway** A new passage boat the *Swallow* and a Steam tug/ferry boat for Port Carlisle.	94
	The launch of the *Corby Castle* at the Canal Basin. Early package holidays. The Solway Lightship	97
	The Jovial Sailor at Carlisle (104) and the Victoria Baths at Port Carlisle. (106)	104
	Silting up of Port Carlisle and the Ravenbank Jetty problem. (108-119)	117
	Closure and conversion to a railway. The Dandy. The Solway Junction Railway viaduct	122
	Artefacts. The back drain. Flying the length of the canal.	125

Conception

In the late eighteenth century canal building was at its height. The industrial revolution, which was sweeping the country at this time, demanded a cheap and reliable method for the bulk transfer of raw and manufactured materials. The south of the country was served by several wide and navigable rivers but in the north the rivers were often too shallow and fast flowing for reliable navigation. Canals appeared to be the answer and several schemes were put forward at this time to link the east and west seas. The main engineer involved was William Chapman, who was eventually to construct the Carlisle Canal.

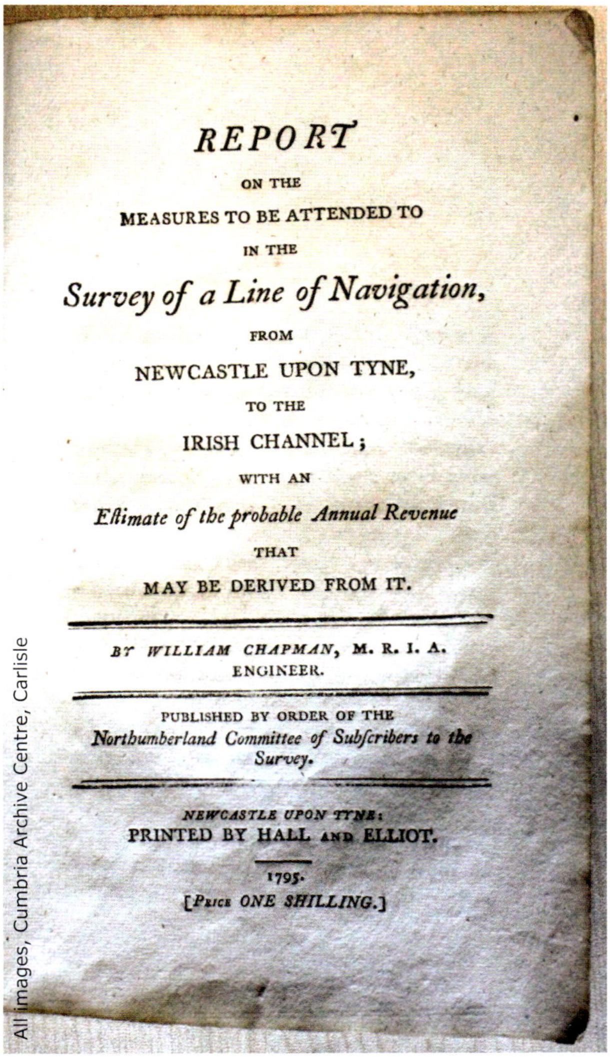

REPORT
ON THE
MEASURES TO BE ATTENDED TO
IN THE
Survey of a Line of Navigation,
FROM
NEWCASTLE UPON TYNE,
TO THE
IRISH CHANNEL;
WITH AN
Eſtimate of the probable Annual Revenue
THAT
MAY BE DERIVED FROM IT.

BY WILLIAM CHAPMAN, M. R. I. A.
ENGINEER.

PUBLISHED BY ORDER OF THE
Northumberland Committee of Subſcribers to the Survey.

NEWCASTLE UPON TYNE:
PRINTED BY HALL AND ELLIOT.
1795.
[PRICE ONE SHILLING.]

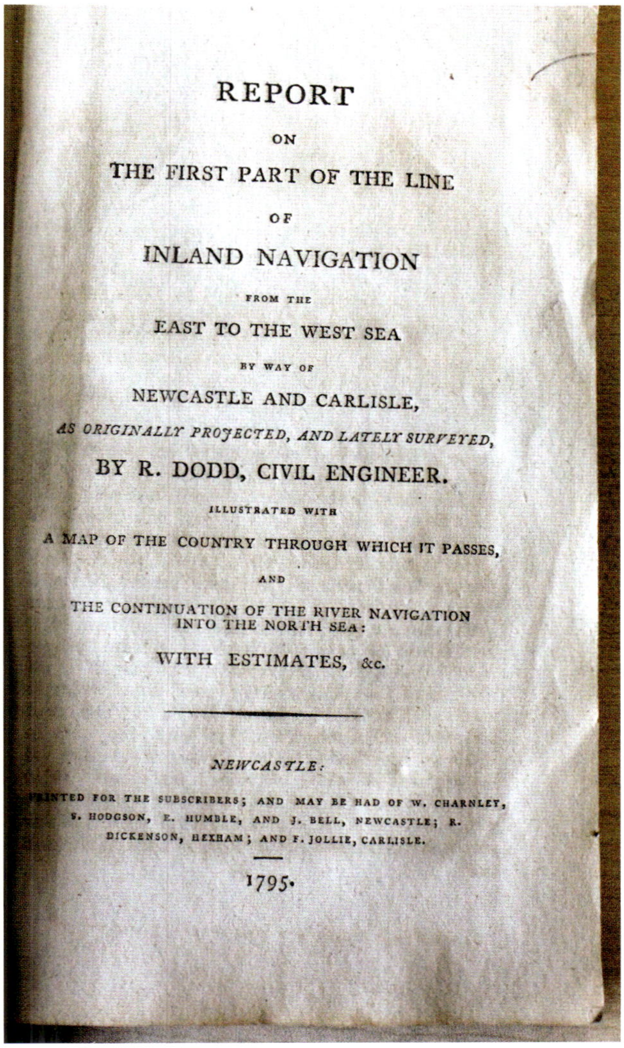

REPORT
ON
THE FIRST PART OF THE LINE
OF
INLAND NAVIGATION
FROM THE
EAST TO THE WEST SEA
BY WAY OF
NEWCASTLE AND CARLISLE,
AS ORIGINALLY PROJECTED, AND LATELY SURVEYED,
BY R. DODD, CIVIL ENGINEER.
ILLUSTRATED WITH
A MAP OF THE COUNTRY THROUGH WHICH IT PASSES,
AND
THE CONTINUATION OF THE RIVER NAVIGATION INTO THE NORTH SEA:
WITH ESTIMATES, &c.

NEWCASTLE:
PRINTED FOR THE SUBSCRIBERS; AND MAY BE HAD OF W. CHARNLEY, S. HODGSON, E. HUMBLE, AND J. BELL, NEWCASTLE; R. DICKENSON, HEXHAM; AND F. JOLLIE, CARLISLE.
1795.

All images, Cumbria Archive Centre, Carlisle

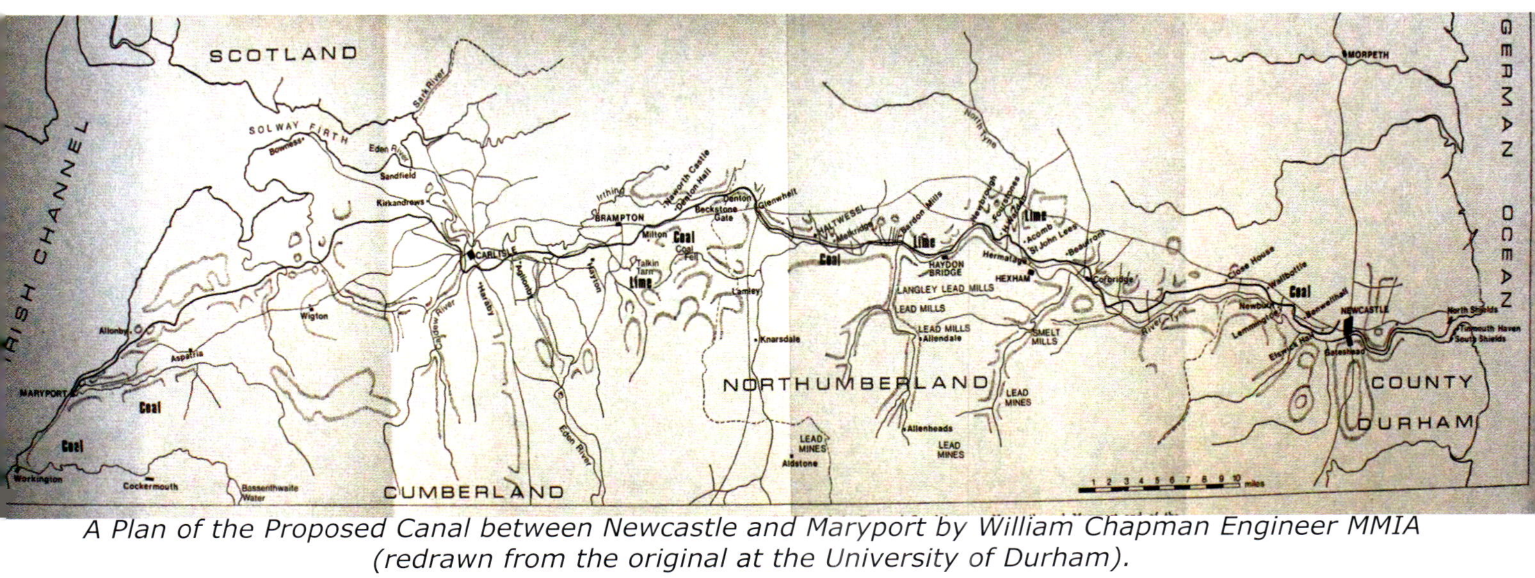

A Plan of the Proposed Canal between Newcastle and Maryport by William Chapman Engineer MMIA (redrawn from the original at the University of Durham).

Unfortunately none of these proposals came to anything in spite of much debate, planning and costing over many years. One such proposition, originally put forward in 1794 and revived in 1802, was a canal to link Newcastle and Maryport.

On 16 February 1802 John Bell, Land surveyor of Newcastle, penned a manuscript entitled 'Copy of Hints to Lord Mulgrave and Colonel Mowbray to form a conversation with the Duke of York on the subject of a canal from Newcastle to Maryport'. This document sets out all the possible advantages of embarking on such a scheme. One interesting advantage that he emphasises is the military one. Perhaps he thought the project stood more chance of Government backing if it could be recognised as a means of improving the defence of the realm. I quote:-

News & Star

Thursday, September 19, 1996

NEWSPAPER OF THE YEAR

EXCLUSIVE: Full report on the Highway of Water on Pages 8 and 9

£6bn DREAM SCHEME TO LINK SOLWAY TO TYNESIDE WITH CANAL

"It may also be stated what great advantage it would be in time of war, for the more immediate conveyance of an army on any emergency, for with the help of this canal, troops might be conveyed from the eastern coast of England to the western coast of Ireland in three days or less."

John Bell concludes his 'hints' with a suggestion as to how the canal might be constructed at the least expense:-

"In the towns of Newcastle, Hexham, Haltwhistle, Carlisle etc. 40,000 soldiers might be conveniently accommodated, who would complete the canal in about three years."

Unfortunately, possibly due to lack of potential investors and commitment from business, the canal linking the west and east seas was never realised, although the proposal was frequently resurrected; the last such proposal for a Tyne - Solway canal being made as late as September 1996.

The Original Port Carlisle

At the end of the eighteenth century Carlisle still had poor transport links to the rest of the country. Bulk goods such as coal, limestone, timber and textiles were traded between the small Cumberland ports and cities such as Liverpool and Manchester using coastal craft. Goods to and from Carlisle had to be transported between the city and the Solway ports by horse and cart along winding, inadequate roads. It was obviously more economic in time and money to reduce this road travel to the absolute minimum.

Five miles below Carlisle the River Eden meets the Solway Estuary, and at Sandsfield, on Burgh Marsh, the Solway was navigable for vessels between 60-80 tons, depending on the conditions. This was the nearest berth to the city for sea-going vessels and timber or other merchandise was landed there and carted the three and a half miles to the city.

At Sandsfield there were two jetties, the old and the new, as well as a bonded

The remains of the jetty at New Sandsfield farm seen in 1953 with the bonded warehouse (later demolished) in the foreground.
Insets: a section of the tithe map (c.1842) showing the bonded warehouse and a view of Sandsfield Farm from the same position as the main picture in 2013.

warehouse in which imported goods were stored until sold, when the import taxes had to be paid. However the tides and the narrow channels made this ancient port unreliable, ships often having to wait days for suitable tides and weather conditions. According to Roger Baker Old Sandsfield on the River Eden was approachable by vessels of up to 60 tons burden. The trade was mainly imported timber, iron, flax, tar, rice and general goods, with a smaller export trade of wheat, butter and alabaster. Goods landed there were carted the remaining three and a half miles into the city which added considerably to the cost.

For example, the retorts and ironwork for the original gasworks in Carlisle (1819) were brought from a manufacturer in Liverpool to Sandsfield by schooner, and from there into the city at double the shipping costs. The building at Old Sandsfield was originally an Inn

Matthew Nutter Painting - small ship unloading on the shingle near Burgh.

called *The Lady Lowther*. It is situated at one of the fords or waths used to cross the Solway at low tide so it probably served cattle herders and travellers as well as sailors bringing ships to the jetty. The shallowness of the Solway Estuary in its upper reaches was the main problem. This is illustrated by Sam Bough's early 19th century painting of cattle crossing the Solway and the fact that the local haaf net fishermen can ford the estuary on foot at very low tide.

Old Sandsfield Farm.
At one time 'The Lady Lowther Public House.'

An engraving after Sam Bough's Painting - Cattle crossing the Solway

The following inquest report from the Carlisle Journal, l4 September 1805, adequately illustrates the difficulties and consequent dangers of using the port of Sandsfield:

"*On Saturday last an inquisition was held upon the body of William Bragg, Captain of the 'Active' a dogger, belonging to Workington, laden with oak timber, from Cardew; before R Mullender Esq., Coroner. It appeared that the said vessel had been lying for some time below Sandsfield, being detained by adverse winds and neap tides; that the deceased being impatient of delay, had made a raft on Thursday se'nnight * and had proceeded some way down the river, and in the evening, having moored the raft, returned to his night's lodging at Old Sandsfield. The next morning as the mate and he were walking down the river in order to proceed with the raft, they were surrounded by the tide: the mate swam on shore, but the captain unfortunately perished. He has left a pregnant wife and eight children, to deplore his loss - Verdict, Accidental Death.*"

* (A week last Thursday)

In spite of the shallow channel up to Sandsfield large ships did occasionally reach the port. It was recorded in 1805 that Post Captain William Mounsey, son of the Mounsey family of Castletown House, Rockliffe, brought his frigate up to Sandsfield on a particularly high tide. He moored in the channel and rowed ashore with his officers for afternoon tea with his mother and family. Afterwards, returning to his ship, he left on the same tide.

When the tides at Sandsfield were favourable and as coal from the West Cumberland coalfield was one of the major imports to Carlisle at this time, such events were worthy of note, as this extract from the Carlisle Journal, 13 June 1807 indicates:-

"The following extraordinary instance of despatch was never remembered to have been equalled. A vessel arrived at Sandsfield from Maryport on Saturday last, with a cargo of coals - returned and arrived again on Tuesday following; with a like cargo, which was sold at 4d a peck."

Indeed, the need for plentiful and cheap supplies of coal and other raw materials was steadily increasing as Carlisle's textile industry expanded. This need was acknowledged at a public meeting on the 21st May 1807 when a committee was formed to :-

"promote a canal from Carlisle to the sea". This committee met to consider the economics of such a venture on 9th June 1807 at the Moot Hall in Carlisle. The Carlisle Journal, 13 June 1807, reported as follows :-

"The price of coals at Maryport is 16s 8d for 25 Cumberland Bushels, to which adding 8d for harbour dues and 4d for incidental expense the charge will amount to 17s 8d. The freight to Sandsfield is 12s which makes the price 4d (the price they have been sold this week at Sandsfield). There are 87 Carlisle Pecks in a waggon. The cartage from thence should not exceed ld per peck, so that the cost in Carlisle should not be more than 6d. Should, however, the project of a canal be put in execution, coals might be sold at Carlisle, at the same price that they are now sold at the vessel, besides ensuring a constant supply, nothing we can conceive, could more effectually, or more speedily promote the increasing importance of Carlisle, than a communication with the sea, which by being the means of augmenting its manufactures and consequent population, aided by its great natural advantages, would render it one of the most flourishing places in the kingdom."

This memorial to Post Captain William Mounsey recording his achievements in the Royal Navy can be seen in Rockliffe church

For those out of touch with the old imperial units I will convert the above costings into a more understandable form. The Peck and the Bushel are imperial units of volume.

Four pecks = 1 bushel. 240d (old pence) = 20s (shillings) = £1.

Assuming that a Cumberland Bushel is the same measure as a Carlisle Bushel.

Hence coal would be sold at Carlisle at about 5d or 6d per Peck which is nearly three times the price charged off the vessel at Maryport. Even allowing for canal dues, coal could be delivered to Carlisle by canal at less than half the price current at that time and supply would be much more reliable.

Price of coals at Maryport				
25 Cumberland Bushels = 16s 8d	=	200d		
Harbour dues	=	8d		
Incidental expense	=	4d		
Cost at vessel per 25 Bushels	=	**212d**	**Cost at vessel per peck = 212/100**	= **2.12d**
Add 12s = 144d freight (from Maryport)	=	144d		
Price of coals off vessel at Sandsfield per 25 Bushels	=	**356d**	**Cost at Sandsfield per peck = 356/100**	**= 3.56d**
Cartage to Carlisle at 1d per peck	=	100d	(approx)	
Price of coals on arrival at Carlisle per 25 bushels	=	**456d**	Cost at Carlisle per peck	= **4.56d**

It was perhaps not surprising that the members of the Canal Committee resolved at their meeting:

"that a survey be immediately made - that Mr Chapman should be employed to make the survey, and that in so doing, he be instructed to consider the line of the canal which can, with the least expense, afford a safe and commodious communication with the sea."

On July 4 1807 a letter was published in the Carlisle Journal from 'One of the Coal Committee' which suggested that:-

"Bowness would be an ideal outlet to the sea as the canal would be short and the expense small, so that the canal could be made wide and deep enough to admit vessels drawing seven or eight feet of water right up to Carlisle. This would open up Carlisle to all the coal ports in the Firth (sic) which, most likely, would fully answer the need of furnishing this city with a plentiful supply of coal."

In the same letter he dismisses Maryport and ports to the south because all have a scarcity of water at neap tides and labour under the disadvantage of so extensive a line of canal, as wholly to preclude all ideas of navigating it with sea boats.

In his report Chapman still preferred to terminate the canal at Maryport, but he was aware that this might be too expensive and suggested an alternative terminus east of Bowness on Solway at Fishers Cross.

At a meeting of the canal committee on Monday l0th August 1807 it was resolved to ask engineer Thomas Telford to examine Mr Chapman's reports of 1795 and 1807. On the 6th February 1808 Telford reported on 'The Cumberland Canal', as he called it. He proposed a canal to link Carlisle with the Solway Firth at Fisher's Cross, a mile east of Bowness. He costed the canal, designed to take coasting vessels, at £l09,393, with a navigable feeder to Wigton, taking smaller boats, for an extra £38,139, if required, and there the matter rested for another ten years.

During the intervening years, however, canal building was continuing apace throughout the country. For example, the Cumberland Pacquet, Tuesday 4 November 1817, reported:- " A canal is to be cut from Portsmouth to London. All the money is subscribed and the work about to be immediately commenced."

The same edition contained a report on the progress of the Kendal Canal:- "The workmen employed in the tunnel through which the canal is to pass at Hincaster, near Kendal, met in opposite directions on Saturday se'night. This extensive perforation is through an eminence, consisting of stones, bedded in cemented gravel."

So, with canal fever gripping the country, it is perhaps not surprising that a meeting was called on Tuesday 7 October 1817 to look once again at the Carlisle - Solway Firth canal proposal. At this meeting Mr William Nanson was appointed Secretary and Mr William Chapman, Engineer. Things now began to move and the Cumberland Pacquet carried the advertisement below on the 28 July 1818.

This was followed a month later with a report on a canal committee meeting which stated that:- "Mr Chapman's report was received with much approbation, and was ordered to be printed."

The report was published and distributed early in September and this time the finance was forthcoming. Lord Lonsdale, Lord Lowther and Sir James Graham were amongst local subscribers, which included Carlisle Corporation and many leading citizens.

berland Pacqu

S WHITEHAVEN ADVERTISER.

PUBLISHED, TUESDAY, 28 JULY, 1818.

s and Matur'd Debate; an Eye Impartial, and an Even Scale.—Hence Wisdom sound, and unrepenting Choice.

On SALE,

A Choice Cargo of TIMBER, imported in the Brig WILLIAM, Capt. WILSON, from MIRAMICHI;

CONSISTING OF

Yellow Pine, Masts, Lathwood, and Planks.

Apply to

WILLIAM PATTERSON & SON.

CANAL.

A General Meeting of the SUBSCRIBERS, and Others interested in the Formation of a CANAL between *CARLISLE* and the *SOLWAY FRITH*, will be held at the Townhall, Carlisle, on TUESDAY the 11th Day of August next, at Ten o'Clock in the Forenoon, to determine upon the Adoption of the LINE of CANAL recommended by Mr. CHAPMAN in his REPORT: and to enter into a SUBSCRIPTION for SHARES, in Order to be prepared to apply for an Act of Parliament in the next Session. (29)

An aerial view showing Old Sandsfield in the top left hand corner. Prior to the opening of the canal, goods from Sandsfield had to be carted up to 5 miles, on very poor roads, through Beaumont and Kirkandrews to Carlisle.

The line taken by the canal between Ratlingate and Kirkandrews can also be seen on this photograph. The canal was level for the first three miles from the basin at Carlisle to Beaumont where the first lock was built.

The thumbnail images below appear full - size in the relevant section of the book

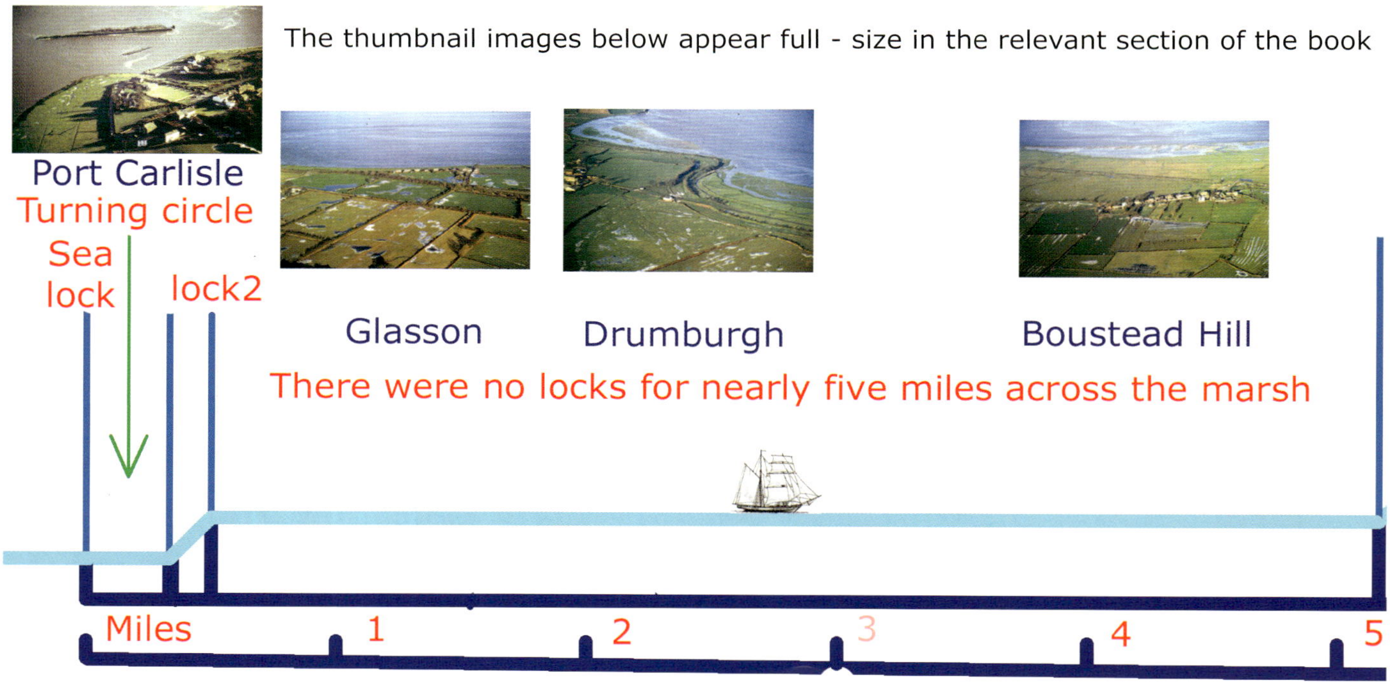

A profile of the Carlisle Ship Canal from Port Carlisle in the west to Carlisle in the east.

Three of the many papers, reports and letters on the subject of a canal from Newcastle to the Irish sea.

By 1807 it was realised that the only likely project to be economically practical was a canal from Carlisle to the Irish sea.

Below is Mr Chapman's original 1795 map revised for the proposed Carlisle to Port Carlisle project in 1807.

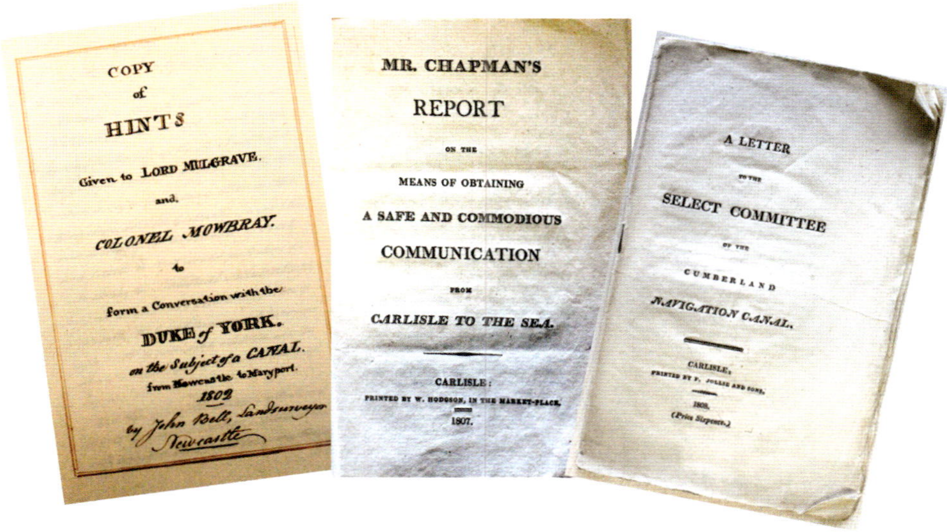

COPY of HINTS Given to LORD MULGRAVE and COLONEL MOWBRAY to form a Conversation with the DUKE of YORK, on the Subject of a CANAL from Newcastle to Maryport. 1802 by John Bell, Landsurveyor Newcastle

MR. CHAPMAN'S REPORT ON THE MEANS OF OBTAINING A SAFE AND COMMODIOUS COMMUNICATION FROM CARLISLE TO THE SEA.

CARLISLE: PRINTED BY W. HODGSON, IN THE MARKET-PLACE. 1807.

A LETTER TO THE SELECT COMMITTEE OF THE CUMBERLAND NAVIGATION CANAL.

CARLISLE, PRINTED BY F. JOLLIE AND SONS, 1808. (Price Sixpence.)

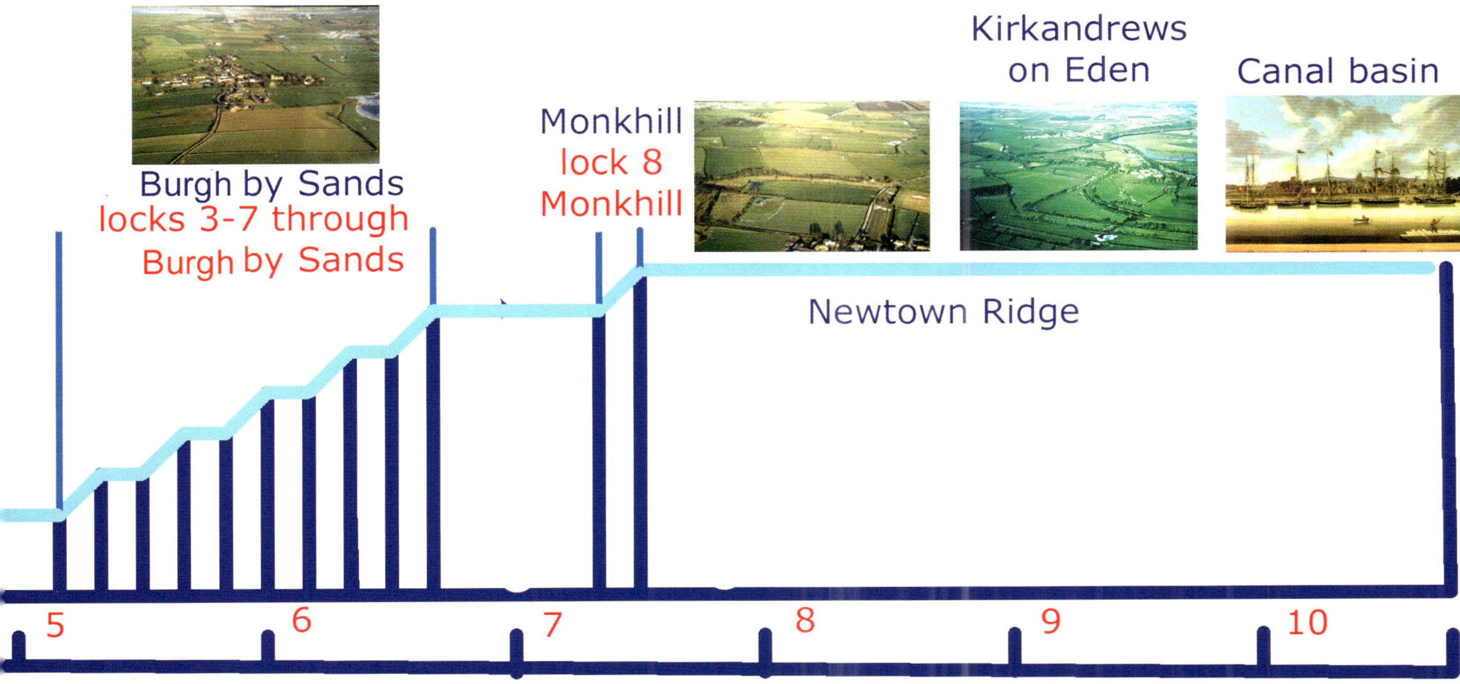

This drawing is based on an original by Denis Perriam in the Cumbria Archive centre, Carlisle

The Beginning of Labour

In 1819 an Act of Parliament was obtained for the construction of the canal. The canal was to be 11½ miles (18.4km) long, 54ft (16.5m) wide and 8ft 6in (2.6m) deep. 16.5m wide and 2.6m deep). It was to have a total of 8 locks, including the sea lock. Each lock was to be 18ft 3in (5.6m) wide and 78ft (24m) long.

The canal was to run from Fisher's Cross, near Bowness. Here there was to be a sea lock, followed by a turning circle and a second lock. The canal would then run level across Burgh Marsh for over 5 miles, before climbing through 6 locks in the next $1^1/_4$ miles. It would then run level again to the Carlisle Basin, which was to be 450ft (138m) long by 120ft (40m) wide.

A profile diagram of the canal can be seen on the previous page.

It was hoped that the canal would provide work for many of the poor of the city, many of whom were destitute.

This hope was expressed in the Carlisle Journal, 12 February 1820 which reported that:- "this week the workmen at the canal have commenced operations. A great number of men have arrived from distant places in expectation of being engaged. We hope, however, that a preference will be given to the poor of our own neighbourhood, who may be out of employ. "

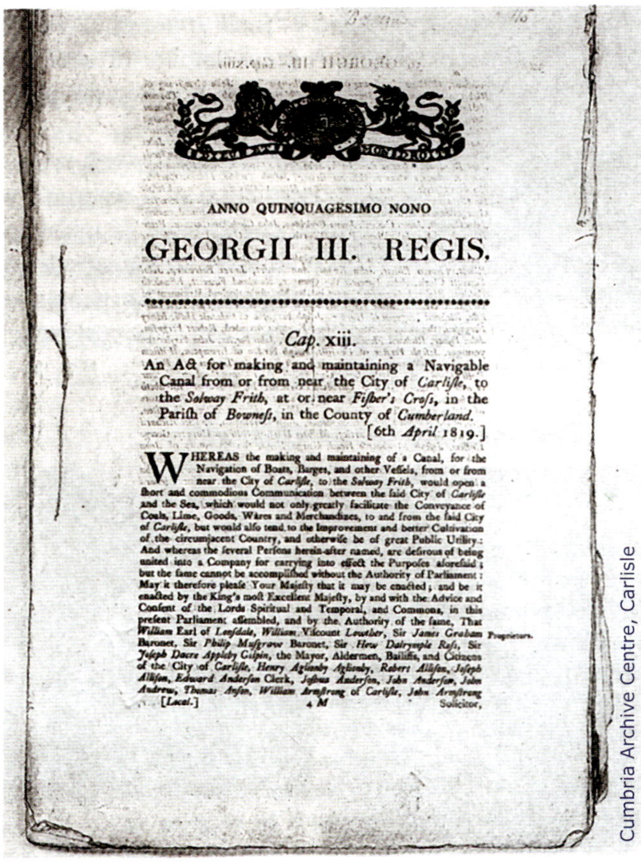

ANNO QUINQUAGESIMO NONO

GEORGII III. REGIS.

Cap. xiii.

An Act for making and maintaining a Navigable Canal from or from near the City of *Carlisle*, to the *Solway Frith*, at or near *Fisher's Cross*, in the Parish of *Bowness*, in the County of *Cumberland*. [6th *April* 1819.]

WHEREAS the making and maintaining of a Canal, for the Navigation of Boats, Barges, and other Vessels, from or from near the City of *Carlisle*, to the *Solway Frith*, would open a short and commodious Communication between the said City of *Carlisle* and the Sea, which would not only greatly facilitate the Conveyance of Coals, Lime, Goods, Wares and Merchandizes, to and from the said City of *Carlisle*, but would also tend to the Improvement and better Cultivation of the circumjacent Country, and otherwise be of great Public Utility: And whereas the several Persons herein-after named, are desirous of being united into a Company for carrying into effect the Purposes aforesaid; but the same cannot be accomplished without the Authority of Parliament: May it therefore please Your Majesty that it may be enacted; and be it enacted by the King's most Excellent Majesty, by and with the Advice and Consent of the Lords Spiritual and Temporal, and Commons, in this present Parliament assembled, and by the Authority of the same, That *William* Earl of *Lonsdale*, *William* Viscount *Lowther*, Sir *James Graham* Baronet, Sir *Philip Musgrave* Baronet, Sir *Hew Dalrymple Ross*, Sir *Joseph Dacre Appleby Gilpin*, the Mayor, Aldermen, Bailiffs, and Citizens of the City of *Carlisle*, *Henry Aglionby Aglionby*, *Robert Allison*, *Joseph Allison*, *Edward Anderson* Clerk, *Joshua Anderson*, *John Anderson*, *John Andrew*, *Thomas Anson*, *William Armstrong* of Carlisle, *John Armstrong* Solicitor, Proprietors.

[*Local.*] 4 M

Cumbria Archive Centre, Carlisle

The 1819 Act of Parliament for the canal

No time was lost after the granting of the Act of Parliament. Early in 1820 contracts had been awarded for the whole of the works. The coming of the canal caused great excitement among the townsfolk and was a source of great pride, as the entry in the Carlisle Directory of 1821 illustrated:

THE CARLISLE CANAL COMPANY

Was established in pursuance of an act of Parliament passed in the same year as the preceding. Their capital is £73,750 in 1,475 shares of £50. There are 305 share-holders. The work is rapidly going forward, and will be the means of connecting this city with the Solway Frith, affording a communication for small sea-vessels, and will contribute greatly to the wealth and prosperity of the city. The length of the cut is 11 miles, and the estimated expense £71,188.

It was at one time proposed to continue the line of navigation across the island to Newcastle, but the immensity of the undertaking caused it to be given up. It is very probable, however, that in time this desirable object may be accomplished.

Keeping the canal filled with water

Advertisements requesting tenders for canal work were regularly to be seen in the local newspapers about this time. One notable contract was for the construction of a reservoir near Ratlingate Woods, Kirkandrews on Eden. This was one of several reservoirs to provide water to fill the canal. The farm owning the land on which the reservoir was constructed is still known as Reservoir Farm to this day. The earthen bank dam of the reservoir is in Ratlingate Woods, the Cumbria campsite of the Guide and Scout Association. A deep gully in the woods, over which scouts and guides for generations have built wooden bridges and swung on their ropes. This gully was the overflow channel for the reservoir. The reservoir itself was in the field to the south of the woods and the brickwork of the outlet sluice, complete with large feedpipe and stopcock is still to be seen to the southeast of the site. The water flowed from here down a channel to the canal, which crossed the field just to the east of Ratlingate farm. Surplus water from the canal, or the reservoir, was also used to feed the watermill at Mill Lough on the other side of the road.

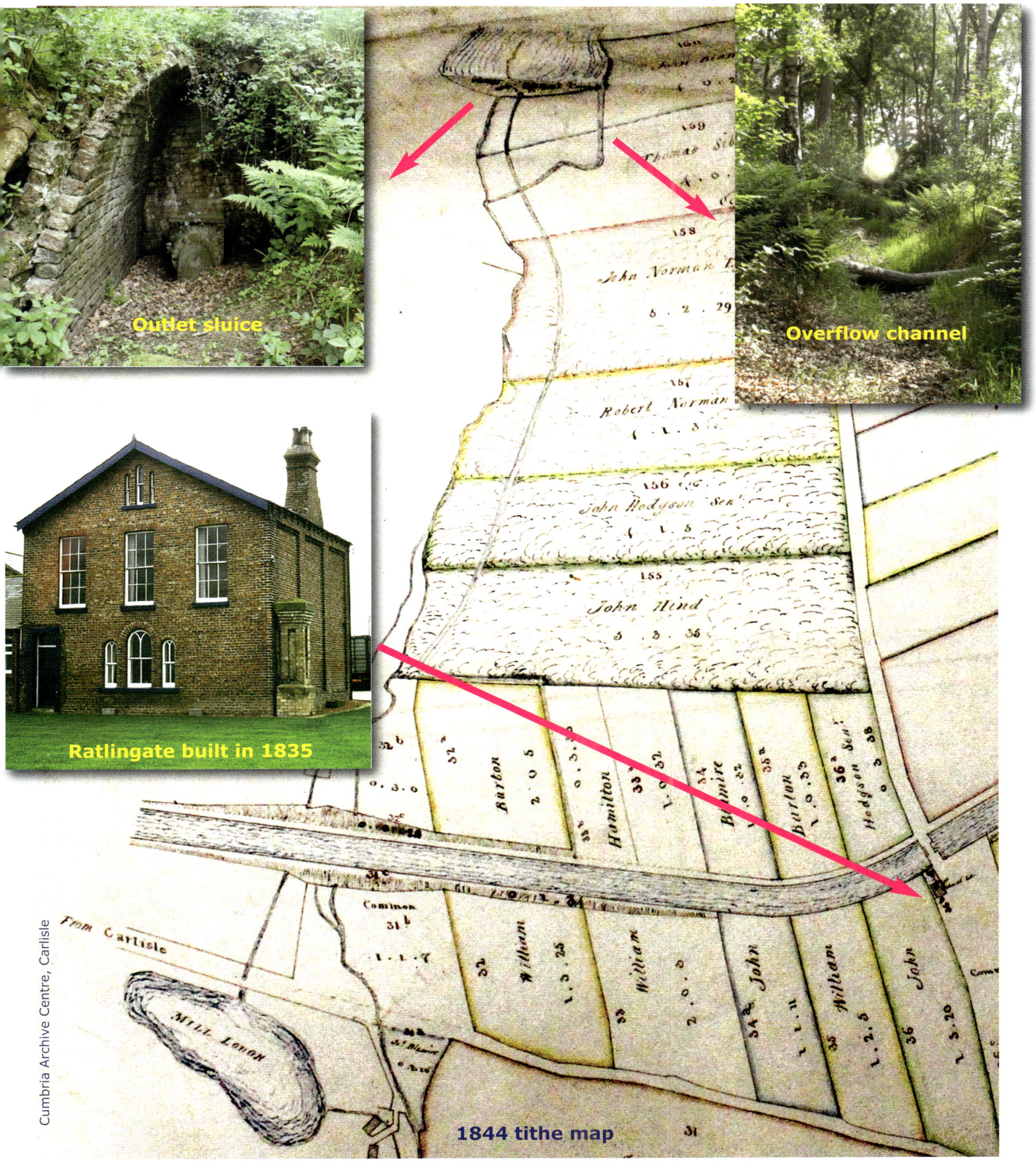

Outlet sluice

Overflow channel

Ratlingate built in 1835

1844 tithe map

Cumbria Archive Centre, Carlisle

Ratlingate Farm, Kirkandrews is rather a commercial looking building and not typical of farmhouses in the area. This is due to the fact that it was built beside the canal in 1835 as a bonemeal works and housed a steam engine. Bonemeal was transported from the works by canal. However the owners obviously overstretched themselves initially because, within a year of completion, the company went bankrupt.

In September 1836 the business was sold at auction.The manufacture of bone meal fertiliser was obviously profitable as there were at least four grinding mills along the line of the canal and in 1837 the advert below was posted in the Carlisle Journal.

BONE MANURE.

BONE MANURE, of the best quality, may be had at DIKESFIELD, in the Carlisle Canal, on application to JOHN SIBSON, of Grinsdale, (if by letter, post-paid,) or on Saturdays, at the King's Head Inn, Fisher Street, Carlisle.
Grinsdale, 15th June, 1837.

Many local people tried to take advantage of the excitement and interest in the coming of the canal. Adverts soon appeared in the local papers advertising property and boats for sale, which made reference to the project. See below.

PROPERTY ADJOINING THE LINE OF CANAL FOR SALE.

TO BE SOLD BY AUCTION, upon the Premises, on THURSDAY, the 1st Day of March next,—All that truly desirable PROPERTY, situate at BURGH, in the Parish of Burgh-by-Sands, in the County of Cumberland; consisting of a Dwelling-House, Barn, Byer, two Stables, Sheds, a Garden, and Croft, and now in the occupation of THOMAS LANGCAKE and others.

The above Premises adjoin the intended Canal Wharf at Burgh, and are well calculated for an Inn.—Apply to Mr. HEWIT, Solicitor, Carlisle.

SLOOP FOR SALE.
TO BE SOLD, BY PRIVATE CONTRACT,

THE SLOOP ROBERT BURNS, of ANNAN, with her Long Boat and Appurtenances. Her Burden, per Register, is 51 91-94ths Tons, but she will carry 60 Tons.—She was built at Dumfries in 1815,—is a very tight and substantial Vessel, and well adapted to the Trade of the Solway Frith, particularly that to Carlisle, as she will pass the Locks of the New Canal now in progress.
Apply to Mr. WILLIAM LITTLE, jun. Merchant, Annan.

BANKRUPT'S ESTATE FOR SALE.
To be SOLD, by PUBLIC AUCTION, on MONDAY, the 26th day of SEPTEMBER next, at the *Crown and Mitre Inn*, CARLISLE, at Six o'Clock in the Evening, (by order of the Assignees of ROBT. JAMES, a Bankrupt,)

ALL that Freehold BONE-DUST MANUFACTORY, SAW-MILL, and PREMISES, situate at or near GRINSDALE BRIDGE, on the Bank of the Carlisle and Bowness Canal. The Works have been recently erected, are on the most improved principle, and well worthy the attention of Persons desirous of embarking Capital in the increasing manufacture of Bonedust.

Also all the said Bankrupt's ESTATE and INTEREST of and in all that MESSUAGE, TENEMENT, and LANDS called BUSH-LEA BANK, situate in the Parish of Abbey Lanercost, in the County of Cumberland; consisting of a Dwelling House, Farm Buildings, and 80 Acres of Arable, Meadow, and Pasture Land, with 20 Stints or Cattlegates on Sidefell.

The Property is of Customary Tenure, held of the Earl of Carlisle, Manor of Askerton.

Also, all the said Bankrupt's Term and Interest of and in the DRAINING TILE MANUFACTORY and WORKS at SEBERGHAM, in the County of Cumberland, with or without a considerable Stock of TILES now on hand.

For particulars apply to Messrs. JOHN LITTLE, HUBERT RAWSON, and WILLIAM RICHARDSON, the Assignees; or to Mr. G. G. MOUNSEY, Solicitor, Carlisle. M. ARMSTRONG, Auctioneer.

Ratlingate woods from the south. The reservoir, of about half an acre and up to eight feet deep was in the dip in the centre ground.

The influx of canal workers into the city at this time brought its own problems. Reports in the local papers record some of the incidents which arose. For example the Carlisle Journal, 18 July 1820, reported:-

"We are sorry to have occasion to notice a circumstance which is highly disgraceful to our city, and if not disgraceful to themselves as injurious and disgusting to the public at large. We allude to that body of men who are brought from a distance (many from Ireland), and employed at the canal. During the whole of Sunday last, the neighbourhood of Caldew Bridge was, disturbed, and passengers (sic) annoyed, by a number of these persons, who, not content with excessive drinking, and fighting in the streets, proceeded to plunder the tavern - keepers of their property. One party took forcible possession of the bar of the Fox and Grapes, Public - House and plundered the place of spirits, ale &c. In fact, the whole day, particularly from five to nine p.m. that neighbourhood was one continuous scene of confusion and uproar. We hope our magistrates, who we know are anxious for the peace and comfort of the citizens of Carlisle, will be upon their alert, and put an end to such disgusting proceedings."

The canal workers did not always get off scott free. The Carlisle Journal of 20 October 1820 reported that:— "three canal labourers were fined 5s each for being drunk on the streets on Sunday, the 8th inst., and, in default of payment, to be placed in the stocks. After waiting a considerable time, a friend came forward and advanced the money, and they were accordingly discharged."

On the 10th November the same paper reported that:- " Last week several sheep were stolen and slaughtered on the line of the new canal. The skin of one was found at Riggstown, near Sandsfield on Thursday morning."

Occasionally the canal workers came into direct conflict with the local inhabitants. On the 29th December 1821, the Journal reported that:- "Thomas Clark of Drumburgh, blacksmith, was committed for further examination on Wednesday last, at the Police office in this city, on a charge of stabbing a labourer at the canal." Such happenings did not endear the canal workers to many of the local population, who felt threatened by their presence and their general tendency to disorderly behaviour.

Carlisle about 1835 *W. H. Nutter.*

However, the canal workers were necessary if the canal was to be built. The population in the city at this time was about 15,500 of whom only half were 'Cumbrian' born. A quarter of the town's population were Irish and a quarter Scots.

According to the Carlisle Journal at the time:-

"One eighth of the population are paupers, living on the contributions of the rest. Three eighths have low wages and live on a pittance. One quarter with difficulty support their families. One eighth, the middle classes, struggle to maintain their place in society. One eighth are exempt from this disorganised state of existence."

At this time Carlisle had four schools and three newspapers. The city had two M.P.'s who were elected by roughly 900 free burgesses of Carlisle, resident and non-resident. The canal workers excesses occasionally brought tragic results. On l4 April 1821 the Carlisle Journal reported:-

"This week, two of the workmen employed at the canal, near Burgh, having swallowed a large quantity of whiskey, and afterwards sleeping all night in the open air, expired next morning, a sad example of the intemperate use of ardent spirits."

The Carlisle Patriot was obviously better informed on this story. it described how:-

"seven or eight canal- men, living on Burgh Marsh, purchased six quarts of smuggled whiskey" (obviously the Irish variety). "Not having sufficient money to pay for it, they showed the illiterate vendor a tradesman's bill-head, which they pretended was a £10 note. The seller not being able to give the required change, it was agreed that on some future day he should bring ten gallons, and the whole should be paid for together. Having now got the whiskey into their possession, they retired in glee, and drank to such an excess that two of them, named Richard Hall and James Johnston, died through suffocation in consequence, and two or three others of the party have not yet recovered. Inquests were held on the bodies of the deceased on Tuesday, - Verdict, Died by excessive drinking of whiskey. "

Smuggled drink was often confiscated by the Customs and Excise, who then sold it as the advert, below opposite, illustrates. (Carlisle Patriot - 7 April 1821). Stress was often a factor then as now for the poor canal worker with a family to support. The Carlisle Journal, 22 September 1821, reported the inquest on John Dodd of Caldewgate. See opposite.

Building the basin

At this time building was continuing at a rapid pace. The Carlisle Journal, 17 March 1821, informed the reader that:- " the first stone of the Bason (sic) of the canal will be laid on Tuesday morning next at 10 o'clock." The following edition reported on the ceremony, which was attended by:- "a great number of persons " and "was performed amid loud cheers. A sum of money was afterwards given to the workmen to drink prosperity to the canal. "

The basin was built adjacent to where McVitties Biscuit Works now stands, in Port Road, Carlisle. The site is now a modern business park and all traces of the canal, apart from the gatekeepers house, have now, unfortunately, been bulldozed. The aerial view, above opposite, taken in1997, shows the Port Road Business Park (seen from the north). The canal basin was on the raised ground where the Business Park now stands. McVitties Biscuit works is to the centre left, the Cumberland Infirmary to the right foreground and

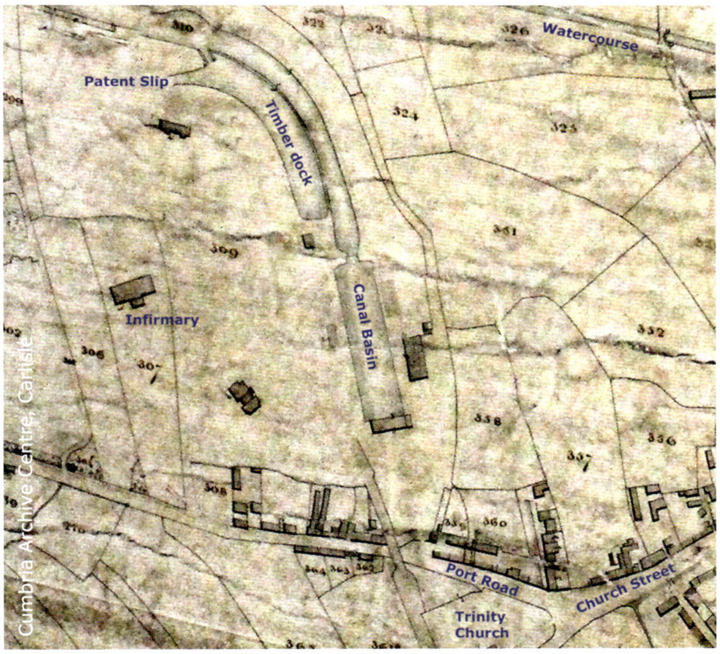

Dixon's chimney to the rear. The adjacent map, of 1842, shows the basin, the timber dock, built in 1838 and the watercourse; which led water from the River Caldew to a 16ft undershot waterwheel. Initially it had been hoped that the upper reaches of the canal would be kept full by the reservoir at Grindsdale, but it was soon realised that an extra supply would be needed. The canal pumping mill was built in 1825 to provide this supply, but as traffic on the canal increased, even that proved insufficient and further provision had eventually to be made.

The last stone of the canal basin was finally laid on 21st December 1821. However on this occasion, due to the inclement

CUSTOM-HOUSE CARLISLE.

5th April, 1821.

THIS is to give NOTICE, that on TUESDAY FIRST, the 10th Inst. at 12 o'Clock, will be SOLD, to the highest Bidder, at the KING'S WAREHOUSE HERE, in several Lots, for ready Money, 80 gallons of Foreign GENEVA, of very superior quality and strength.

On Tuesday morning last, John Dodd, a labourer at the canal, and a resident in Caldewgate, left his house between three and four o'clock, but not returning, his wife became alarmed, and arose from bed; however her alarm was increased by searching in vain for him about the premises. He had not put on either his waistcoat or handkerchief. About seven o'clock he was found drowned in the river Eden, opposite the Sheep-mount, and adjoining Etterby-scar.—A coroner's inquest was held on the body—verdict, *found drowned*.—The poor man had been observed to labour under a depression of spirits for some weeks—he has left a wife and four small children in a destitute condition.

weather, the Canal Committee did not assemble to celebrate the event, but resolved to do so at a later date. Little heed appears to have been taken at this time to health and safety considerations, as the following items from the local newspapers indicate.

Carlisle Patriot, 23 June 1821 :- "A boy, the son of one of the men employed on the canal, was so much crushed by the wheel of a wagon, in a narrow pass at the works, that he is not expected to recover."

Carlisle Patriot, 28 July 1821:- "A canal-man was nearly killed last week, near Beaumont, by the falling of earth: one of his thighs was broken, and he was otherwise much injured."

Carlisle Patriot, ll August 1821:- "On Saturday last a canal man was killed by a fall of earth which he was undermining, on the same spot where one of his fellow labourers had his thigh broken so lately. He has left a wife and seven children. One of his sons was working at his side when the accident happened."

The canal workers were obviously under great pressure to meet deadlines.

Carlisle Patriot, 26 January 1822:- "The canal-men on a part of the line near Newtown, are now working by lamplight in order to complete a contract by the stipulated time. "

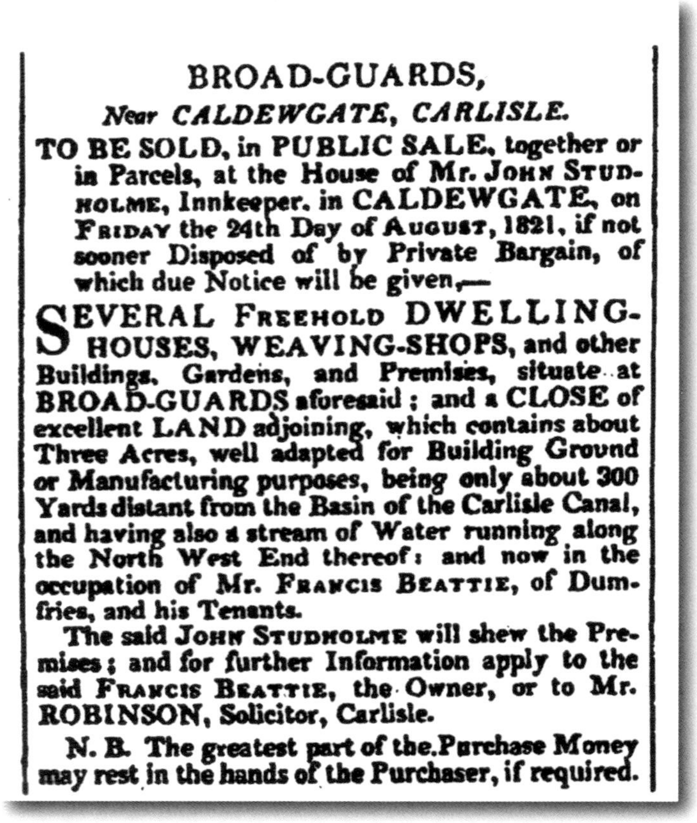

BROAD-GUARDS,

Near CALDEWGATE, CARLISLE.

TO BE SOLD, in PUBLIC SALE, together or in Parcels, at the House of Mr. JOHN STUDHOLME, Innkeeper, in CALDEWGATE, on FRIDAY the 24th Day of AUGUST, 1821, if not sooner Disposed of by Private Bargain, of which due Notice will be given,—

SEVERAL FREEHOLD DWELLING-HOUSES, WEAVING-SHOPS, and other Buildings, Gardens, and Premises, situate at BROAD-GUARDS aforesaid; and a CLOSE of excellent LAND adjoining, which contains about Three Acres, well adapted for Building Ground or Manufacturing purposes, being only about 300 Yards distant from the Basin of the Carlisle Canal, and having also a stream of Water running along the North West End thereof: and now in the occupation of Mr. FRANCIS BEATTIE, of Dumfries, and his Tenants.

The said JOHN STUDHOLME will shew the Premises; and for further Information apply to the said FRANCIS BEATTIE, the Owner, or to Mr. ROBINSON, Solicitor, Carlisle.

N. B. The greatest part of the Purchase Money may rest in the hands of the Purchaser, if required.

The potential for increased business due to the coming of the canal probably enhanced property values in the Caldewgate area as illustrated by this advertisement.

Correspondents to the newspapers at this time were keen to offer their help and advice. One writer, who described himself as:- ' a subscriber to the canal ' was most concerned that the project be completed as soon as possible and suggested offering a premium to the contractors to complete early. He saw no difficulty in completing the work in twelve months :-

"300 spade men would cut it with ease in that time, allowing 8 yards per day for each man."

One correspondent in particular wrote a series of letters to the Carlisle Patriot under the pen name 'A Practical Man. ' He argued that the canal should be extended to the head of Ullswater, where large supplies of blue slates were available (presumably from the Hartsop and Patterdale quarries). From here, following the north side of the Tyne, he proposed that very few locks would be needed between Ullswater and Newcastle, perhaps no more than seven or eight. The only great expense, he maintained, would be a high aqueduct to carry the canal over the Eden. The benefits however would be immense; much desired blue slates at a reasonable price for the north-east and London and coal, lime and merchant goods for the Eden valley.

The letters were very persuasive giving costings, potential profits etc., they also discussed inland navigation westward to Workington. However, nothing came of them and the identity of ' Practical Man ' was finally revealed as one R S Stephenson Esq.. I have not been able to ascertain whether or not this gentleman had holdings in the slate quarries!

As the building work progressed the work had to be financed and shareholders were periodically required to honour their commitment to provide additional funds as required. Notices were posted in the local papers as shown here.

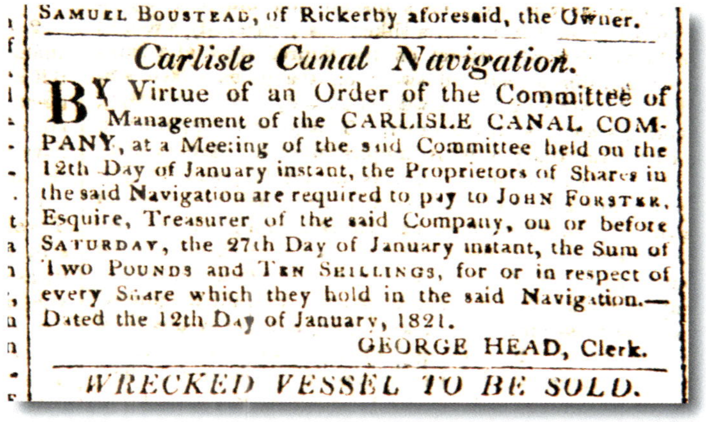
SAMUEL BOUSTEAD, of Rickerby aforesaid, the Owner.

Carlisle Canal Navigation.

BY Virtue of an Order of the Committee of Management of the CARLISLE CANAL COMPANY, at a Meeting of the said Committee held on the 12th Day of January instant, the Proprietors of Shares in the said Navigation are required to pay to JOHN FORSTER, Esquire, Treasurer of the said Company, on or before SATURDAY, the 27th Day of January instant, the Sum of Two Pounds and Ten Shillings, for or in respect of every Share which they hold in the said Navigation.—Dated the 12th Day of January, 1821.

GEORGE HEAD, Clerk.

WRECKED VESSEL TO BE SOLD.

The weather was particularly bad early in 1821, causing problems both for the Canal Company and their workers. The Carlisle Patriot, 7 April 1821, recorded that :-

"On Tuesday last, the Solway Firth rose to a greater height than had been known for a number of years. It overflowed the whole of Burgh Marsh; and inundated the huts of some of the workmen employed in the formation of the canal from this city to Bowness, to the imminent danger of the lives of the women and children who occupied these frail dwellings at the moment, - particularly of one poor woman in child-bed. The water also damaged the works of the Canal upon the Marsh. We have not heard of any great injury sustained on this side of the Firth. At Whitehaven, the market place was covered to a considerable extent, which caused a suspension of business for a few hours."

Digging the canal uncovered occasional surprises.

Early in January 1821 the remains of a female human skeleton was found at Newtown, on the line of the canal. The Carlisle Patriot reported :- "The soil being peaty, the colour of every part was completely altered by carbonaceous depositation, excepting the enamel of the teeth, which retained it's pristine whiteness. Some parts of the face and temple appeared to have been bent in and fractured, but their decayed state render any conclusion of that kind uncertain. All conjectures concerning the the time of deposition must be vague; yet, unlike bones of great age, they did not moulder on exposure to the atmosphere. No remains of sepultural (sic) enclosure were discernible; they were about three feet from the surface of the earth in a boggy hollow, which had formerly been one of the fossae of Hadrian's line of fortification, part of which is commonly known as the Picts' Wall."

This was not the only archaeological find in the area. In later years when the canal had been converted into a railway (and this area was known as 'Engine Lonning' there were two more 'finds':-

In 1860 a solid gold Roman necklace was found in the area where the engine sheds and workshops were to be built. This now resides in the British Museum and is one of the finest ever found.

In 1861 a pot containing Roman gold coins was found where foundations were being dug for the Waverley viaduct.

What did the canal bridges look like?

Baggage Waggons approaching Carisle *Sam Bough 1849*

Very little evidence of the canal now survives in the area of Newtown as it was landscaped several years ago. The bridge shown on old maps over the canal at Engine Lonning is no longer to be seen.

However, the bridge was recorded for posterity by Sam Bough in 1849 as a detail in his painting 'Baggage Waggons approaching Carlisle', reproduced above

Looking at the detail in the left of the picture, the canal at Newtown can be seen with a two - leaved drawbridge raised and a steam tender passing along the canal.

Canal Bridge at Bonnybridge

Carlisle Castle, the Cathedral and Dixon's chimney can be seen on the horizon in the main painting above. This is probably a good example of artistic licence because Coalfell Hill at Belle Vue would make it very unlikely for one to see all three of these edifices from the Moorhouse road.

The design of the locks, bridges and other furniture of the canal was modelled on that used on other canals, particularly the Forth and Clyde Ship Canal. So I contacted Guthrie Hutton author of books on the Forth and Clyde Canal and he sent me a photograph of the Bascule bridge at Bonnybridge. This appears to be similar to the bridge in Sam Bough's painting (even including the steam tender!).

Unlike the bridge at Newtown, the stonework of most of the canal bridges has been preserved. When the canal closed the railway bridges were created by building extra stonework, to increase the height, directly onto the existing canal bridges. This picture shows the old railway bridge at Knockupworth (a listed structure), just outside Carlisle. The dressed canal stonework is clearly distinguishable from the more modern stonework above it. The second picture shows the original canal stonework, on the western abutment, complete with inscribed date of construction.

The aerial photograph below shows the bridge in the field at Knockupworth with the adjacent bridgekeeper's cottage. The canal curved round the base of the hill towards

Grinsdale Bridge and Ratlingate. The straight depression in the terrain is the vallum of Hadrian's Wall. There was a berth at Knockupworth Farm on the left. The inset photo is of a sandstone mooring post removed when the farmer levelled one of the canal banks to help drain the field.

As physical signs of the coming canal began to appear so public interest and speculation increased. Around this time the first Carlisle Gas Works was being constructed to light the city streets and buildings. It was a time of great change and led some to poetry. The public excitement and anticipation engendered as a result is caught in the adjacent poem; written at this time:-

' Aye ! Lads, what think ye has happen'd,
I fackins the world's upside down,
They're cutting a long ditch frae Boness
And diggin' greet holes i' the toon,
They say that yen's a canal
For bwoats and for ships and sich things
And t'other's for what they ca gas
For cockspurs, and flying bat's wings.
Whey my lads, they are ganing, I fear,
To mek Carel aw fly away.
Ships will sail through meadows, I hear,
And night be far brighter than day,
Tallow chandlers are aw fearcely swearing
And say that their trade will be done,
The carriers, too, are despairing -
They're finished as sure as a gun!

CANAL SHARES FOR SALE.

TO BE SOLD, TWO SHARES in the CARLISLE CANAL.—Apply to the PRINTERS of this PAPER.——Carlisle, March 27, 1821.

CARLISLE CANAL.

THE PLANS and SPECIFICATIONS for the WOOD and IRON WORK of the WAREHOUSE at the CANAL BASIN, will be ready for inspection, at the CANAL OFFICE, in CASTLE-STREET, CARLISLE, on TUESDAY, the 26th MARCH inst.; and Sealed Proposals, for the Execution of the Work, will be received at the Canal Office until Monday, the 1st Day of APRIL next.
Carlisle, March 22, 1822.

By this time the canal share scheme was fully subscribed, so anyone wanting shares had to purchase them from existing shareholders. Shares were thus advertised from time to time as shown.

At regular intervals advertisements inviting tenders for canal buildings appeared in the press. The warehouse referred to above is probably the open structure that features prominently in J W Carmichael's sketch of the canal basin in 1835 (see page 28).

Towards the end of 1821 some of the first boats specifically built for use on the canal neared completion. The Carlisle Journal, 13 October 1821 carried the following report:-

" On Monday a very handsome sloop, burden 50 tons and intended for the canal, was launched from the stocks at Bowness amidst a large concourse of people. She was built by Mr William Bell for Messrs Pickering, Allison, Elliot and Rothwell. William Jackson Esq. of Carlisle, performed the ceremony of breaking a bottle of rum, and named her 'The Crown'. A number of ladies witnessed the spectacle, who were placed upon an eminence and added considerably to the beauty of the scene, with which every person present seemed delighted. Mr Wm Rae is appointed master. In the afternoon the owners, and a party of gentlemen sat down to an excellent dinner at Mrs Hodgson's, The Ship Inn, where they spent the remainder of the day in the greatest harmony."

Work went on quickly and by late May 1822 the first section of the canal was filled between Carlisle and Beaumont (the last lock before Carlisle was at Monkhill, near Beaumont). On the 25th May the Carlisle Journal recorded the first commercial use of this stretch of water:-

"The new Carlisle Canal being partially filled with water, on Saturday last a load of corn, butter, hams &c. was conveyed from Beaumont, by the Messrs: Hodgson of that place, to our market; being the first cargo of provisions brought to Carlisle by water.

On the evening of the same day, it was announced in, our good city of Carlisle, by din of bell, that the Bellerophon would convey passengers, the next day, at two o' clock in the afternoon, to Beaumont. This announcement, of course, invited no little stir among the dashing Daphnes and Strephons in humble life, some hundreds of whom mustered their 'thruppence' a piece to enjoy the delectable novelty of a four mile voyage in a mud boat, reckless of the sore discomfiture and soiling of their Sunday paraphenalia. "

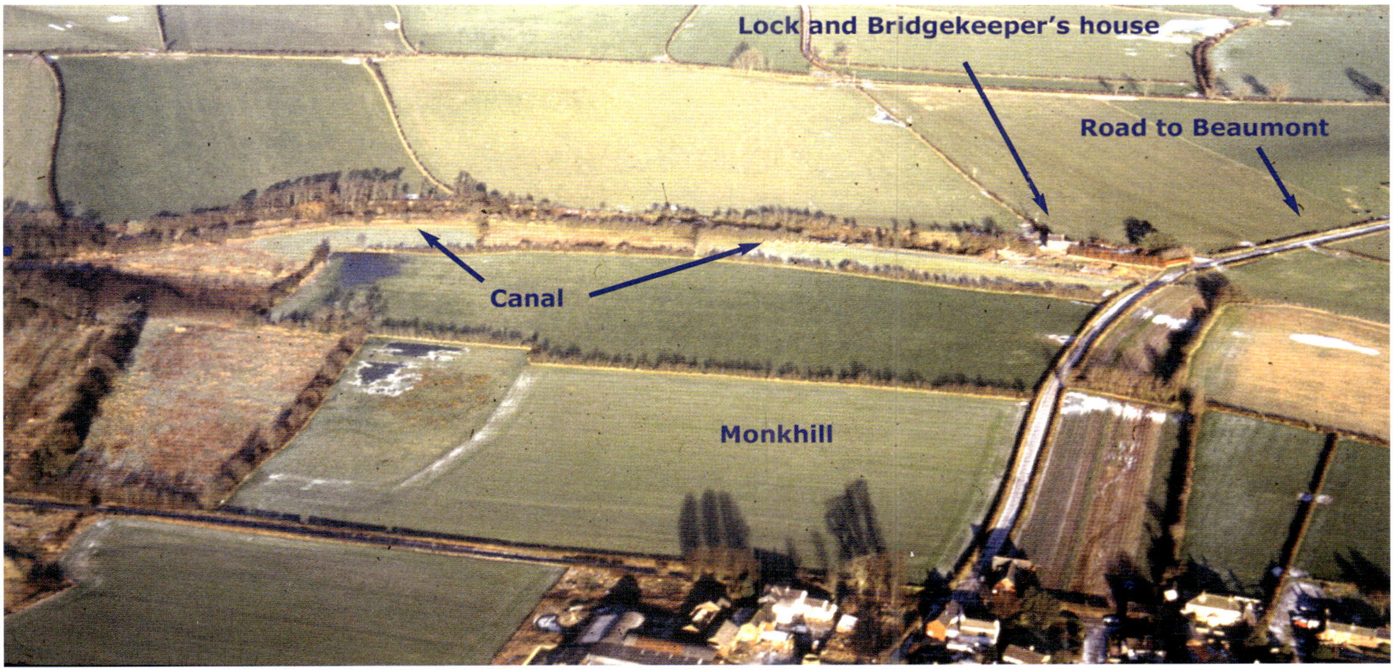

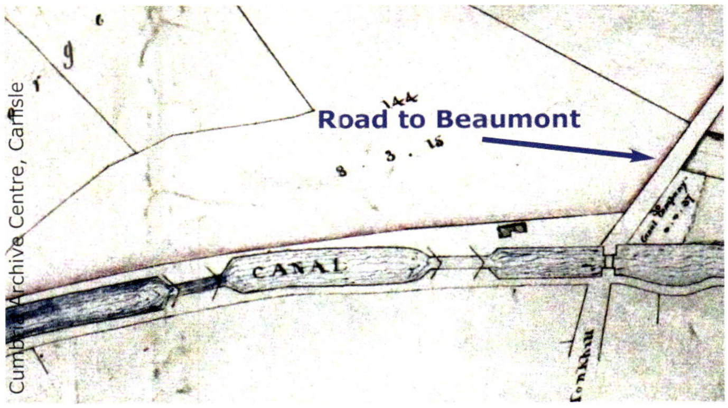

This is an excellent example of the contractors taking advantage of the popular interest in the canal. As it was a Sunday no work was being done so they decided to offer the better-off in society a rather expensive trip in the Bellerophon, which was a dredger. Hence the reference to a 'mud boat'. The first lock after the Carlisle basin was at Beaumont so, as soon as that lock was built, the section could be filled from the reservoir at Ratlingate.

The aerial picture above shows the first lock out of Carlisle between Monkhill and Beaumont. The lock keeper here had to operate the Bascule bridge on the road as well as the lock.The tithe map shows the lock, bridge and house. The lock house, bottom left, was re-slated in 1830 (according to the canal company minutes). The house has recently been re-built and no longer looks anything like the original (taken in 1997).

The Birth and the Early years

Early in June 1822 the Canal Committee met to propose to shareholders that a sum of money, not exceeding £10,000, should be borrowed under interest for the purpose of completing the undertaking. Mr Halton explained that £4000 was needed to purchase land and a deficiency of £2600 had arisen. A sum was also needed for other buildings not included in Mr Chapman's report, such as coal vaults and :-

"a new and commodious inn, which it is proposed to erect close to the termination of the canal at Knox Cross."

The coal vaults, shown to the right, were demolished in 1987. The view shown is from below, on the east side of the canal basin. Ships would unload bulk materials directly into the vaults from the quayside. Horse-drawn carts would then back into the vaults and the coal (or other bulk material) would be discharged directly from the hopper into the cart.

The inn referred to was the Solway Hotel (now a private house) at Port Carlisle. In 1822 Port Carlisle was still known by its old name of Knox Cross. In fact in 1819, before building of the canal commenced, there was very little at Knox Cross (or Fishers Cross as it was also known) apart from the Custom House. The Georgian village of Port Carlisle developed very quickly with the arrival of the canal. That is what makes it so special. Almost all of the buildings date from the same era. During the 32 years or so of its existence the canal company built houses, a bowling green, tennis courts and sea-water baths. All of this served to make the village a weekend retreat from the city for the better-off, as well as a working port.

Although the canal was not yet finished, ships were being built that were designed for use on the new navigation, as the item below right from the Carlisle Journal, dated 11 May 1822, shows. The note about potatoes orders received by shippers in the Dumfries area to be shipped direct to Ireland obviously relates to the famine in Ireland at that time.

The need for the canal was emphasised by adverts for timber from abroad available at Bowness, Rockclife and Carlisle. The goods would only get to Carlisle by horse and cart from either Sandsfield or Rockliffe at this time and would cost considerably more than if they had arrived directly at the canal basin.

TIMBER ON SALE.

NOW Landing at BOWNESS, from the Brig BRITANNIA, Captain M'DOWELL, an Excellent Cargo of MIRAMICHI, NORTH AMERICA, RED, and YELLOW PINE TIMBER, BLACK BIRCH, PLANK, and LATHWOOD, ASH STAVES, &c.—For Particulars apply to HEWITT & NELSON;
Who have on Sale at CARLISLE and ROCKLIFF, MAHOGANY in PLANKS, Dantzic & Quebec OAK STAVES, Heart and Sap LATHS, and an Assortment of Well-seasoned BOARD of every Dimension; also a Large Quantity of Lancashire and Welsh SLATE of all descriptions. Likewise a well-assorted Stock of Swedish and English BAR IRON, NAIL RODS, &c. &c. all of which they are selling on reasonable Terms.
Carlisle, July 27, 1821.

On Tuesday last, a vessel of about 90 tons burden, called the Irishman, the property of Messrs. Robert Ferguson and Sons, of this city, was launched from the building-yard of Messrs. J. N. Wood & Co. Maryport.—This vessel has been built expressly for the navigation of the canal, and it is intended that she shall be employed in trading between Belfast and Carlisle.

Orders to an extensive amount for potatoes have been received by the different shippers in the county of Dumfries, from Liverpool, to be sent direct for Ireland.

Carlisle Journal 11 May 1822

The Opening Ceremony

Cumbria Archive Centre, Carlisle

Carlisle Canal Basin on the opening day. This etching is from one of the original canal share certificates. Note the smoke from the ship on the left, firing a salute with cannons loaned from Carlisle Castle. (Coloured by the author)

The official opening of the canal was on Wednesday 12 March 1823, amidst scenes of joy and and celebration, the like of which had not been seen in Carlisle in living memory. All of the local papers carried long and detailed reports of the day, which give us today an insight into the pride and rejoicing of the local population at the completion of this major venture. The report by the Patriot was by far the most colourful and descriptive account and some of it is reproduced below:-

"The opening of the Carlisle Canal on Wednesday last was one of those events which claim a conspicuous station in local history................the day was looked forward to with great anxiety by all classes of people. Much was expected; but we may venture to assert that the imagination of the most sanguine had failed to depict anything equal to the reality. There was nothing wanting to render the gratification complete - the weather was delightful.

At eight o' clock the Committee breakfasted at the Bush,* and a musical band played a variety of favourite airs in front of the inn. Soon after nine, the Committee proceeded in carriages to the village of Burgh, about five miles from Carlisle, where eleven sea-going vessels, and several small craft (freighted with coals, peat &c.) had arrived in the course of the day previous. The vessels were highly decorated with flags.............. the departure of the Committee was a signal to the inhabitants of the City to bear their part in the business of the day. Nearly all the shops were shut up, and every house poured its quota to the immense masses which before mid-day had congregated around the Basin, or crowded the banks of the canal, nearly all the way to Burgh. .... a short time after ten, the Robert Burns, belonging to Messrs. J M Head & Son, having on board the Committee, and a large party of ladies and gentlemen began to move onwards for Carlisle, and about eleven had passed the locks

** The Bush Inn stood in English Street where the entrance to Victoria Viaduct is now. It was demolished in 1877 to make way for the new road over the railway and was rebuilt to the right of the original building. The National Westminster Bank now occupies these premises. Bush Brow on Victoria Viaduct used to emerge onto English Street through an archway at the front of the inn.*

at Beaumont; the other vessels followed in succession. About half-past eleven the whole of Messrs Dixon's work-people arrived in Carlisle from Warwick Bridge, preceded by two flags and a band of music, belonging to the Friendly Society of that place. They formed themselves into a column opposite the Bush Inn; and after a short halt, marched to the Canal, and joined the vessels near Beaumont, where the band was taken on board the Irishman. At Knockupworth, the vessels were saluted and cheered by a numerous party, with drum and fife, and several flags belonging to the City guilds. As the fleet proceeded, in gay and gallant trim:- decked out in all the pride of marine ornament, and crowded with beauty -- the masts and rigging completely covered with temporary jack-tars in longcoats -- guns were fired at intervals on board each of the vessels, and the spectators on shore loudly greeted. The Board of Ordnance very readily acceded to the request of a loan of cannon, and men to work them. Two 6-pounder field pieces were stationed on a slight eminence near the Basin. The flag was also hoisted at the Castle flag-staff as on public occasions. Another flag decorated the warehouse roof.

About ten minutes before three, the first vessel, the Robert Burns, belonging to Messrs. J. M Head & Son, entered the Basin, preceded by a band of music in an open boat, amid a royal salute (21 guns) and the cheers of the surrounding thousands, and the enlivening strains of Hearts of Oak, Rule Brittania and God Save the King. Then followed the Irishman, belonging to Messrs. Robert Ferguson & Sons; the Menai, the property of Messrs. Head & Son; the Crown, belonging to the Carlisle Shipping Company; the Miss Douglas, of Carlisle; the John, of Carlisle; the Nancy, of Carlisle; the Henry Brougham, of Annan; the Sarah, of Carlisle; the Rosina, of Carlisle; the Mary, of Liverpool."

The reporter from the Carlisle Journal estimated that there could not be less than 18 or 20 thousand persons present:-

"Every yard of ground for a considerable distance round the Basin was densely covered with people present upon this memorable occasion, men, women, children all dressed in their holiday clothes, while vast numbers had proceeded some miles down both sides of the canal to meet the vessels coming up .... the spectacle was grand and imposing and the multitude of people truly astonishing; among whom were hundreds who had never seen a masted vessel, and many of them not even a boat."

Tullie House Museum & Art Gallery Trust

The Canal Basin in 1835 *by John Wilson Carmichael*

William Farish, a native of Carlisle, recorded in his autobiography, published about 1889, that his father and brother both worked as navvies on the canal. He recollected being on his father's shoulder in 1824 (?) at the opening, and seeing:-

"our John on the topmast of the first ship that entered the Basin."

He obviously got the year wrong, but that is quite understandable considering his tender age at the time. His book graphically describes the social deprivation and harsh living conditions in the early 1820's. He writes:-

"The subsequent winter was a terrible one for the working people everywhere, and the hardships fell with unwonted severity on the north-country weavers. The benevolence of the gentry was taxed to its utmost to preserve their poorer neighbours from actual starvation. To utilise these gifts they used the weavers to construct the walk leading from the castle to Eden Bridges, which still remains as a memorial to the honour of some and a reproach to those others who wickedly helped to maintain the iniquitous bread tax in the face of a starving community. Unsound barley meal that year sold for as much as four shillings a stone; while wheat flour and butchers meat were wholly beyond the reach of the ordinary workman. It was no uncommon thing for our house to be without bread for weeks together; and I cannot remember to have ever seen in my very early years a joint of meat of any kind on my father's table, oatmeal porridge and potatoes, with an occasional taste of bacon, being our 'principal food."

However the worries of everyday living appear to have been forgotten for the opening day of the canal and everybody was determined to enjoy themselves. The Carlisle Journal described how the ' Nancy,' leading the second flotilla of ships, arrived at 3.30 p.m. in:-

" .... fine style, superbly ornamented with a great variety of elegant colours that nearly covered the whole of her rigging; at this moment, and during the most animated cheering from the surrounding multitude, a signal was fired from one of the cannon placed near the canal, which was promptly answered by 21 guns from the batteries of the Castle, producing a very grand and enlivening effect."

By four o' clock all 14 vessels were moored in the basin and completely overrun by the excited and curious public. Luckily no accidents occurred apart from a few unexpected dousings in the canal; as inexpert amateur sailors attempted to board or leave vessels, and a gun burst on board the Menai; but luckily no one was injured. Refreshments were provided for the local gentry. The Canal Committee opened up two floors of their warehouse and over two thousand were admitted, by ticket, to be regaled with wine and cake.

This oak-beam crane (seen in 1937 when the canal basin had become railway sidings) appears to be in the same position as that in Carmichael's drawing on the opposite page (102 years earlier).

The Carlisle Patriot commented at length on the reaction of the population to the spectacles:-

"The scene was so new, so unexpected, that it astonished. Some could hardly credit the evidence of their senses, when they saw so many sea-going vessels sailing

The canal warehouse built in 1821 and demolished in 1973 was situated where the Co-operative Pharmacy and Doctors Surgery is now.

along a track where, till lately, they were in the habit of beholding corn in ear, or grazing cattle. An old man, ninety-seven years of age, resident in Caldewgate, on hearing that ships had come up to Primrose Bank, declared that nothing but seeing them would be sufficient to induce him to believe the fact: and he was on Thursday actually carried by two friends to the Basin, where he was obliged to resign his incredulity to the reality."

The workers were not forgotten in all of this excitement:- "In the evening, Messrs Dixon & Sons opened ten public houses, at which every man in their employment, who chose, was allowed ale and bread and cheese to the amount of two shillings. Mr Slater of the New Mill, gave each of his workers one shilling and the women sixpence each. Messrs. J. R. & J. Ferguson also gave their weavers one shilling each; the warpers and warehousemen dined at the Crown, in Botchergate, the females had a tea party. Mr Paul Nixon also treated the people in his employment." At 5 o' clock about 160 shareholders sat down to 'an elegant and sumptuous dinner' in the assembly rooms at the Bush Inn. The celebrations went on well into the late evening with speeches, congratulations, toasts and more speeches. One of the interesting points that emerged was the fact that the Canal Basin was situated on the site of the battery that the Duke of Cumberland set up against Carlisle Castle in 1745, when it was occupied by rebels. The fire from this battery led to the speedy surrender of the castle. Nearly one hundred years later, at the opening of the canal, the same castle loaned two cannon to be fired from that same ground."

It was at this dinner that the name of Fishers Cross (now Port Carlisle) was discussed :- "Mr. Dixon:- It has been suggested to me that as we have made a new port, that we should have a new name for it. I am aware that Carlisle is the most ancient port in the county; but I believe it will be found necessary now to alter the name of 'Port Sandsfield as we shall no longer be dependent on its uncertain tides. The line of canal embraces and, as it were, unites both ports - and if it meet with your approbation, I propose that the entrance at Fisher's Cross be called 'New Port Carlisle.' Names indeed are not of much consequence - but if my proposition is approved of I beg to propose 'success to New Port Carlisle. Mr Pearson suggested that the Basin, from the fact of the Royal Duke's battery having been erected on the spot in 1745, should be called Port Cumberland, or Port William.

Mr Halton:- I am sorry to differ with gentlemen. Let us recollect that the Old Port is mother of all the rest-and, yet, you are going to christen the bairn, and do away with the name of the mother altogether. I hope no one will suffer the bairn to insult the mother. (Laughter and applause.) I'll support the mother of all the ports in Cumberland. I propose the old one- 'Port Carlisle' (Great laughter, and cheers)."

And so they went on discussing, wining and dining into the night. Thus it was that the coming of the canal was celebrated in Carlisle. An event that was truly momentous and unforgettable to the citizens of that time. The immediate benefits were obvious to all. On that opening day Carlisle was seen to become a bustling commercial port. Mr Dixon, speaking at the opening dinner, commented that no fewer than one hundred horses were busily employed in unloading and loading vessels which had brought in cargoes of :-

"cottons, linens, salt, sugar, wine and spirits, dye-woods, copperas, cheese, soap, oranges, oil, coal, peats, stone, paper, staves and bar-iron."

Perhaps the most significant pointer to the instant success of the canal was the price of coals. At $3^1/_2$ pence per Carlisle Peck this was half the price charged three years previously when construction of the canal commenced. Now Industry had access to a cheap and ready supply; as had the public. Mr Dixon remarked:-

"It was yesterday highly pleasing to see the poor people supplying themselves with coal and peats, The latter is allowed by the purchasers, as well as the coals, to be only half the usual retail price."

Due to the competition from imported coal and peat the local peat suppliers were obliged to reduce their prices. This was commented on rather cruelly in a poem on the 'Opening of the Carlisle Canal,' published in the Patriot of 23 March 1823.

Verse 7 of the poem is quoted below :-

There's one noble captain above all the rest,
Whose manly exertions will long be caressed,
Peat-cadgers from Scaleby may all bid farewell,
While brave Bellerophon sails up our canal.

Once the opening celebrations were concluded the city and canal got back to work. The Canal Basin became a very busy place indeed. Merchandise from all over the world became much more readily available in the city and the export of home produced food, and manufactured goods became much cheaper and easier. Advertisements such as those shown on the next page were regularly to be seen in the local press.

The Carlisle Patriot reported an event which illustrates quite well the enthusiasm felt by local people for the canal and its benefit to local industry:-

SLATES ON SALE.

JUST landed from on board the JANE, and now on SALE, at J. LONSDALE'S SLATE YARD, on the West Side of the CANAL BASIN, a choice CARGO of LIGHT and DARK BLUE SLATE, of the very best quality; being from the much approved and most extensive Quarries of CONISTONE and KIRBY, the Proprietor of which intends keeping ups regular and well-assorted Supply, which will be Sold at very reduced prices.

For Particulars apply to Mr. LONSDALE, Caldewgate, who is appointed Agent to the above Concern.

P. S.—The JANE has sailed for another Cargo.

CARLISLE, July 10, 1823.

TIMBER ON SALE.

NOW landing, at BOWNESS, from the Brig NANCY, Capt. MAC CARTNEY, an excellent cargo of MIRAMICHI PINE TIMBER, BLACK BIRCH, PLANKS, and LATH-WOOD.

For Particulars apply to CARRICK & BIRRELL, who have on Sale at CARLISLE, PENRITH, ROCKLIFF, and SARKFOOT, a good assortment of Baltic Timber, St. Domingo and Honduras Mahogany, in Planks; Dantzic Oak Boards and Staves; Heart and Sap Laths; and a large quantity of well-seasoned Boards, of different dimensipns.

Also a large assortment of LANCASHIRE and WELCH SLATES, all of which they will Sell on the most reasonable terms.

Carlisle, 10th July, 1823.

AMERICAN PINE TIMBER for SALE.

NOW Landing at BOWNESS, at the CARLISLE CANAL BASIN, and at ROCKCLIFF, from the Brig JANE, Captain ASBRIDGE, an excellent Cargo of RED and YELLOW PINE TIMBER, BLACK BIRCH, PLANKS, LATHWOOD, &c.

For Particulars apply to THOMAS WAUGH, who has on SALE at his TIMBER YARD, Foot of Scotch-Street, CARLISLE, an excellent Assortment of Memel Crown Timber and Planks; likewise Mahogany ia Planks, and Veneers, Dantzic Oak Boards, Memel Pipe Staves, Heart and Sap-Laths Also, a Quantity of well-seasoned Boards of different dimensions, all of which he is selling on reasonable Terms.

Carlisle, 9th July, 1823.

"Messrs Cowen, Heysham and Co., of Carlisle, had a lot of cotton on board the Miss Douglas. She sailed from Liverpool on Sunday evening, the 9th inst., about seven o' clock, and arrived in the Canal Basin about three on the following Wednesday, the 12th; on Thursday l3th, about half past twelve, the cotton was disembarked and sent to Messrs Cowen, Heysham, and Co's manufactury, where a part of it was almost immediately converted into yarn, by eight the next morning this yarn was sent to Mr. John Ferguson, who caused cloth to be made from it sufficient for a lady's dress by ten on the morning of the 15th; and if a mantuamaker (dressmaker) had been set to work, some blooming Cumberland damsel might have appeared in it at church on Sunday 16th. This curious fact exhibits in a strong point of view the wonderful perfection of our manufacturing system."

It was towards the end of 1823 when the canal basin in all of its glory was captured on canvas for the first time by the artist William Brown. The painting is on permanent display in Tullie House Museum, Carlisle. William Brown's painting faithfully depicts the ships which regularly used the canal. From left to right they are the Rosanna, Robert Burns, Crown, Miss Douglas, Nancy and Ellen. Old Carlisle, including the Castle and the Cathedral is clearly visible in the background. The man in the foreground, poling a plank raft, is probably using this mode of conveying his wood into the basin in order to avoid having to pay berthing dues for his ship.

Tullie House Museum & Art Gallery Trust

Carlisle Canal Basin *William Brown (1823)*

The painting was well received by the people of Carlisle in December 1823 as the following entry in the local periodical 'The Carlisle Citizen', 5 December 1823, illustrates:-

"Our clever townsman, Mr. Brown, has just finished his painting of the Carlisle Canal Basin. It adds much to his former well-eamed fame, and does, we think, credit to our city. The picture is very large; in the basin are all the regular trading vessels; and the city of Carlisle and the distant mountains make a noble and very interesting back-ground. Perhaps a true critic would say that the town is too close on the edge of the basin, of the niceties of the drawing, however, we do not pretend to judge, and shall give it as our opinion, that the effect of the whole is uncommonly pleasing, and that those connected with the Canal ought to be proud of the painting, and the public grateful for the delight it must yield on viewing it. It is to be seen at Mrs. Hetherton's, Old Grapes Lane. We trust the artist will be rewarded for his labours. - A correspondent."

Little is known of William Brown, the artist. An article in the Cumberland News by local historian Denis Perriam reviewed the life of the ' mystery artist from Maryport' and the following information comes from that source. William Brown was first recorded in Jollies Cumberland Directory, 1811, as a water colour painter of Maryport, although all of his surviving paintings are in oil. In 1815 he advertised in the Carlisle Journal:-

"William Brown, Landscape, Portrait Sign and Ornamental Painter, begs leave to inform the inhabitants of the City of Carlisle and its vicinity that he has commenced business near the English Gates .... house painting and painting in all of its branches neatly executed."

His largest and most successful painting was of the newly completed canal basin at Carlisle. Not only did he depict vessels on canvas, but he also painted the actual ships. In 1824 the local press commented:-

"Mr Brown, the artist, has been this week actively employed in ornamenting the stern of the Isabella', which, when completed, will have a fine appearance."

This ship had been launched at Liverpool and was used by the Carlisle Grocers Shipping Company for work on the Carlisle Canal. William also painted other marine scenes such as those depicting launches at Maryport Harbour. This fascinating figure from the past has left us a legacy of paintings which, because they relate to a time before the invention of the photographic camera, have proved extremely valuable in aiding our understanding of maritime life and technology in Cumbria during the first half of the nineteenth century.

Only one week after the opening of the canal a long report in the Carlisle Journal captured the new sense of optimism following the official opening of the canal:-

"Since our last a considerable quantity of grain of different kinds, has been embarked at this port for Liverpool, Glasgow &c. and continues to be shipped daily. The arrival and departure of sea vessels, a spectacle so novel in this place, the increased number of carts, horses and labourers, and the frequent appearance of sailors in the streets, all tend to give a representation of the bustle and activity of a sea-port, and have imparted a new and vigorous impulse to industry, which must eventually prove highly advantageous to this city and its neighbourhood."

Another section of the same report illustrated the very real hazards that sailors of that time experienced almost daily:-

“The sloop *Menai*, Captain T Geddes, belonging to J.M. Head and Son, a constant trader between this port and Liverpool, and the third vessel in the Procession on the opening of the canal, after discharging her cargo at the basin and taking in another for Liverpool, arrived at that port on the 19th inst. after weathering a severe gale in both passages; in the first of which the Captain was twice washed overboard, but succeeeded in regaining his post at the helm.”

By the following year new ships were being launched on a regular basis. On 12 June 1824, the Carlisle Journal reported:-

"The *Carlisle*, Capt. Geddes, belonging to the New Shipping Company, built at Liverpool, intended for the Carlisle Trade, is expected in the Canal Basin in the beginning of the next week." (Is this the same intrepid Capt. Geddes from the *Menai*, one year earlier?) "A band of music is engaged for the occasion, the Committee intending to meet her in their boat, which will be fitted up for the occasion; the *Isabella* belonging to the Grocer's Company, to be launched this day, is expected in the course of a fortnight, when no doubt the same honours will be paid to her. The coal trade is now become very considerable, and likely to increase, and we are rather surprised that the act of Parliament has not been acted upon in giving a ticket, stating the quantity, to every person leading coals from the canal, to be delivered to the purchaser. We would suggest to the committee to have standard measures for the satisfaction of buyers."

The *Isabella* is the ship that William Brown decorated (See page 33).

The Carlisle Grocers Union Shipping Company listed four vessels on their leaflet, reproduced here. These are the Schooners *Miss Douglas* and *Nancy* and the Smacks *John* and *Crown*, three of which feature on William Brown's painting of the canal basin.

If one looks in detail at the flags on the vessels in William Brown’s painting the ships can be identified.

The Crown

Miss Douglas

The Nancy

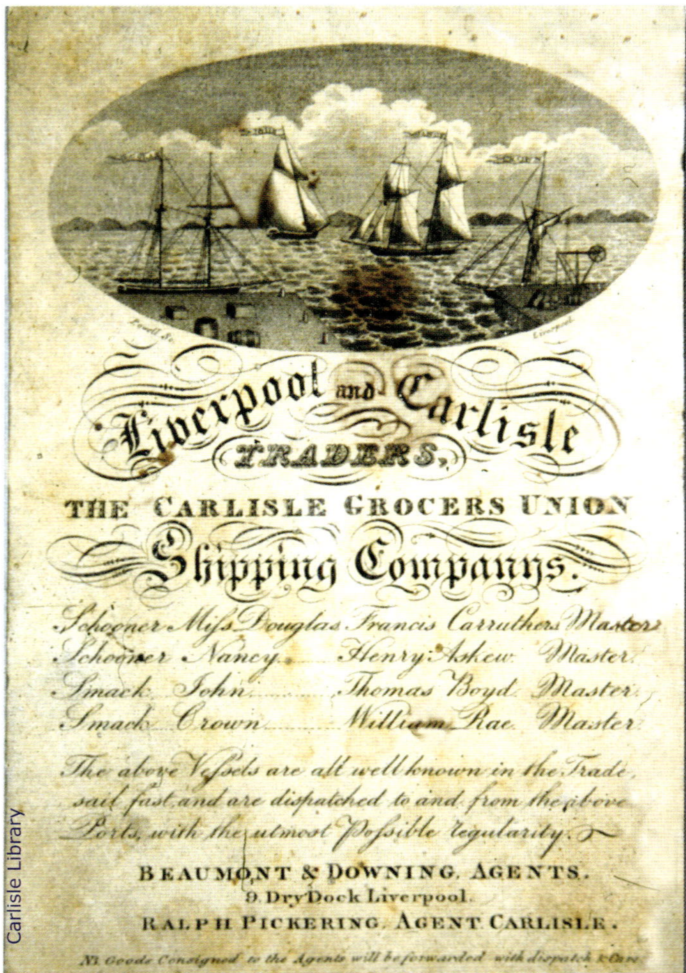

Liverpool and Carlisle Traders,

THE CARLISLE GROCERS UNION

Shipping Companys.

Schooner Miss Douglas Francis Carruthers Master

Schooner Nancy .... Henry Askew Master

Smack John .... Thomas Boyd Master

Smack Crown .... William Rae Master

The above Vessels are all well known in the Trade, sail fast, and are dispatched to and from the above Ports, with the utmost Possible regularity.

BEAUMONT & DOWNING, AGENTS.
9. Dry Dock Liverpool.
RALPH PICKERING, AGENT CARLISLE.

NB Goods Consigned to the Agents will be forwarded with dispatch & Care

Carlisle Library

Problems with water supply

The increasing trade of the canal soon led to the realisation that water supply, particularly in the summer, might become a problem. Every time Monkhill lock was used, water was lost from the upper level. In times of drought the reservoir at Ratlingate (Page 15) might not cope. In order to avoid this eventuality the Canal Committee, decided in April 1824 to cut a channel from a branch of the Caldew "near Mr Donald's Mill" from which water could be lifted to the canal, when required, by an engine. Little did they know at that time how much of a problem this was to become and how long it would take to solve.

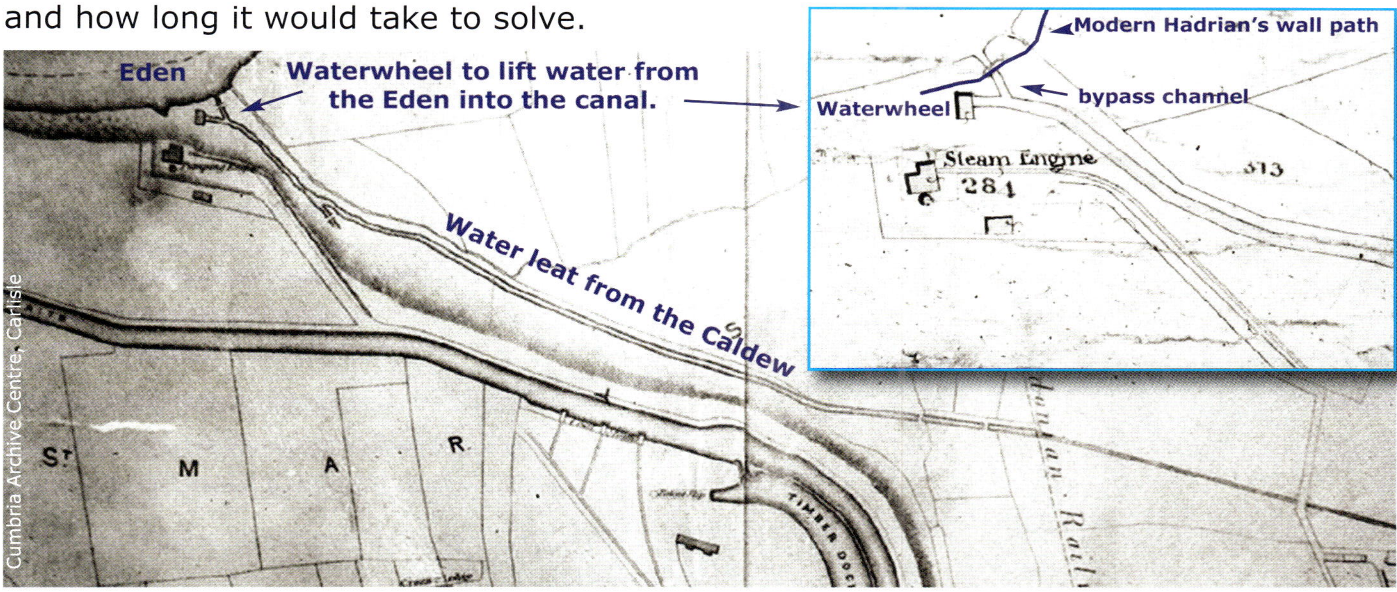

For example - the arrival of the *Carlisle* in June 1824 was an auspicious occasion:-

" ..... a great concourse of people lined the banks of the canal during the greater part of the day, notwithstanding the incessant rain and a strong easterly wind. In the afternoon, the Committee's boat, containing the Mayor and several other gentlemen, proceeded down the canal, and on reaching Burgh it was announced to them that the *Carlisle*, **from her depth in the water**, could not proceed further that day. In order therefore to lighten the vessel, and enable her to move forward, a boat-load of merchandise was taken out of her, and sent up to the Basin, by which she was able to reach her destination on Tuesday. .... Two bands of music were stationed on board the *Carlisle* which during her passage played 'God Save the King,' 'Rule Brittania,' and other national airs, adding not a little to the enlivening scene. When several miles below the Basin, the vessel (decorated with a profusion of colours) was met by many hundreds of persons of every description, who returned on the line of the canal, accompanying the sloop in her progress. After many obstructions, occasioned by her being still too deeply laden, she arrived safe in the Basin, with a number of gentlemen on board, about half-past four o' clock, - when her arrival was announced by the discharge of two pieces of small cannon. In the evening, the owners and a numerous party of friends partook of a profusion of good cheer on board the vessel, where part of the company remained in much conviviality until a late hour.- The *Carlisle* is 82 tons burden, and on entering the Basin drew 8 feet 6 inches water. She is commanded by Capt. Geddes."

The same paper reported that:- " the work had commenced cutting the water course from the head of the Willow Holm, near Mr Donald's Mill, for the purpose of supplying the Canal with water in droughty seasons, like the present."

As Carlisle got used to being a port and familiarity with ships increased, the locals obviously developed their appreciation of good looking craft. The correspondent for the Journal commented that the boat had been:- "highly approved of by the admirers of symmetry and neatness in naval architecture."

The annual general meeting of the Carlisle Canal Navigation Company was held at the Town Hall on Tuesday 6 July 1824. Mr Nanson's report makes very interesting reading as it illustrates the day to day problems associated with a venture of this kind. He reported on the good progress that had been made completing various works that were unfinished at the opening of the canal. The towing path was now complete and in such good condition that no further expenditure on it was likely for many years to come. Much of the railing and fencing of the banks had been completed; more than 100,000 "quicks" (cuttings) having been planted over the winter. Parts of the bank which were weak and tended to leak, such as at Kirkandrews and Monkhill, had been strengthened and leaks were now minimal. The inside slopes of the banks had been much improved by "tampering sods in those parts that were broken by the agitation of the water; a plan that has been found very effectual, and it will be desirable to act upon in other places. Stone pitching for securing the entrance to the sea lock and two overflows, one upon Burgh Marsh level, and the other upon the high level, for carrying off surplus water were the main masonry works carried out during the year. It had been found necessary to make the overflows considerably wider than originally intended, due to the sudden increase in water to which the canal was subjected due to rain or high winds.

The majority of the locks and bridges had been put into the care of the keepers who resided in the houses attached to them. Most of these houses had been constructed during the course of the year and the remainder would soon be completed. It appears that some damage must have been caused to the locks and bridges by passing vessels as Mr Nanson reported that:- "The fifteen bridges constructed on the Forth and Clyde Canal plan have been effectually protected from damage by passage vessels, by strong fenders of timber; so that in a few months the locks and bridges will want no other attendance than that of the men who occupy the houses."

Work on the intended graving dock (dry dock) had been deferred due to all of the above activity, although the site had been excavated as they had an opportunity to dispose of the soil to advantage. The masonry work had yet to be done. A carpenter and smith's shop were being erected on the site and it was intended to start the building of a new vessel before the end of the summer.

The previous year the Committee had expressed dissatisfaction with dock and lock machinery erected under the original engineer's directions. This dissatisfaction had been fully confirmed by the experiences of the past year. The only two bridges constructed on his plan (Grinsdale and Kirkland) were now in a dilapidated condition and were soon to be replaced by bridges of the Forth and Clyde type (See page 22). In addition the faulty lock gates at the entrance to the canal were to be altered to the same construction as the others.

Mr Nanson reported with some pride that there had been no interruption of the navigation since opening, but there were concerns, enhanced by the current dry weather, that such interruption might occur due to scarcity of water. He went on to describe the mill race being constructed and that Mr Lennox had been awarded the contract to build a wheel and machinery for £800 to raise water into the canal. Any surplus capacity of the mill would be put to other use.

The Committee observed that the receipts of the Canal were :- "fully equal to what might have been expected in the first year after the opening of the navigation."

The canal millrace (or water leat) today

Import tonnage had doubled since the first quarter of the preceding year and a considerable increase in income was predicted for the coming year. Finally the Committee reported that they had insured the warehouse against fire for £1500 against the property deposited in it so that the public would have additional confidence in it as a depository.

Possible extension of the canal to Newcastle

The success of the undertaking soon raised the question once more of extending the canal to Newcastle and Mr Chapman was asked to carry out a survey to establish the cost of such a venture.

His report, published in November 1824 costed the scheme at £888,000. This compared badly with the cost of a railway at an estimated £252,000, see below. Chapman commented towards the end of the report as follows:-

"This calculated expense, which I conceive to be materially under what it would prove to be, on an actual survey, must, exclusive of the annual charge of 117 lock-keepers, and 96 bridge-keepers, between Newcastle and Carlisle only, clearly show to every dispassionate mind, the impropriety of any longer entertaining the idea of a ship canal, and that only practicable for those with striking masts."

(i.e. the canal would only take ships which could lower their masts).

horses, and fences, gates and stiles 1 0 9

Equal to 2,205l. 10s. per mile. 5 0 3

Approximate estimate of a railway from Newcastle to Carlisle :—

64½ Miles of Rails, as in the preceding statement, at 2,205l. 10s. per mile	£142,255
Cuts and batteries (excavations and embankments), under the variations admitted by stationary engines, inclusive of the portions nearly sufficiently level for horses and loco-motive engines, admit of no accuracy without an actual survey, assumed at an average of 600l. per mile on the whole distance	38,700
Short tunnel at Lemington, wooden bridge at Rytonhoughs, over the North Tyne, the Eden, &c. under the same predicament as above, but may be assumed at	20,000
Land, inclusive of fences, embankments, and cuts, average width 40 feet on 64½ miles, equal to 310 acres, at 60l.	18,600
	219,555
Temporary damage to land, superintendance, incidents, &c. 15 per cent.	32,933
	£252,488

In the present uncertain state of information as to the whole localities of the way, it would be futile to make any estimate of the cost of stationary engines, with their appendages, or of loco-motive engines; because it has already been shown that the suggested charge of 1d. per ton per mile will be an ample reimbursement on the expense they may require.

...ing and descending navigation, in preference to the shorter, more level, and less expensive line between the Forth and Clyde.

Approximate estimate of a continuation of the Ship Canal from the basin at Carlisle, to the river Tyne at Redheugh, above the bridge at Newcastle :—

117 locks of about 7 feet rise, including gates, difficulty of foundation, &c. at an average of £3,000	£351,000
Aqueducts over the Tyne and Eden	32,000
Aqueduct over the Derwent	7,000
Smaller aqueducts and culverts over lesser rivers, viz. the Caldew, Petteril, Tipple, Devil's water, at an average of £3,000, and about 25 small brooks, at £450	24,500
96 draw-bridges, viz. three in every two miles, at £500 each	48,000
About 32 miles on an average of level cutting, with towing paths, fences, &c. viz. £2,640 per mile..	84,480
20 miles of deeper cutting and embankment, at an average of £4,000 per mile	80,000
10 miles more difficult	60,000
2 miles, viz ; 3520 yards, £10 per yard	35,200
Reservoirs in the high country, on the vales of the Irthing and Tipple, with purchase of land, probably not less than	6,000
Compensation for mill property on the Irthing and Tipple, uncertain, may assume it as	3,000
Incidents superintendence, &c. 15 per cent	109,677
Land at an average width of only 84 feet, will require 10 1-6th acres per mile, viz. on 64½ miles, equal to 655 acres, at an average of £60 per acre	39,300
Temporary damage to Land 1-5th of the above..	7,860
	£888,017

This calculated expence, which I conceive to be material-

Another landmark event for the canal at this time was the laying of the keel of the first ship to be built at the Canal Basin. The vessel was to be built for the Carlisle Grocers' Shipping Company by ship-builder Mr William Bell of Bowness. The Carlisle Journal reported as follows:- " She is calculated to carry upwards of 100 tons burden, measures 54 feet in length, and when completed will be the third vessel to be built expressly for the trade between this port and Liverpool, since the opening of the Canal; besides the *Eden* and the *Curwen*, which were purchased. Including the old traders, there are now twelve vessels engaged in this employ, all of which perform their voyages in little more than half the time that was occupied when the cargoes were delivered at Sandsfield. This important circumstance, added to the the greater number of shipping and the vast increase of tonnage, sufficiently evince the rapid improvement which has taken place in the trade and commerce of Carlisle."

This increased commercial activity depended very much on the city receiving adequate supplies of coal. This was catered for by the *New Coal Company*. Their vessel the *Rebecca* was reported as arriving from Maryport on Wednesday 10th November carrying 41 'waggons' or about 90 tons of coal. The company's vessel *Mary* was intended for the same trade so that the city might, in the words of the Journal correspondent:-

"expect a pretty regular supply of the essential article of coal during the winter months. We would again recommend to the Committee to enforce the Act of Parliament, which compels every person sending coals from the Canal to deliver a ticket, stating the quantity to the purchaser."

There was obviously concern at the possibility of short measures being delivered by unscrupulous traders. The same paper mentioned that Mr Lazonby of Oughterby, who had run a pacquet-boat (passengers, goods and mail) during the summer months between Bowness and Carlisle, was discontinuing it during the winter due to the lack of adequate accommodations for his passengers. It is not clear from the report whether this was just the lack of cover provided on the boat or the lack of a hotel and other facilities at Port Carlisle. Although plans were in hand, the Solway House Hotel had yet to be built near the canal entrance.

The canal and its works still suffered from vandalism from time to time. In November 1824, John Lawson of Thurstonfield was charged with "having wilfully wasted the water of the canal, by drawing one of the sluices near to Moorhouse Road." A similar offence had been committed previously and so the Canal Company employed two men to watch and caught the accused in the act. He was fined 20 shillings with expenses as he was of previous good character and said that he did it out of curiousity. He was very lucky as the maximum fine could have been £20 and according to the Carlisle Canal Act:-

"If any person or persons shall wilfully, maliciously, and to the prejudice of the said navigation, break, throw down, or destroy any bridge, bank, lock, erections of buildings, or other works, created or made by virtue of this Act, every person so offending, being lawfully convicted, shall be transported as felons for a term not exceeding 14 years."

A harsh penalty indeedI

1823. Quarters ending	£	s.	d.
June	197	0	9
September	323	9	1
December	372	19	6
1824.			
March	263	15	1
June	403	3	2
September	373	16	0
December	388	10	6
1825.			
March	414	3	3
June	494	16	2

Improving the water supply

In July 1825 the pumping machinery built to supply the canal with water was tried for the first time and found to operate very satisfactorily. It was reported to be lifting more than a million gallons of water into the canal every 24 hours. However, there were some teething problems The Carlisle Patriot mentioned that:- "The wheel worked well; but the experiment was rendered incomplete by the breaking of a chain and the bursting of a wood pipe, or conduit. The damage was soon repaired; but the duct again burst in a second experiment on Wednesday. Some persons are of opinion that the pressure of the water will be found too great for anything but a metal conduit."

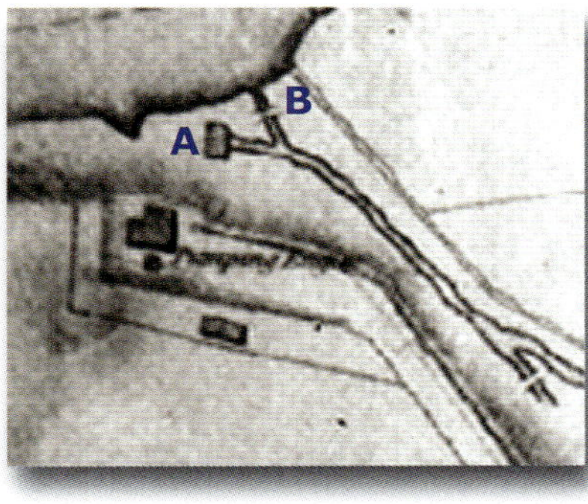

Left: *the water wheel and bone mill seen in winter when there is little vegetation to obscure it.* ***A*** *on the map.*

Below: *a view of the wheelpit from above.*

Above Left: *The wall of the bone mill can still be seen and the archway to the wheel pit is visible at the end of the millrace.*

Left: *the overflow sluice for when the wheel was not in use.* ***B*** *on the map.*

At the annual general meeting of the Canal Committee the chairman reported on the good progress that had been made during the last year. The bridge at Grinsdale Lane had been re-modelled without interruption to the navigation and that at Kirkland was nearly complete, so that all would soon be of the Forth & Clyde type, which had been proved to be sound (see page 22). The waterwheel and pumping machinery had been completed and there was 'no doubt' that it would be more than sufficient for the purposes of the canal. The jetties at the sea locks had caused problems for shipping entering the canal. Damage had been caused to both the jetties and vessels and so they were to be removed and re-sited to improve safety. The cost would be little more than that required for the removal of the materials and the work should be finished before the winter.

By agreement with the Carlisle and Liverpool steam Navigation. Company a small dock was to be built for the use of the steam vessels proposing to establish services between Liverpool and the Solway Firth, the expense of which was to be recovered by an annual rent over a period of five years. The report concluded with a statement of the improvement of revenue of the canal, which had fully equalled the expectation expressed in the previous year's report. The comparative incomes for 1823 and 1824 are reproduced on the left.

Shipbuilding in Carlisle

On Tuesday 17th October 1825 the largest vessel that had ever entered the canal basin The *Linnet* arrived with American Deal. She was described in the Carlisle Patriot as:- "a fine new brig" registered at 90 tons but actually carrying 120 tons.

On Monday 23rd October 1825 'The City', the first ship to be built in Carlisle, was launched at the Canal Basin. The day, according to the Carlisle Journal, was fine, except for two or three slight 'flying' showers and:- "on the whole well suited to the assemblage of a vast concourse of people which gathered together about twelve o' clock, and the place around the canal was very crowded until sun-set."

The vessel was built by Mr William Bell, of Bowness, and launched from his timber yard at the Basin. A bottle of 'spirits' was "thrown at her" immediately she hit the water to cries of "Success to the *City*." The Bell family built ships in Carlisle throughout the life of the canal. Indeed the gravestone shown on this page remembers William Bell; a son of the original Mr William Bell, who carried on his father's business at the Basin and died in 1894. The 1841 census shows that William Bell (Shipbuilder) lived at Canal Cottages with his wife Sarah and children including Dorothy, who is also remembered.

A churchyard survey, made in 1929-1930 of Holy Trinity Church, Carlisle, recorded that William Bell of Bowness-on-Solway died 24 April 1837 aged 82. His wife Mary died five months earlier, also aged 82.

Ships built by William Bell

The Crown - launched Bowness 50 tons -built for the canal.

The City - 23 October 1825

The Albion - November 1826

The Jane - (Smack) April 1829

The Fortuna - July 1827

The Elizabeth - *4 August 1832*

The Blenkinsop - *1838*

Once the launching ceremony was completed the company, consisting of the "principal gentlemen of the vicinity of Carlisle", sat down to the usual "gratifying repast" singing and toasting the night away.

The City was registered at 81½ tons but could carry about 110 tons.

The Formative Years and Middle Age

As related earlier in this book the Solway could be a dangerous navigation for ships. The Carlisle Patriot of 19 November 1825 had a tragic event to report and a severe criticism to make of the authorities:- "Our readers will observe by the shipping news in another column, that the *Linnet*, the beautiful vessel which we lately spoke of as having entered our Canal Basin, was lost on the 10th inst. on her voyage to Maryport, under melancholy circumstances; she struck on the Robin Rig (sic.) sand—bank abreast of Beckfoot, and immediately upset: she was launched only five months ago from the building-yard of Messrs. Peat & Co. of Maryport, was their property, and will be a loss to these gentlemen of at least two thousand pounds: the vessel has not been seen since the accident.

Preparatory measures were sometime ago adopted for buoying the Firth. What occasions the delay? It is of the utmost moment to the trade and navigation of the Firth that those indispensable sea-marks should be laid down forthwith; and the establishment of a light on the shore, near Skinburness, would be likewise found of great advantage. Our trade is rapidly on the increase, we are soon to have steam vessels; and it would be an impolicy, almost amounting to criminality, to neglect what is so necessary to convenience, safety and prosperity. No less than eleven vessels arrived in the Carlisle Canal Basin on Monday last."

Details of the accident were related (as stated above) in the shipping news:-

"The *Linnet*, Daniel, from Carlisle for Maryport, laden with oak timber, struck upon a bank off Beckfoot, on the 10th inst. and upset, and we regret to add, that two passengers, a woman and a girl, were drowned. The crew succeeded in getting into the boat, and landed at Maryport the same day. The sufferers were a poor woman and her child about nine years old, named Thomlinson, daughter of Sergeant Skinner, formerly of the staff of this district; she resided in Caldewgate, Carlisle, but was proceeding to Maryport to receive her rent which was paid by that parish, her husband having deserted her some time ago, leaving her with three children, two of whom she left until her return. At the time of the mishap, she was below asleep; in that state she was surprised by death. Her child was running about the deck, and was washed overboard; she was picked up soon after near Allonby."

In January 1826 Cumbria suffered a long cold spell and the canal became completely frozen over. Trade was brought to a halt but others took advantage of the recreational potential this event offered; in one case with a nearly fatal result. The Patriot, 21 January 1826, reported:-

"On Friday, we understand, some artillery officers, stationed here, and others, skaited (sic.) the whole length of the canal (eleven miles) in about an hour and a half. On Saturday, a man named Tinning, set off from Burgh, on the ice, in skaits, with his market basket. Gliding onwards with great velocity, he suddenly came to a breach in the

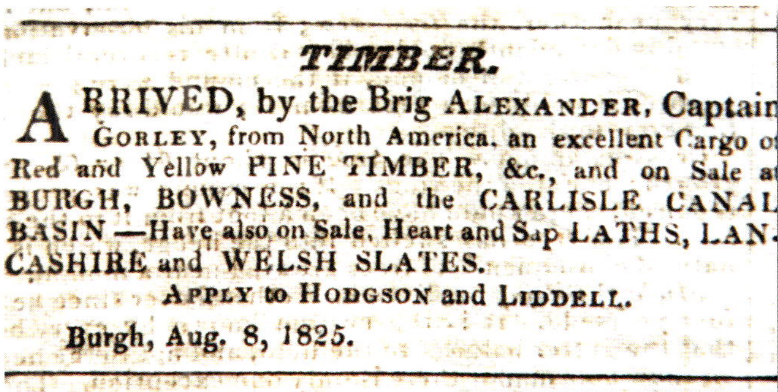

TIMBER.

ARRIVED, by the Brig ALEXANDER, Captain GORLEY, from North America, an excellent Cargo of Red and Yellow PINE TIMBER, &c., and on Sale at BURGH, BOWNESS, and the CARLISLE CANAL BASIN.—Have also on Sale, Heart and Sap LATHS, LANCASHIRE and WELSH SLATES.

APPLY to HODGSON and LIDDELL.

Burgh, Aug. 8, 1825.

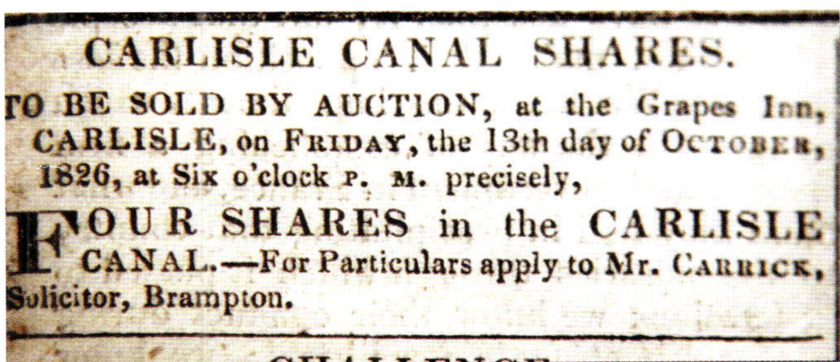

CARLISLE CANAL SHARES.

TO BE SOLD BY AUCTION, at the Grapes Inn, CARLISLE, on FRIDAY, the 13th day of OCTOBER, 1826, at Six o'clock P. M. precisely,

FOUR SHARES in the CARLISLE CANAL.—For Particulars apply to Mr. CARRICK, Solicitor, Brampton.

ice, caused by the opening of the reservoir sluice, not being able to check himself in time, he plunged into the water, overhead, and narrowly escaped drowning. The navigation is again open. Immense masses of ice, from 2-4 inches thick, have passed down the Eden in the last three days."

Shipping.

The Prosperity, Irving, from Whitehaven, at this port, with slate.

The navigation of the canal is completely stopped up, owing to the intense frost of last week; and the vessels in the basin have been detained for the last fortnight.

The Albion, Fisher, sailed from Dublin for Whitehaven on the 26th ult.; about 12 o'clock P. M., the

The next edition of the paper apologised for its premature statement that the canal was open again. Apparently due to the large thickness of ice (eight inches in some parts) the canal remained effectively closed for a further week.

CARLISLE, JANUARY 21, 1826.

So very dense was the frost which we mentioned in our last, that on Saturday and Sunday last, the Eden and the Carlisle Canal were thronged with gentlemen engaged in the delightful exercise of skating. And we hear that one person who ventured on some white ice fell in the Eden, and a lad ventured on some white ice in the Canal, but they were fortunately rescued from their impending fate. The frost continued until Monday night, when a gentle thaw, succeeded by rain, ensued, and rendered the air comparatively mild. The ice was broken up in the rivers on Wednesday. A gentle frost has now succeeded.—The cold was felt during last week very intensely in London, and the frost was so severe that the Thames was frozen over at Blackfriars' Bridge, and we lament to hear that two unfortunate boatmen were drowned, in consequence of their vessel coming in contact with some large blocks of ice. The fog was so very dense that the merchants in the City were obliged to burn candles all day.

The end of January 1826 brought more bad news with the loss of *The City*, the first ship launched at the Canal Basin, less than three months before. She had sailed from Dublin on the 2l January with a cargo of barley for Glasgow and had not been heard of since. The Journal commented that Captain Scott was a single man, but that two of the crew had families dependent on them for support. They hoped that a subscription would be entered into for the benefit of their families. The crew consisted of the master, four or five men and a boy.

NEWCASTLE AND CARLISLE RAILWAY.

THE Directors hasten to inform the Subscribers to the intended RAILWAY between NEWCASTLE and CARLISLE, that they have been induced to defer their application to Parliament for the necessary powers for executing this great public Work until the next Session.

It is their confident expectation that this delay will, in the result, be productive of improvements on many parts of the line, alike beneficial to the public and acceptable to the Proprietors of Lands through which the Way has to pass, and at the same time will effect a considerable saving of expense.

Newcastle, 13th February, 1826.

Plans were proceeding for the proposed Newcastle-Carlisle Railway but, due to the need to consult and negotiate with landowners etc. along the route, it was decided that more time was needed and the adjacent advertisement was placed in the Carlisle Journal to inform the subscribers to the scheme of the delay in applying for the Act of Parliament.

The next event of note regarding the canal was the arrival of *The Cumbria*, a new vessel built at Liverpool for the Carlisle New Shipping Company. The Carlisle Journal, 11 March 1826 recorded the arrival and the subsequent inevitable celebrations that followed, in its usual charmingly descriptive manner:-

"She left Liverpool, under favourable auspices, on Friday morning, (the 3rd inst.,) and arrived at the foot of our canal on Sunday evening, outstripping, at the commencement of her voyage, another vessel which had often floated on the ocean. Her burthen being very heavy, it was found impracticable to tow her along the canal without lightening her of part of her cargo, and accordingly forty tons were transplanted from the infant vessel into the sturdy veteran, Bellerophon, which followed the Cumbria at a respectful distance; the latter laden with a cargo far more volatile than that of which she had just been lightened. Her approach to Burgh-by-Sands was honoured by the presence of many of the principal gentlemen in Carlisle, who celebrated her arrival into the canal with many a joyous shout, and continued enthusiastic cheers. At intervals, loud discharges of powder from the vessel signalised the arrival of the inexperienced sailor safely to her destination. She came into the basin at exactly 25 minutes past four o' clock, amid tremendous cheers from all on board, and the witnesses on shore, succeeding the enthusiastic toast of "THE CUMBRIA." A cold collation had been previously prepared, of which the company partook, highly gratified with the hospitality of the owners, & we believe we can venture to say that there was not one present who did not participate in the pleasure which the proprietors must have experienced, at beholding the flattering reception of the completion of the first voyage of the second new vessel which the New Shipping Company have started:- And we may add, with the same feeling with which it was given and received on Wednesday last, SUCCESS TO THE CUMBRIA."

At the end of March in 1826 a part of the puddle (a thick watertight barrier made with clay), which retained the water in the graving dock adjoining the Canal, gave way. The water in the graving dock escaped into the mill dam below in a great rush. This happening led to rumours that the canal bank had given way, draining the summit level of the canal. However this was not so and the Carlisle Journal repudiated the rumour by stating in their issue of 1 April 1826 that:-

"on the following day seven of our largest and regular traders, with valuable cargoes from Liverpool, took their births along the Canal basin quay, and that since that time arrivals and departures have gone on regularly as usual."

A civic ceremony was held by the City Corporation on Monday 22 May 1826 at which the owners of the ship *Carlisle* (the New Shipping Company) were presented with a set of colours, in honour of the vessel being named after the city. As usual the Carlisle Journal reported on the festivities that followed the presentation:-

"-the company partook of some refreshment, and afterwards did honour to the occasion by the timely quaffings of good punch, accompanied by very appropriate toasts."

The opportunity to celebrate even quite minor events with food, drink, speeches and good company was never missed.

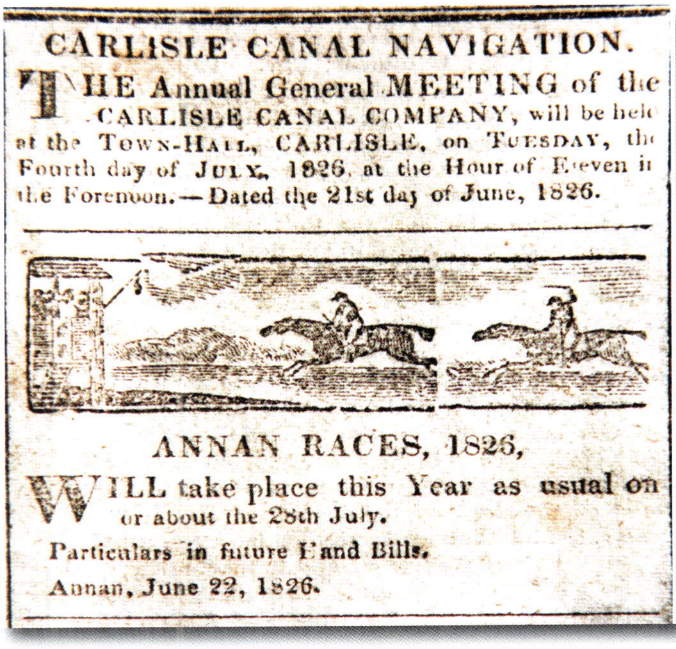

CARLISLE CANAL NAVIGATION.

THE Annual General MEETING of the CARLISLE CANAL COMPANY, will be held at the TOWN-HALL, CARLISLE, on TUESDAY, the Fourth day of JULY, 1826, at the Hour of Eleven in the Forenoon.—Dated the 21st day of June, 1826.

ANNAN RACES, 1826,

WILL take place this Year as usual on or about the 28th July.

Particulars in future Hand Bills.

Annan, June 22, 1826.

Meanwhile the canal continued to further the trade of Carlisle. Weekly shipping notices of the movements of vessels at all of the local ports appeared in the local press. Every now and again an event a little out of the ordinary would occur which justified a more detailed report such as that of the arrival of the *Ellen* described in the Carlisle Patriot of 3 June 1826.

"On Wednesday last, while the wind blew from the west, and consequently favourable, a laden vessel (the *Ellen*) sailed all the way up the Carlisle Canal, in the usual time, without the aid of horses."

Joseph Osborne 'Tracker' and later 'Seed Merchant'

This was most unusual as invariably boats required the help of 'trackers,' the men with horses who were employed to pull the boats along the canal. One of these trackers was Joseph Osborne, who reputedly did well in the tracking business because he had better and faster horses than his competitors. He lived in the bridge-keepers house at Kirkandrews-on- Eden. After the closure of the canal in 1853 Joseph went into the landscape gardening business. Then, when the railway opened in 1854, he took on the job of looking after the new railway station at Kirkandrews-on-Eden. Apparently this did not pay very well (about 3 shillings a week) and to help make ends meet Joseph kept a few pigs. A letter exists from Joseph to the Railway Company in which he asked for a rise "as the pig trade was not, very good."

Apparently no rise was forthcoming because he soon left that job and went into producing and selling seeds to farmers; a concept that was quite new at the time and the firm of 'J Osborne and Sons, Seed Merchants' was born. Joseph was a colourful character, carrying his fiance, Mary, on his back across the Solway Sands to a Gretna Green wedding. The business prospered and Joseph eventually built Eden House at Kirkandrews in a style that "showed he had a bit of brass."

Teddy Robinson (now deceased); was his great grandson and former boss of Carlisle Racecourse. He told me that before Joseph died in 1895, aged 71, he built a small warehouse next door which is still there today. Joseph left two sons James and Henry in the business. James became very well-known over the year for his interest in country sports. He judged wrestling and was involved with hound trailing. James carried on in business until he was 90. His daughter, Evelyn, died in December 1996 at the grand old age of 98, and it was her son and James' grandson, Teddy Robinson, who took over the company in 1946. The firm finally closed in March 1995 after 175 years in business.

When the railway replaced the canal in 1854 it was laid along the bed of the canal. However the railway by-passed the sharp bend in the canal just north of Kirkandrews station leaving a section of canal untouched. This section retained some water and became a pleasant nature walk from the bridge in Kirkandrews, with water hens and other wildlife giving the beholder a feeling of what the canal must have been like. Unfortunately, in recent years this section has been used for landfill and is no more. The pictures below show how it looked in the 1970s.

Cumbria Archive Centre, Carlisle

Baillie Nichol Jarvie - the first Pacquet Boat

Since the opening of the canal there had been a need for a pacquet boat to carry passengers from Carlisle to Bowness to meet the Liverpool steamers. On 17 June 1826 The Carlisle Patriot announced the arrival in the Basin of the *Baillie Nichol Jarvie* a pacquet boat for the Carlisle Canal, purchased by the Canal Company, 'at second hand', in Scotland. The report went on :- "She is advertised to be let; and we think that a spirited innkeeper might make her a source of profit as well as of amusement and utility to the inhabitants of Carlisle, in the Summer Season. Her Accommodations are most ample, with conveniences for a proper division of the company; so that every class of persons may at the same time repair to the Solway in her, inhale the sea-breezes, or perform their ablutions and return home before nightfall."

The article amply illustrates the perceived importance of maintaining and observing the social class distinctions of the time. A couple of weeks later a further report announced that Mr Alexander Cockburn had taken the passage boat for the season. The report continued :-

"On Thursday last, the boat made her first trip down the canal, and returned the same evening, having on board a considerable number of passengers, whom are much gratified by the comfortable accommodation she affords. A band of music was on board, and the attention of Mr Cockburn gave great satisfaction. We are certain that the boat will be found to be a great acquisition to this city and neighbourhood, not only on account of the pleasant mode of enjoying a country excursion, but also will add much to the health of the inhabitants, by the facilities it will afford them in visiting the sea coast."

PASSAGE BOAT TO LET.

THE CARLISLE CANAL COMPANY having purchased a PASSAGE BOAT, are desirous of having the same employed in TAKING PASSENGERS TWICE A WEEK, (or oftener if found requisite,) between CARLISLE and BOWNESS Any Persons inclined to take the same during the Summer Months, are requested to apply at the Company's Office, where the Boat may be seen, and further Particulars given.

N.B.—Several LOTS of GRASS, along the Canal Banks, to be disposed of. Apply as above.

(Not to be repeated.)

PASSAGE BOAT.

BETWEEN CARLISLE & BOWNESS.

THE PASSAGE BOAT which sails between CARLISLE and BOWNESS, will leave the Canal Basin at Eight o'Clock on TUESDAY Morning next, for the Conveyance of Passengers to the SOLWAY STEAM VESSEL, which sails on that day.—The Public are respectfully acquainted that the Passage Boat will ply between the two places whenever the Steam Boat arrives or sails, at hours which will afford the greatest facility of communication.

On 4 July 1826 the Annual General Meeting of the Carlisle Canal Company was held at the Town Hall. Mr Nanson's report recorded with pleasure the increase in Canal dues over the year from £1671 5s. 11d. to £1815 12s. 6d. With a corresponding increase of the warehouse dues the increase in total receipts was £32l 7s. 6d. However, the chairman reported that this would have been considerably larger but for several serious interruptions to the navigation which were not likely to occur again. The principal work had involved the improvement of the entrance of the canal into the sea and the putting of the water wheel and machinery for supplying the Canal with water into an effective state. The jetties at the entrance to the sea lock had been altered by placing them in a direct line along the west side of the cut outside the lock in order to make the entrance perfectly safe for all vessels in all tides. This had proved very successful.

In addition a dock, which had been excavated at the entrance to the canal from the sea in a joint project with the Steam Navigation Company, was now ready for the reception of steam vessels. Mr Nanson also commented on how the design of the dock made use of the ebb tide to scour both the dock and entrance from the sea.This effect can still be seen to this day with the stone dock built ten years later. Large stones are piled in the middle of the dock making it shallower there.

On the ebb tide this causes the retreating water to swirl around the centre, thus scouring the sides of the dock where deep water is needed for the berthing ships.

The chairman's comments re-the work on the water wheel were less upbeat. I quote:-

"With respect to the. water wheel, it has been a considerable source of much regret to your Committee, that the Canal was left by the engineer to depend even partially upon a supply of water from machinery. From the defective manner in which the wheel and machinery had been executed, and partially also from defects in the plan of construction, a very considerable delay took place before they could be brought in to operation. Your Committee were in consequence obliged to call in the aid of a skilful millwright, under whose advice and assistance the pump and machinery have been put into a working state, and are now supplying the Canal with water, there being also a considerable quantity in reserve in the reservoir."

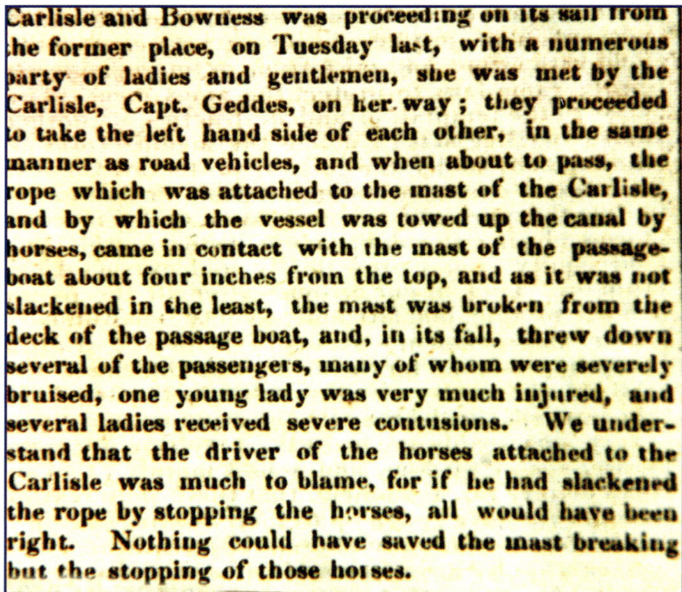

Carlisle and Bowness was proceeding on its sail from the former place, on Tuesday last, with a numerous party of ladies and gentlemen, she was met by the Carlisle, Capt. Geddes, on her way; they proceeded to take the left hand side of each other, in the same manner as road vehicles, and when about to pass, the rope which was attached to the mast of the Carlisle, and by which the vessel was towed up the canal by horses, came in contact with the mast of the passage-boat about four inches from the top, and as it was not slackened in the least, the mast was broken from the deck of the passage boat, and, in its fall, threw down several of the passengers, many of whom were severely bruised, one young lady was very much injured, and several ladies received severe contusions. We understand that the driver of the horses attached to the Carlisle was much to blame, for if he had slackened the rope by stopping the horses, all would have been right. Nothing could have saved the mast breaking but the stopping of those horses.

The newspaper carrying this report also described a serious mishap involving the new passage boat, which had occurred on the previous Tuesday; the same day as the Annual General Meeting of the Canal Company.

Another interesting item in that paper described the forthcoming introduction of a steamboat service between Carlisle and Liverpool. The boat to be called the *Solway* was described as being "very handsome" and intended for goods and passengers.

Two weeks later the *Solway* arrived at Bowness on its first voyage from Liverpool. The arrival was greeted with great pomp and ceremony. From half-past seven to half-past nine, conveyances were continually leaving Carlisle for Bowness. The report in the Journal makes amusing reading as it comments on the effects these events had on the villagers along the route:-

"Among them (the conveyances) may be mentioned two stage coaches, the Herald & the Royal Sailor, with the conveyance by which Messrs. Fairbairn & Wilson generously and gratuitously gratified their friends, both as a compliment to them and in celebration of the event of the day. On the road, Colquhoun, the guard, readily entertained - the company with some of his best tunes on the key bugle; and so great a rarity was it to see two stage coaches on that road, that at every house they passed by - the inhabitants seemed to contemplate the wonder with eyes and mouths both open"

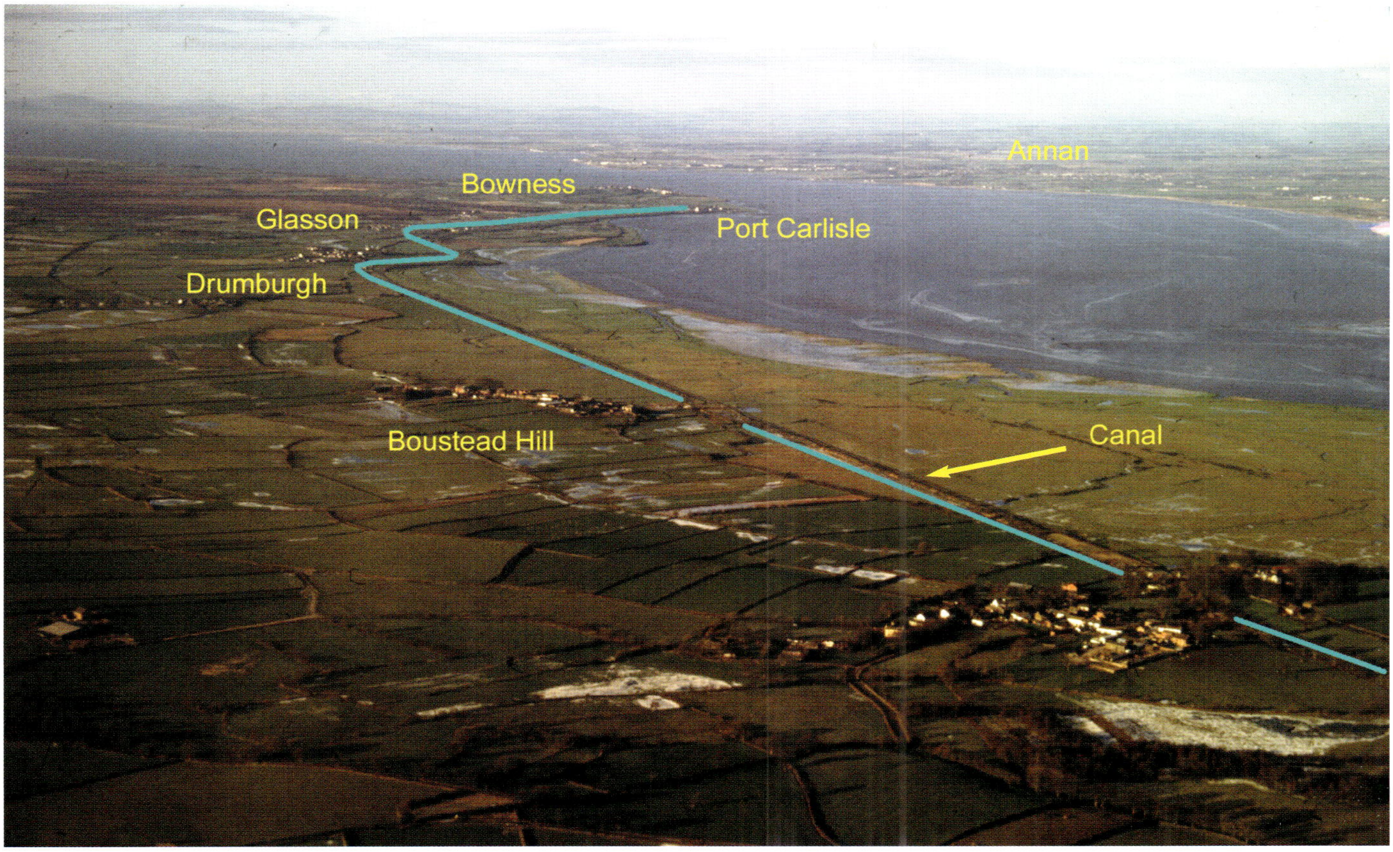

An aerial view of the line of the canal between Brough and Port Carlisle

In addition about 140 people travelled to Bowness on the passage boat for the celebrations. The weather was terrible, raining heavily for most of the day, but, in spite of that several parties went out in sailing boats to meet *The Solway*. The report continued:-

"The humble sailors followed at a respectful distance when the wind being against them, kept the little vessels out at sea for a length of time; so that they were not able to reach land for some time after *The Solway*. On her approach to the jetties, she was accompanied by loud and long continued cheering; and immediately on her arrival, she became literally crowded with visitors, every one bearing testimony to Mr. Ferrier's improvements in the harbour.

She is a fine, handsome, well-built schooner. Her length, from stem to stern, is 133 feet; the beam, 21 feet, 6 inches; and her length, over all, about 140 feet. Her depth, 15 feet, She is registered at 190 tons burthen; but according to carpenter's admeasurement, she is capable of 288 tons burthen."

The article went on to describe in great detail the interior layout of the vessel, the fittings, furniture and the engines. Refreshments were provided in the dining room for all present "patricians, plebeians and fair ladies." In all of the bustle two or three parties were reported to have had very narrow escapes:-

"As one of the small sailing vessels, mentioned above was returning, the crew found that she had leaked, and 'every hand on board buckled to' to lighten her. For want of pumps, hats, shoes &c., were called into requisition; and the vessel just kept her equilibrium, and no more. She however reached shore, bringing her passengers safe. On coming near the shore, a gallant officer of this town was borne on a sailor's back from the bark, and (oh, luckless stars) was spilt from off the wicked tar's back:- a genteel dip was the consequence, and, we are glad to say, *all* the consequence."

Two weeks later the canal was in the news again. The Carlisle Journal, 12 August 1826 reported an accident in the Canal Basin:-

"On Wednesday last, an accident happened at our canal, which had well nigh been attended fatal consequences; but which we are very glad to learn, caused very little more than mere alarm. *The Allonby*, Henney, master, was unloading a cargo of' coals, and a cart, belonging to Messrs. Porter, of this city, was receiving some of the cargo, when the horse attached, being plagued with flies, and the reins, at the same moment, being caught by the shaft, the animal backed; and running against the Allonby, broke the ropes by which the vessel was secured. The ship immediately shoved into the middle of the basin, and the horse and cart were instantly precipitated into the water, with about 21 pecks of coal, which had just been put into the cart. The poor animal, almost drowned, was, as soon as possible, dragged out of the basin into the canal, and then brought on shore; and is now in a fair state of recovery."

It was a very wet day in November 1826 when Messrs. Bell launched their next ship into the Canal Basin *The Albion*, built for the Carlisle Grocer's Union. In what by now was becoming the usual tradition the population turned out in large numbers to witness the scene and to partake of the refreshments served in the hold of the vessel afterwards. After the feast the toasts began as reported by the correspondent of the Carlisle Journal:-

"When the cloth was moved Dr. Blamire proposed 'The King,' `Better Health to the Duke of York,` `Duke of Clarence, and the Navy,' 'The Members,' 'Dean and Chapter,` 'The Bishop,` 'Mr Howard of Corby, and family,' three times three, &c. &c. &c. (i.e. three times three cheers) Capt. Birch proposed 'Mayor and Corporation,` three times three. Mr Blamire, in returning thanks, assured the company that at all times and in all cases the Corporation would be eager to do all the good in his power for Carlisle. ---- 'Success to the Albion, and may she always be victorious!' - three times three and loud huzzas! - 'Commodore Pickering.` 'Captain Boyd, master of the Albion. 'Mr W. Bell, the builder of the Albion.' 'The Canal trade' All these toasts were duly appreciated and met with great applause. - 'Messrs Allison & Martindale, who were the first to build vessels of British oak on Primrose Bank. Mr Martindale, for himself and Mr Allison, declared, that so far were they from being discouraged, in consequence of the early melancholy fate which attended their first unfortunate vessel, The City, that this day was the exact anniversary of the day when the City was launched. It was to be hoped, however, that better success would attend this vessel! He then proposed 'the memory of the late Capt. Scott, who perished with The City!' 'The Grocers Union Shipping Company,' and success to it three times three etc.."

The Mr Martindale mentioned here is the Carlisle pharmicist, famous for his Pharmacopoeia, see the box on the opposite page.

As with previous such events the speeches, toasts and general celebrations continued late into the night. The gentry of those times certainly knew how to enjoy themselves. The Solway steam pacquet was by now a routine visitor to Bowness and did not generally give cause for comment in the local press. However on Monday lst January 1827 the weather was bad. The report in the Carlisle Journal is interesting in that it gives a full breakdown of the cargo carried :-

"*The Solway* came up to her birth (sic) at the entrance of the Canal, in a heavy gale of wind, on Monday last, performing well. She had four cabin and eleven deck passengers, and the following cargo of goods:- 266 bales cotton, 20 barrels flour, 1 iron cistern, 38 ditto pipes, 45 trusses, manufactured goods and yarn, 31 boxes and bags, sundries, 4 casks madder; 5 puncheons iron water, 5 boxes soap, 8 firkins and 4 half-firkins soap, l box, 1 chest lac dye, 3 chests starch, 1 chest indigo; 100 bags salt, 1 cask tobacco, 4 bags coffee, 1 barrel apples, 1 sack nuts, 10 sacks linseed, 27 boxes and chests fruit, 734 bars iron, 22 tierces scrap ditto, l hhd sugar, 1 pun. oil."

For those not acquainted with all of the above measures and items:-

truss -	a bundle weighing about 60 lbs or 27 kg.
barrel -	relates to quantity packed in a barrel (about 32 imperial gallons).
cask -	a barrel of any size.
puncheon -	a cask with a capacity of between 70 and 120 gallons (320 and 550 litres).
chest -	relates to the quantity packed in a tea-chest sized container.
tierce -	a former measure of liquid capacity equal to a third of a pipe or 42 wine gallons
hhd -	half hundredweight (4 stone or approx. 30 kg.)
pun -	probably short for puncheon.
madder -	a red dye from the Madder root
iron water -	ferric acetate (a brown compound) dissolved in water and used as a dye mordant (i.e. used to fix the dye to the material). It was also used as a tonic! (The soft drink 'Iron Brew' contains ferric citrate).

The list gives an interesting insight into the type of goods that were important and of value in Carlisle at that time, particularly raw materials for the textile industry, the building industry, salt for food preservation and luxury items for the shops.

Sawyers 'List of Cumberland Shipping' which was published in 1840 records the *Fortuna* as registered at Carlisle in 1827 and that the ship was owned by 'W. R. Martindale and others. W. R. Martindale ran a pharmacy business in Carlisle, which provided medicines for both human and veterinary use. His interest in the canal trade obviously reflected his need to import a large variety of different raw materials for his pharmacy business. The advertisement on the next page is from Steele's Guide to the Lancashire and Carlisle Railway, published in 1841. W. R. Martindale was the Great Uncle of William Martindale, who was subsequently to produce *The Extra Pharmacopoeia,* first published in July 1883 (see previous page). William, who came from a Cumbrian farming family, became apprenticed to his Great Uncle at the shop in Carlisle, where he worked for 6 years. He then moved to London where, through his business acumen, academic brilliance and pioneering work in pharmacy, he quickly became very successful. And respected in his field. His Extra Pharmacopoeia, is still extant, although now much enlarged, and in its thirtieth edition.

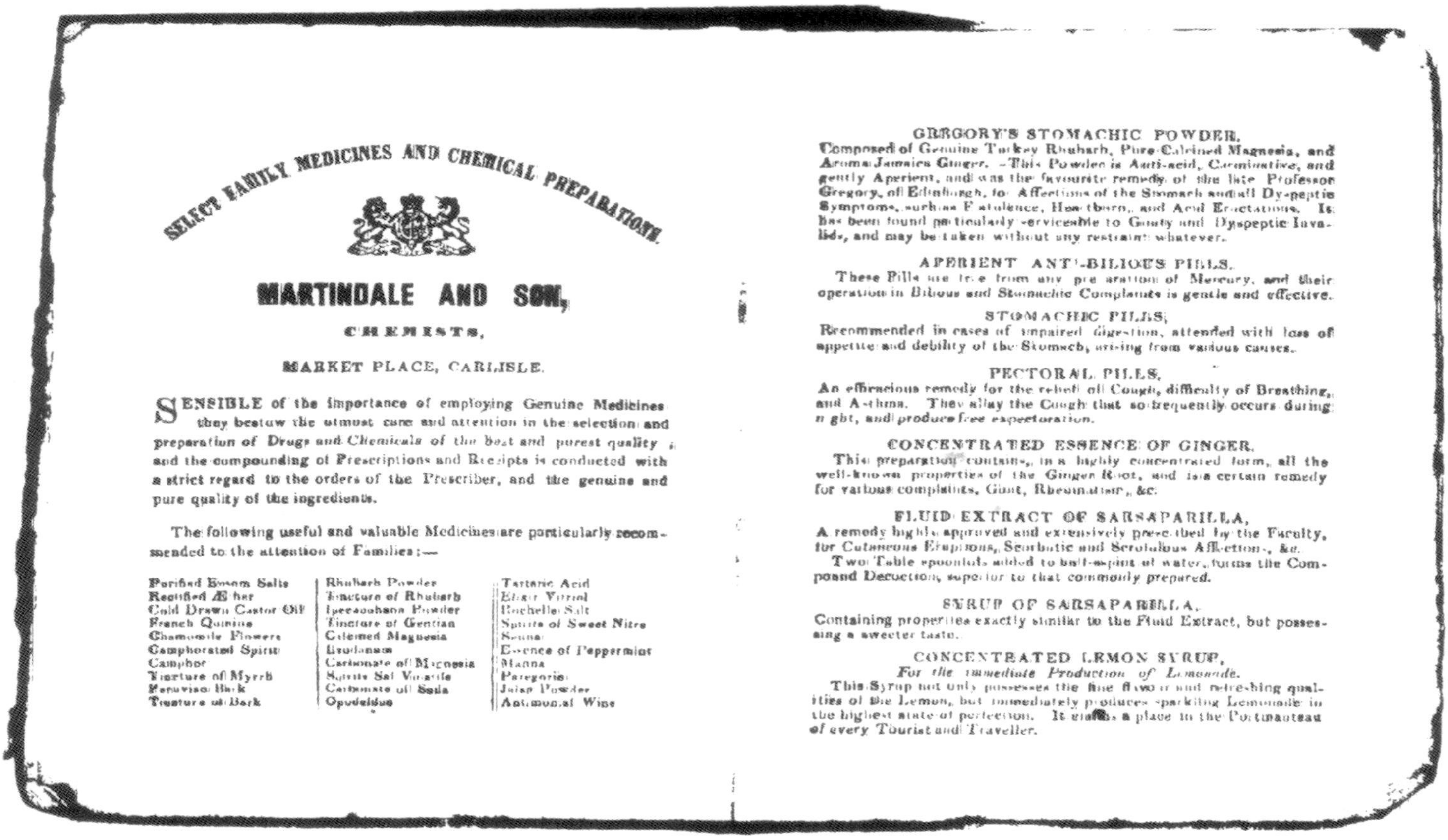

SELECT FAMILY MEDICINES AND CHEMICAL PREPARATIONS

MARTINDALE AND SON,

CHEMISTS,

MARKET PLACE, CARLISLE.

SENSIBLE of the importance of employing Genuine Medicines they bestow the utmost care and attention in the selection and preparation of Drugs and Chemicals of the best and purest quality; and the compounding of Prescriptions and Receipts is conducted with a strict regard to the orders of the Prescriber, and the genuine and pure quality of the ingredients.

The following useful and valuable Medicines are particularly recommended to the attention of Families:—

Purified Epsom Salts	Rhubarb Powder	Tartaric Acid
Rectified Æther	Tincture of Rhubarb	Elixir Vitriol
Cold Drawn Castor Oil	Ipecacuanha Powder	Rochelle Salt
French Quinine	Tincture of Gentian	Spirits of Sweet Nitre
Chamomile Flowers	Calcined Magnesia	Senna
Camphorated Spirit	Laudanum	Essence of Peppermint
Camphor	Carbonate of Magnesia	Manna
Tincture of Myrrh	Spirits Sal Volatile	Paregoric
Peruvian Bark	Carbonate of Soda	Jalap Powder
Tincture of Bark	Opodeldoc	Antimonial Wine

GREGORY'S STOMACHIC POWDER.

Composed of Genuine Turkey Rhubarb, Pure Calcined Magnesia, and Aroma Jamaica Ginger. —This Powder is Anti-acid, Carminative, and gently Aperient, and was the favourite remedy of the late Professor Gregory, of Edinburgh, to Affections of the Stomach and all Dyspeptic Symptoms, such as Flatulence, Heartburn, and Acid Eructations. It has been found particularly serviceable to Gouty and Dyspeptic Invalids, and may be taken without any restraint whatever.

APERIENT ANTI-BILIOUS PILLS.

These Pills are free from any preparation of Mercury, and their operation in Bilious and Stomachic Complaints is gentle and effective.

STOMACHIC PILLS,

Recommended in cases of impaired digestion, attended with loss of appetite and debility of the Stomach, arising from various causes.

PECTORAL PILLS,

An efficacious remedy for the relief of Cough, difficulty of Breathing, and Asthma. They allay the Cough that so frequently occurs during night, and produce free expectoration.

CONCENTRATED ESSENCE OF GINGER.

This preparation contains, in a highly concentrated form, all the well-known properties of the Ginger Root, and is a certain remedy for various complaints, Gout, Rheumatism, &c.

FLUID EXTRACT OF SARSAPARILLA,

A remedy highly approved and extensively prescribed by the Faculty, for Cutaneous Eruptions, Scorbutic and Scrofulous Affections, &c.

Two Table spoonfuls added to half-a-pint of water, forms the Compound Decoction, superior to that commonly prepared.

SYRUP OF SARSAPARILLA.

Containing properties exactly similar to the Fluid Extract, but possessing a sweeter taste.

CONCENTRATED LEMON SYRUP,

For the immediate Production of Lemonade.

This Syrup not only possesses the fine flavour and refreshing qualities of the Lemon, but immediately produces sparkling Lemonade in the highest state of perfection. It claims a place in the Portmanteau of every Tourist and Traveller.

On 3rd March 1827 The Carlisle and Liverpool Steam Navigation Company proudly announced the introduction of their new steam pacquet; The *Cumberland*. The Steam Pacquet Office was in the Main Guard and is the building to the right of the painting by W. H. Nutter on page17.

In the same edition of the Carlisle Journal an inquest, held on the previous Tuesday, was reported on George Lamb, aged 13 years:-

"The youth had left his father's house on Monday of the previous week to go sliding on the ice. He had imprudently ventured on the canal proceeding on a part of the ice too weak to bear him, he fell in, and was drowned. His body was found about 150 yards below the Basin. Verdict; Accidentally Drowned."

A meeting was held at this time regarding the proposed new railway between Carlisle and Newcastle. At this meeting came the first indications that shareholders generally were not very happy with the performance of the canal shares to date. Several of the

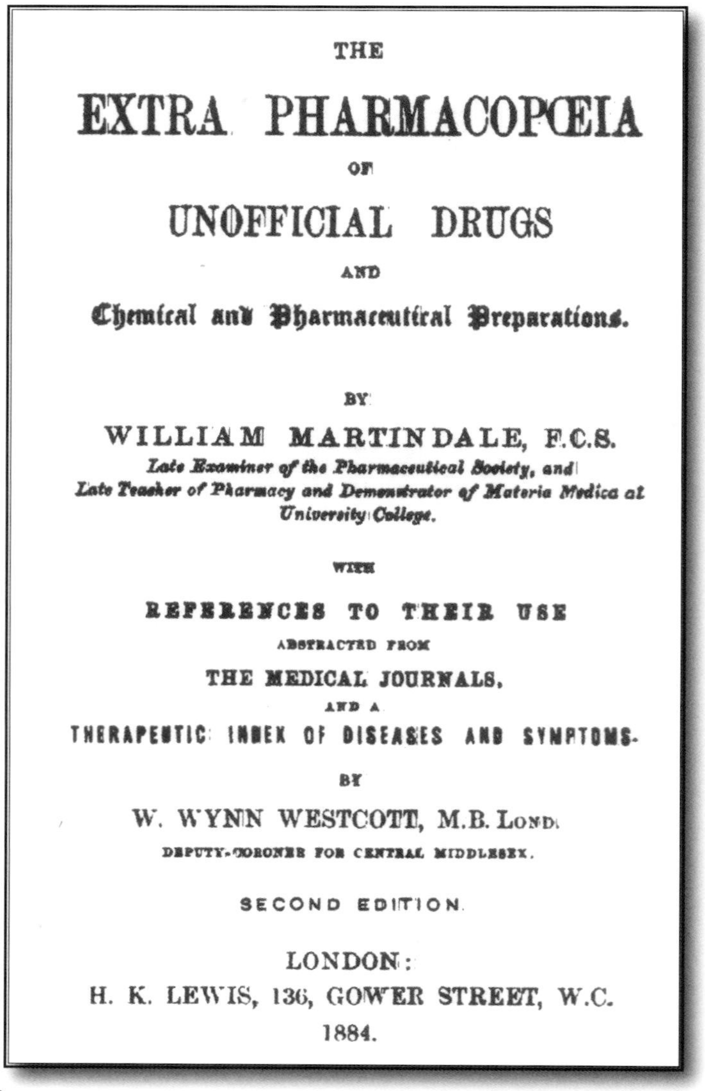

THE

EXTRA PHARMACOPŒIA

OF

UNOFFICIAL DRUGS

AND

Chemical and Pharmaceutical Preparations.

BY

WILLIAM MARTINDALE, F.C.S.

Late Examiner of the Pharmaceutical Society, and
Late Teacher of Pharmacy and Demonstrator of Materia Medica at University College.

WITH

REFERENCES TO THEIR USE

ABSTRACTED FROM

THE MEDICAL JOURNALS.

AND A

THERAPEUTIC INDEX OF DISEASES AND SYMPTOMS.

BY

W. WYNN WESTCOTT, M.B. LOND.

DEPUTY-CORONER FOR CENTRAL MIDDLESEX.

SECOND EDITION.

LONDON:
H. K. LEWIS, 136, GOWER STREET, W.C.
1884.

Canal shareholders urged that a public meeting be called in the city :-

"for the purpose of urging the concurrence and support of the people of Carlisle, in purchases (of railway shares) . There was a demand of shares this day by some Carlisle gentlemen; but it was rather a matter of surprise that the canal shareholders did not eagerly embrace the opportunity of supporting so admirable and lucrative an undertaking. The Carlisle canal was, at present, rather a dead weight than a source of profit. Indeed profit was out of the question. But if the rail-road were once completed, the experience of a few months, nay, a few weeks, would amply prove its benefits. Carlisle and the villages of the neighbourhood would be supplied with fuel at half the price; the basin would become a place for exportation at a great profit, instead of importation at a great expense; a rail-road might afterwards be thrown from Carlisle to Penrith, so that the latter town might also be supplied at a low rate."

The Carlisle and Liverpool Steam Navigation Company were obviously experiencing some difficulty with their accounting procedures for the goods carried on their steam pacquets The Solway and The Cumberland. In June 1827 their advertisement in the Carlisle Journal contained the following statement:-

"The above Company, taking into consideration the liability to errors in the accounts, where freight is received for any distance further than Liverpool, or from thence to Carlisle or Annan, have come to the resolution of taking payment for the Carriage of **Goods betwixt the above ports only, and not as formerly, to Manchester, London, &c.;** and to reduce the rate of all Manufactured Goods to ls. 9d. per Cwt., (gross weight.) in place of 2s., the rate hitherto charged. - They have also reduced the rate of carriage for all Grain and Flour, where the parties find their own sacks; where this is not the case, the rate will be the same as stated in a former list."

Steam vessels in the canal basin were the subject of some controversy at the Annual General Meeting of the Canal Committee in early July 1827. Steam barges were lying for up to a week in the basin acting effectively as floating warehouses for goods coming into and out of the port.

Mr Head complained about the effect this practice had on the income of the Canal Company's warehouse. Mr Dixon maintained that the steam barges had brought much more trade to the canal and that their revenue would not have been anything like what it was, had it not been for the steam vessels. These steam barges were generally used to ferry goods between larger ships berthing at Port Carlisle and the canal basin.

TIMBER ON SALE.

ON Sale, at the CARLISLE BASIN, CARLISLE, and ROCKLIFF, two Cargoes of American PINE TIMBER, of the best quality; likewise a few Thousand Feet of excellent MEMEL TIMBER; also a quantity of Black BIRCH, Heart and Sap LATHS, and Seasoned BOARDS of all dimensions.—Apply to WILLIAM SOWERBY, 14, George-street.

Carlisle, June 5, 1827.

THE CARLISLE GROCERS' UNION SHIPPING COMPANY

RETURN their grateful Thanks to their numerous Friends for the liberal support they have hitherto met with, and beg leave to acquaint them that they have appointed Messrs. J. & R. THOMSON, Strand Street, to be their Agents in Liverpool; in whom the fullest confidence may be placed, & that Goods entrusted to their care will be forwarded with the strictest punctuality.

The undermentioned Vessels are despatched to and from Liverpool with the utmost possible regularity.

Schooner, MISS DOUGLAS, *F. Carruthers* Master.
Schooner, ALBION,.......... *Thos. Boyd...* Master.
Smack,... ISABELLA,....... *Henry Askew* Master.
Smack,... JOHN,.............. *John Rae.....* Master.
Smack,... CROWN....... .... *Wm. Rae.....* Master.

RALPH PICKERING, Agent for Carlisle.

The Steamers at Port Carlisle

The Carlisle and Liverpool Steam Navigation Company was now established with regular sailings from Port Carlisle as shown in the advertisement below. They carried goods and livestock as well as passengers and were very competitive as the "nota bene" N.B. in the last sentence in the advert shows:- "The above Company have come to the resolution of carrying Iron and Grocery Goods at the same rate of Freight as the Sailing vessels out of this Port, after this date."

The service provided by the two vessels was comprehensive serving Lancashire, the south of Scotland and the north-east of Britain and timetabled to suit the Lancashire livestock markets.

Passenger tickets could be purchased at the Carlisle office. An example is shown below.

In spite of the dissatisfaction of some shareholders regarding the profitability of the Canal Company the canal was certainly successful and trade for the city was expanding quickly. New ships were being commissioned and at the end of July 1827 the Fortuna was launched; another vessel from the yard of Mr Bell. Once again there were the usual celebrations with "an ample supply of both solids and liquids" (Carlisle Patriot).

It was six months later in January 1828 when tenders were invited for the surveying and levelling of the Newcastle to Carlisle Railroad. See opposite.

The New Steam Packet

CUMBERLAND,

JOSEPH SEWELL, Master.

HAS now commenced to ply between the CARLISLE CANAL, at BOWNESS, and LIVERPOOL, and Sails every TUESDAY, about half an hour before high water, from the former place, and every FRIDAY, at the same time, from Liverpool.

The SOLWAY is now being repainted, and will again take the birth on the 12th JUNE, from which date the communication by Steam will be twice a week, betwixt the Carlisle Canal, Bowness, and Liverpool, calling off Annan, Maryport, and Whitehaven, to leave and take on board Passengers, sailing from the two Ports respectively, every TUESDAY and FRIDAY.

These Vessels will take Goods from Liverpool to Dumfries, Kirkcudbright, Roxburgh, Selkirk, and Berwick Shires, by way of Annan; and for Northumberland, Durham, Westmorland, and Cumberland, by way of Carlisle; and *vice versa*.

The CUMBERLAND and SOLWAY have Cabins, commodiously fitted up for Passengers, and are attended by Male and Female Servants: Refreshments also of every kind may be had on board, on moderate terms.

This mode of Conveyance is particularly eligible for Persons travelling to Liverpool, Manchester, Bristol, and most parts of Ireland.

These Conveyances will be found very convenient for transporting live Stock to the Lancashire Markets, particularly the Boat that sails on FRIDAY, as it arrives at a suitable time for the Kirkdale and Manchester Markets.

All Goods addressed to Messrs. THEAKSTONE & Co., the Agents at Liverpool, or to the Subscriber here, will be received and forwarded free of Commission, and dispatched by the first Boat after arrival.

For Freight or Passage apply to JAMES BIRRELL, Steam Packet Office, Carlisle.

N.B.—The above Company have come to the resolution of carrying Iron and Grocery Goods at the same rate of Freight as the Sailing Vessels out of this Port, after this date.

Carlisle, 1st June, 1827.

No.

Name

Packet

To

Date

No.

Carlisle & Liverpool Steam Navigation Company's Office.

No. has engaged Cabin Berth from to pr. Steam Packet to sail on

AGENT

The Canal Company was obviously doing its best to maximise profits. The annual general meeting of Ist July 1828 reported that the Committee had:-

"avoided entering upon any work of permanent outlay and had limited their expenditure to maintaining the navigation in an effective state."

Income from canal dues was £2893 2s. 7d.., being an increase of £318 16s. 5d. above those of the previous year. Warehouse dues also increased from £101 18s. 1d. to £141 8s. 10d.

The gross receipts for the year were a grand £3004 12s. 9d. The Committee considered that the canal was in a good state of repair and that the future annual expense for repairs would be "extremely moderate." The proposed railway to link "the East and the West seas" was seen by the committee to be of great importance to the canal and continued:- "- that, the Canal navigation which has hitherto been unprofitable, will rapidly rise in importance, and become, at no distant period a source of profit to the shareholders."

Mr. P. Dixon spoke in very flattering terms of the prospects held out to the Canal proprietors by the proposed railway to Newcastle and moved the following resolution; which was unaminously carried:- "That it appears to this Meeting of the utmost importance to the interest of this Company, that the proposed Railway between Carlisle and Newcastle should be carried into effect, and that every possible exertion should be used in Carlisle and the neighbourhood to promote that object"

The passage boat plying between Carlisle and Port Carlisle only ran on weekdays and Mr A. Graham wished to "direct the attention of the meeting to the proprietary and advantage of allowing the Passage Boat to run on Sundays." Mr. A. Halton stated the reasons which caused the Committee to refuse such permission:- "When the boat was allowed some time ago to run, so much riot and confusion took place on board, from the number of passengers who crowded the boat, that the persons in command lost all control, and great risk was thus run both to the lives of the passengers and to the boat and works on the canal. From a pecuniary point of view the advantage of running the boat on the Sunday was very trifling - £20 being the difference offered by the persons who had the boat for the desired permission." No motion was made and the subject was dropped.

In April I829 the smack *Jane* was launched at the Canal Basin, the fourth boat to be built

NEWCASTLE AND CARLISLE RAIL-ROAD.

THE DIRECTORS are ready to receive PROPOSALS for SURVEYING and LEVELLING the LINE of the intended RAIL-ROAD from NEWCASTLE-UPON-TYNE to CARLISLE. It is proposed to divide the Work into 2 Parts, at a point between the Summit Level and Haltwhistle. The Eastern portion, commencing at Newcastle, and extending to the point of Division, will embrace the extent of about 40 Miles; and the Western portion, extending from the point of Division to Carlisle, will embrace an extent of about 20 Miles.

Persons desirous of undertaking either of the Portions, are referred, for Particular Information, as to the nature of the work, and the Conditions upon which Tenders must be made, to Mr. THOMPSON, at the Pelaw Main Office; if by Letter, post-paid; or personally, on *Tuesdays* and *Saturdays*.

The DIRECTORS will meet to open the Tenders on *Tuesday*, the 5th of *February* next, at 12 o'Clock, up to which time they will receive Sealed Tenders, under covers, addressed to the Directors of the Newcastle and Carlisle Railway, Newcastle-upon-Tyne.

N.B. Tenders may comprise one or both Portions of the Survey.——January 17, 1828.

NEWCASTLE-UPON-TYNE & CARLISLE RAILWAY.

WANTED, 300 Tons of No. 2 BAR IRON, the Scantling to be 3 Inches by 1 Inch, and in Lengths about 15 Feet, to be delivered One Half upon Newcastle Quay, and One Half at the Canal Basin, at Carlisle, before the 25th of MARCH next. Proposals will be received at the Office of the Railway Company, 16, Newgate-street, Newcastle, until the 21st of JANUARY next.

Payment at Three Months after delivery.

Newcastle, 17th Dec. 1830.

by William Bell at Carlisle. By this time such events appear to have lost their novelty as the news item only warranted four lines in the Carlisle Patriot. However the same edition of the paper recorded robberies from boats in the Basin:-

"A few days ago while the Mary Isabella, of Annan was lying in the Carlisle Canal Basin, some person entered her, during the temporary absence of the crew, and took away a silver watch. The Ranger, of Allonby, was also entered whilst lying at the same place, on Friday night last, and robbed of a silver watch, and some wearing apparel."

An interesting item in the Carlisle Patriot (2 May 1829) reported that the Carlisle Steam Navigation Company had completed and brought into operation a telegraphic communication from Bowness to the Canal Basin for the purpose of announcing the arrival and sailing of the Cumberland steamer. The intelligence of the arrival was reported as being conveyed in less than five minutes. This must have been some form of semaphore or flag signal as the first electric telegraph transmission in Britain was demonstrated in 1844 using Morse code. The most likely form the telegraph took would be a flag being hoisted up a flag pole. My reason for supposing this is that the drawing below of lock gates at Burgh - by - Sands was executed by the Rev. W. Ford in October 1830; after the new telegraph system had been set up. The large flagpole seen on the lock keeper's cottage was probably the 'telegraph pole.' One of these on every lock and bridge keeper's house between Port Carlisle and Carlisle would have enabled the signal to be sent by the raising or the lowering of a flag. The only other reference to this system I have been able to find to date was in 'The Citizen', 1 May 1829, which reported:-

"The arrival of the *Cumberland* steamer at Bowness is now made known at the Canal Basin in five minutes by means of telegraphic communication."

The same edition of the Patriot carried the information that:-

William James Blacklock appears to have sketched the same lock from a different position.

"The Canal passage boat will again be set in motion for Bowness, for the season, on Wednesday next, under the same management which gave so much satisfaction last year."

Another item in the same newspaper illustrated the growing importance of Carlisle as a trading port. A meeting of the principle tradesmen in the city with Sir James Graham, Bart, their Member of Parliament, discussed the steps necessary to obtain a bonded warehouse for Carlisle.

Forty one vessels belonged to the port, many of which went to other ports to discharge their cargo. Traders in Carlisle had to pay immediately for their full stock and were thus unable to compete with traders who did not have to pay the duties until the articles were taken out for actual consumption. It was commented that several vessels which were built for the canal had gone direct from the basin to Spain, Portugal, St. Petersburg and other foreign ports. They would have come directly back if a bonded warehouse had been available, so that the merchants would not have been compelled to pay the duties immediately on importation. It was argued that such a provision would not cost the Board of Customs and Excise any more as the existing coast guards at Bowness, Skinburness and Annan would be sufficient to guard against fraud. Another small item in this most interesting edition of the newspaper illustrated the added dangers of living in an age without vaccination protection against Tetanus:-

"On Thursday last, as two boys, of the name of Smith and Hope, were amusing themselves near the Canal Basin making small boats, one of them, while in the act of cutting a piece of wood which the other held in his hand, slipped the knife and cut off the end of Smith's thumb. The accident produced locked jaw, of which it is feared the unfortunate youth will not recover."

One week later, on 9 May 1829, the Journal reported on a further meeting about the proposed bonding warehouse. In support of the proposal it was stated that the annual excisable goods arriving in Carlisle would be at least:

"1200 hhds of sugar, 200 tierces of coffee, 400 puns of rum, 60 pipes of brandy, 250 pipes of wine, 1000 tons of cotton, 250 casks of tallow and 180 tons of tar"

(For an explanation of the units of measurement see page 49).

Good news about the Newcastle to Carlisle Railroad was broken to the population of the city on Saturday 16th May 1829, when the Carlisle Journal reported that the Parliamentary Bill for the project had been passed in the House of Commons. The report continued:-

"To Carlisle it will be of incalculable advantage, leading, as beyond all doubt it will, to a great increase of` trade and commerce. When the work is commenced we trust the Directors will not overlook the superior claims of our native labourers to those of the swarms of Irish paupers, who will probably flock here to take of its benefits."

A racialist comment if ever there was one! Of course the building of the railway was eventually to ensure the final demise of the canal. Nine months later an event was reported that could be viewed in retrospect as being rather ironic:-

"One of Stevenson's locomotive engines, intended for the Liverpool and Manchester Railway, was passed through this town this week, to be shipped at the Canal Basin for Liverpool. The boiler, the only part which could be seen, is very small and compact. Four of Mr Stevenson's locomotives have now been forwarded by our canal."

The weather was quite severe in February 1830. Soup and coal were distributed by the Committee for the relief of the poor and the county's roads were blocked by snow, but the Canal remained open. The Carlisle Patriot 6 February 1830 reported;-

"The canal navigation from Carlisle to the Solway has suffered no impediment. The ice boat passes up and down daily, and thus the canal is kept open, to the great accommodation of the town and neighbourhood"

After more than two years of relatively trouble free sailings the 'Cumberland' steamer ran into trouble in February 1830.

The report in the *Carlisle Journal*, 20 February 1830, ran as follows:-

"The Cumberland Steamer - This vessel had a most dangerous and unfortunate passage to Liverpool on Sunday last. She sailed from Bowness with a large cargo of sheep and cattle, about ten-o-clock, a heavy squall came in, in the course of which the cattle in the hold broke loose, some of them were smothered, and the vessel was thrown on her beam ends. While in this situation the sheep on deck also broke loose, the sea was running mountains high, and the vessel for a while perfectly unmanageable. A heavy sea breaking over the deck, carried the master (Sewell) overboard, together with a great number of sheep; the rudder wheel was destroyed, one boat carried away, and the other rendered useless. In this perilous state the vessel remained for some time, but when the gale a little abated, she righted again, but the concussion threw down the chinmey, which killed some more sheep. During all this time (nearly half an hour) the Captain remained in the water, holding by a rope to the vessel, the crew, in the confusion on board, being unable to render him any assistance. Fortunately he was saved and is now quite well. This is the third escape of a similar kind he has had since he took the command of the *Cumberland*. His wife, to whom he had been married only about a week, was on board at the time. The vessel arrived at Liverpool on Sunday evening, her damage has been repaired, and she arrived safe at Bowness yesterday."

This was not the end of the matter, however. The Carlisle butcher who owned the stock sued the Carlisle and Liverpool Steam Navigation Company for compensation. According to the summons the claim was for 150 sheep, 12 cows, 12 oxen, 12 heifers, 12 steers, and 12 bulls to the value of £500. They maintained that the various animals were not adequately secured. The case was due to be held on Tuesday 17th August 1830 at the Cumberland Summer Assizes. The Carlisle Journal, 21 August 1830 reported:-

"Matthews vs Dixon and others. This was an action against the proprietors of the *Cumberland* steam vessel for damage sustained by the plaintiffs, by the loss of sheep and cattle during a storm, when a great number were lost overboard. On the case being called on Mr Brougham stated that it had been settled out of Court, the defendants agreeing to pay £375 damages and costs. The case had excited considerable interest, and the court was much crowded on Tuesday morning."

The Pacquet Boat Cumberland - Storm on the Firth *Joseph Heard (1840)*

Indeed, such was the interest in the event that the artist Joseph Heard later painted his interpretation of the scene entitled 'Storm on the Firth'. The captain, Mr Joseph Sewell, who was washed overboard, can be seen in the water at the stern of the boat.

During the next few years there was intense competition between the pacquet steamers, each trying to outdo the other for service and reliability. In 1834 the Carlisle Grocers' Union sold their fleet of sailing ships and purchased the *City of Carlisle* for their newly created Carlisle and Annan Steam Navigation Company. The advertisements below indicate how intense the competition was and this continued right up to the closure of the canal many years later.

TO MERCHANTS, GROCERS, AND THE PUBLIC IN GENERAL.

THE CARLISLE GROCERS' UNION SHIPPING COMPANY beg leave to state that in the course of two or three weeks they will discontinue their line of Sailing Vessels between this Port and Liverpool;—and return their most grateful acknowledgments for the very liberal support they have received in the trade, which they trust will be continued to their successors, the Carlisle and Annan Steam Navigation Company.

THE CARLISLE and LIVERPOOL STEAM NAVIGATION COMPANY'S PACKET, *CUMBERLAND*, having received new Boilers and other considerable Improvements, will be on the Station again on SATURDAY the 16th inst., and for the accommodation of the Public will run *Three Trips in the Fortnight*, in place of Once a Week, as formerly.

The above Vessel has excellent accommodation for Passengers in the Cabin and on Deck, and is attended by Male and Female Servants. Refreshments also of every kind may be had on board, on reasonable Terms.

Fares from Liverpool to Whitehaven and Maryport, and vice versa.

CABIN 10s. DECK 4s.

Do. do. *Liverpool to Annan & Bowness, & vice versa.*

CABIN 15s. DECK 5s. Steward's fees included.

The following are the Hours appointed for her Sailing:

FROM LIVERPOOL.

July 16,	Saturday, ...	4 o'Clock,	Afternoon
22,	Friday, ...	9	Morning
27,	Wednesday, ...	1	Afternoon
August 1,	Monday, ...	4	Do.
6,	Saturday, ...	9	Evening
11,	Thursday,..........	1	Afternoon
15,	Monday, ...	4	Do.
20,	Saturday, ...	9	Evening

THE

CARLISLE AND ANNAN STEAM NAVIGATION COMPANY

BEG leave to inform the Merchants, Manufacturers, Cattle Dealers, and all concerned in the Liverpool and Manchester Trade, that their splendid New Steam Packet, the

"*CITY OF CARLISLE,*"

JOHN HUDSON, Master,

Will Sail from LIVERPOOL, on WEDNESDAY Morning, the 28th of MAY, with Goods and Passengers, and from PORT CARLISLE, on THURSDAY Afternoon, the 29th.

FARES.

From Liverpool to Port Carlisle and Annan Waterfoot, and *vice versa*,

Cabin, 15s. Deck, 5s. Steward's Fees included.

This Company have made arrangements with Mr. BENSON, Queensberry Arms, Annan, to forward Passengers from the Vessel to Mr. FRASER'S, King's Arms Inn, DUMFRIES, from whence there are Coaches to all parts of the North daily; and with Mr. FRASER, to forward Passengers from Dumfries to the Vessel at Annan Waterfoot on her day of Sailing.

The following additions to the Whitehaven Steam Company's Advertisment came to hand after our front page had been put to press:—"CONVEYANCE BY THE SAINT ANDREW, STEAM BOAT, TO CARLISLE ASSIZES:—At Five o'Clock on Monday morning, the 11th August next, the Steam Boat, St. Andrew, will sail from Whitehaven for Carlisle Canal Foot, direct, calling off Workington and Maryport, for the purpose of taking Passengers. The Fly Boat on the Canal will be in readiness to take the Passengers forward to the City immediately on the arrival of the St. Andrew.—Magistrates, Solicitors, Jurors, Witnesses, and others having business at the Assizes, will find this by much the pleasantest, cheapest, and most expeditious means of accomplishing their Journey to Carlisle.—Should a sufficient Number of Passengers from the Assizes offer, the Saint Andrew will sail from the Canal Foot on Sunday the 17th of August, at Three o'Clock, for Whitehaven, calling off Maryport and Workington. The latter Voyage will offer an excellent Opportunity to Parties from Whitehaven desirous of viewing the beautiful Scenery on the Borders of the Solway.

Fares to the Canal Foot, Cabin 10s., Deck 5s.

Parties going up and returning the same voyage will be charged the above Fare only.

☞ The St. Andrew will Sail from this Port for Dublin on Friday Morning at Half-past Three o'Clock."

Apart from the regular timetabled services steamship specials were organised for events such as horse-racing or the Assizes in Carlisle. See the advertisement for the *Saint Andrew* at the bottom of page 58. Note that the fare includes free passage along the canal from Port Carlisle to the Canal Basin and that the chance to view the beautiful scenery along the route is emphasised.

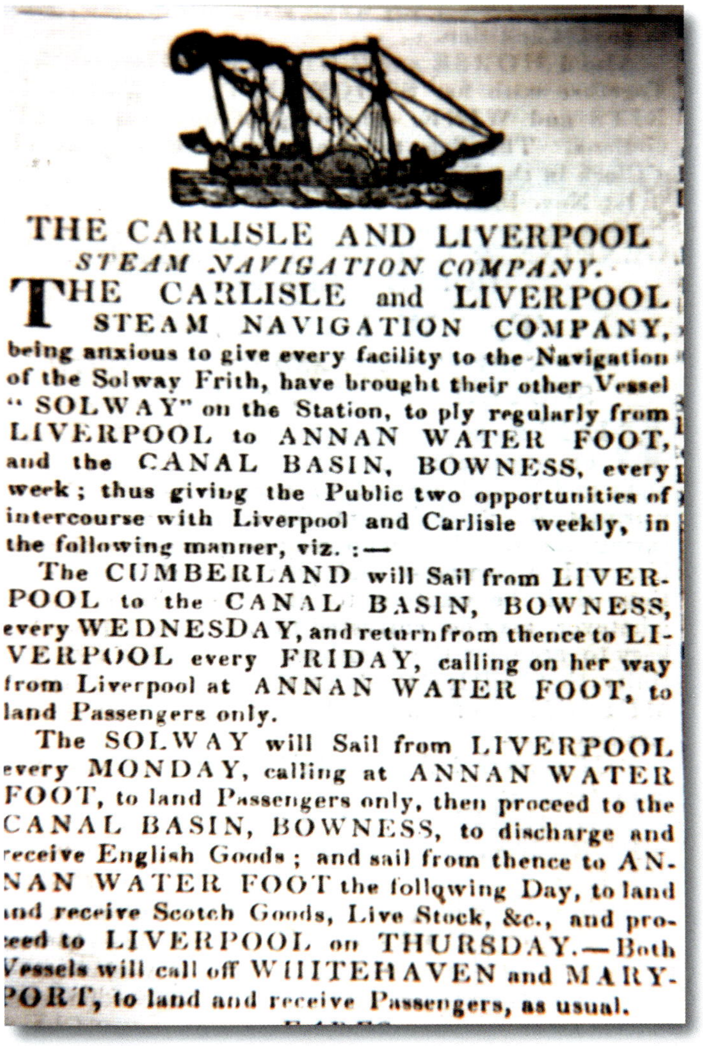

THE CARLISLE AND LIVERPOOL
STEAM NAVIGATION COMPANY.

THE CARLISLE and LIVERPOOL STEAM NAVIGATION COMPANY, being anxious to give every facility to the Navigation of the Solway Frith, have brought their other Vessel "SOLWAY" on the Station, to ply regularly from LIVERPOOL to ANNAN WATER FOOT, and the CANAL BASIN, BOWNESS, every week; thus giving the Public two opportunities of intercourse with Liverpool and Carlisle weekly, in the following manner, viz. :—

The CUMBERLAND will Sail from LIVERPOOL to the CANAL BASIN, BOWNESS, every WEDNESDAY, and return from thence to LIVERPOOL every FRIDAY, calling on her way from Liverpool at ANNAN WATER FOOT, to land Passengers only.

The SOLWAY will Sail from LIVERPOOL every MONDAY, calling at ANNAN WATER FOOT, to land Passengers only, then proceed to the CANAL BASIN, BOWNESS, to discharge and receive English Goods; and sail from thence to ANNAN WATER FOOT the following Day, to land and receive Scotch Goods, Live Stock, &c., and proceed to LIVERPOOL on THURSDAY.—Both Vessels will call off WHITEHAVEN and MARYPORT, to land and receive Passengers, as usual.

Remains of the original steamer pier at Port Carlisle

In March 1831 an incident occurred in Caldewgate which illustrated the antagonism between the keepers of law and order and the common people who inhabited that place. The Patriot reported as follows:-

"DISGRACEFUL OUTRAGE - Last week, upon the occasion of Mr Batty, late superintendent of police here, leaving Carlisle for Manchester, a most scandalous attack was made upon him by a gang of weavers and others, composed of men, women and boys, as he proceeded to the lighter at the Canal Basin, which was to convey him and his family to the steam-pacquet for Liverpool. They had obtained information of Mr Batty's intended departure, and had collected in groups prepared to assault him as he passed to the Canal. After being pursued by them along a part of Caldewgate, Mr Batty with some difficulty succeeded in taking refuge in the lighter, where the infuriated mob instantly followed him, and but for the exertions of the crew, who hastened to secure Mr Batty in the cabin, they would, in all probability, have laid violent hands on him. As it was, they followed the vessel for a considerable distance, throwing stones at it, and assailing those on board with the most hideous yells. It need scarcely be added, that it was Mr Batty's vigilance as an officer of police which had excited this disgraceful feeling of rage and violence towards him."

Benjamin Batty was the first superintendent (chief officer) of the newly formed Carlisle Police Force. He was in post from 3 February 1827 to 9 March 1831. In 1829, writing about the city's new police force, the compiler of the *History, Directory and Gazetteer of the Counties of Cumberland and Westmorland* wrote:-

"so successful have been his (Mr Batty's) efforts, that Carlisle now ranks as one of the most peaceable cities in the kingdom, though Mr Batty and the officers under him met with serious resistance from the Irish, Scotch and other weavers in Shaddongate unused to the interference of an effective police. The officers have since exercised their functions without opposition, and peace and property are now as well preserved here as in any other place in his Majesty's dominions."

This explains the animosity of some of the less celubrious residents of Caldewgate to Chief Batty after he had retired. The full history of the Carlisle City Police Force is recorded in 'Watching Over Carlisle', published by the author of this book.

Deaths from infectious disease were common and quarantine was often the only protection available. The Patriot, 2 July 1831 reported :-

"The walls of this city were, on Tuesday last, plastered with copies of the King's proclamation, ordering the laws of quarantine to be punctually obeyed by the masters and owners of all vessels containing goods and passengers from the Baltic."

The article went on to express the hope that we would be protected from the fatal malady currently affecting the countries bordering the Baltic. Many of the ships using the canal basin brought in cargoes of timber from the Baltic ports.

The Carlisle Journal, 2 July 1831, advertised the sale of the yacht *Elizabeth* and, more interestingly, a notice of commencement of business in Castle Street by a recently arrived baker to the city named Jonathan Dodgson Carr. A few years later, as we shall see, he was to open his biscuit works and flour mill adjacent to the Canal Basin. The Carlisle and Liverpool Steam Navigation Company were obviously prospering at this time. They had refurbished the *Cumberland* and fitted new boilers and they were to run three trips a fortnight instead of one a week between the two ports.

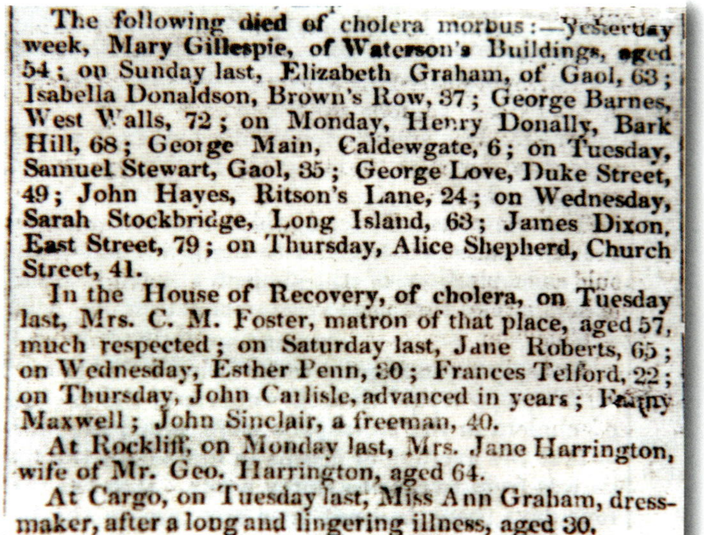

The following died of cholera morbus:—Yesterday week, Mary Gillespie, of Waterson's Buildings, aged 54; on Sunday last, Elizabeth Graham, of Gaol, 63; Isabella Donaldson, Brown's Row, 37; George Barnes, West Walls, 72; on Monday, Henry Donally, Bark Hill, 68; George Main, Caldewgate, 6; on Tuesday, Samuel Stewart, Gaol, 35; George Love, Duke Street, 49; John Hayes, Ritson's Lane, 24; on Wednesday, Sarah Stockbridge, Long Island, 63; James Dixon, East Street, 79; on Thursday, Alice Shepherd, Church Street, 41.

In the House of Recovery, of cholera, on Tuesday last, Mrs. C. M. Foster, matron of that place, aged 57, much respected; on Saturday last, Jane Roberts, 65; on Wednesday, Esther Penn, 30; Frances Telford, 22; on Thursday, John Carlisle, advanced in years; Fanny Maxwell; John Sinclair, a freeman, 40.

At Rockliff, on Monday last, Mrs. Jane Harrington, wife of Mr. Geo. Harrington, aged 64.

At Cargo, on Tuesday last, Miss Ann Graham, dress-maker, after a long and lingering illness, aged 30.

Just a small example from the newspaper of the vulnerability of the population at this time to death from infectious diseases.

Vaccines were not common although smallpox could be prevented by immunisation with a cowpox vaccine.

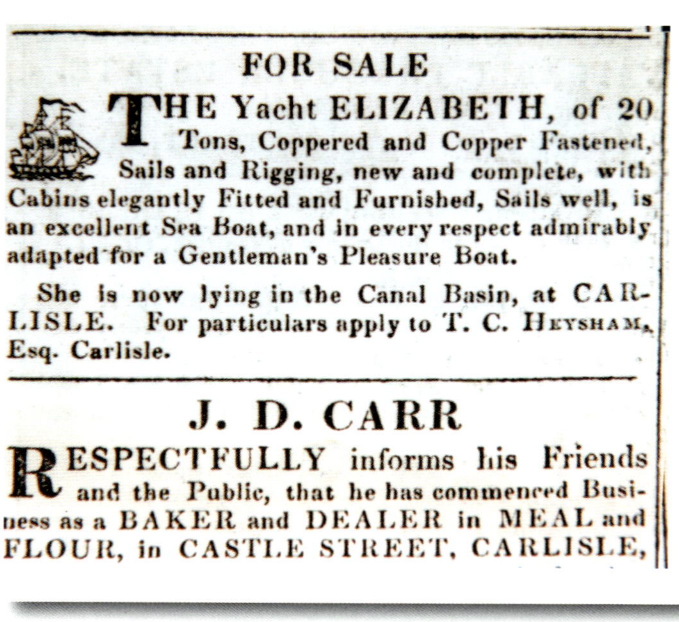

FOR SALE

THE Yacht ELIZABETH, of 20 Tons, Coppered and Copper Fastened, Sails and Rigging, new and complete, with Cabins elegantly Fitted and Furnished, Sails well, is an excellent Sea Boat, and in every respect admirably adapted for a Gentleman's Pleasure Boat.

She is now lying in the Canal Basin, at CARLISLE. For particulars apply to T. C. HEYSHAM, Esq. Carlisle.

J. D. CARR

RESPECTFULLY informs his Friends and the Public, that he has commenced Business as a BAKER and DEALER in MEAL and FLOUR, in CASTLE STREET, CARLISLE,

Emigrants to the New World via the Carlisle Canal

The canal was an obvious route for those leaving to seek their fortunes in the New World. Many Cumbrians took the route along the canal to catch the Liverpool steamer, from where they would depart for the Americas. This report in the Carlisle Journal (23 July 1831) illustrates the numbers involved :-

> Several families from this city and neighbourhood, and also from Penrith, passed down our Canal during the early part of this week, to embark at Annan Waterfoot for the Canadas, as emigrants.

> EMIGRATION.—A number of Prussians from Magdeburgh, some time ago purchased a tract of land in Upper Canada, lying between Montreal and Quebec, to which they are now emigrating. About a fortnight ago, 130 of the party passed through this city, on their route. On Thursday last 218 more of the emigrants arrived here by the Newcastle and Carlisle Railway, and were conveyed in the lighters to Port Carlisle, where they embarked on board the City of Carlisle steamer, for Liverpool.

"The number of families which has (sic) emigrated to America this season from this city and the neighbourhood is truly astonishing. During the last month upwards of 60 individuals have gone from Botchergate and Warwick Bridge, and bid adieu to their native land; and we are informed that several others are preparing themselves to follow this example. An agency has been established in the city for some time by which intending emigrants can now arrange everything necessary for their departure and be put in possession of that information here which could formerly be got only at the port of embarkation; and hence many, no doubt, have been led to emigrate who, probably, in other circumstances, would not have thought of it."

Once the Newcastle to Carlisle Railway was fully opened in 1838 many people from Europe travelled overland to the coast where they embarked on ships for Newcastle. They then took the train to London Road Station from where they travelled by horse-drawn omnibus to the canal basin (as the line from London Road to the canal was only a goods line). They then took the passage boat or a lighter belonging to the steamship company to Port Carlisle. They could then take a steamer to Annan, Whitehaven or Liverpool depending where their emigrant ship to Upper Canada or the Americas was sailing from.

The canal offered a quick method of dispatch for those poor souls who wished to end their lives for whatever reason. On 9th July 1831 the Patriot reported:-

"ATTEMPTED SUICIDE" - On Thursday morning last, about five o' clock, a respectable female, who resides in Scotch Street, was observed, at that early hour, walking on the banks of the canal. At a period when she thought she was unobserved by any one, she took off her bonnet and shawl, which she hung upon a thorn tree, and immediately threw herself into the water of the canal. Two men who witnessed the transaction instantly ran to her assistance, got her from the water, and conveyed her to an adjoining house, where she shortly afterwards recovered. Disappointment in marriage is said to be the cause of this rash act, and, if we are rightly informed, this poor female, who is yet but young in life, has been the victim of as much perfidy and ill-usage as any unprincipled lover had ever to atone for."

The Carlisle Journal reported the incident in like fashion under the title 'Effects of Love.' In that report the 'adjoining house' mentioned above, was:-

"Mr. Wm. Underwood's, Green Dragon Inn, Newtown, where the usual means for restoring suspended animation were used."

The increase in frequency of the sailings of the steamer *Cumberland* appeared to have paid off. On 17 September 1831 the Journal reported:-

"The *Cumberland* steamer, after a most successful season, having - rarely, if ever, failed in accomplishing her extra trip between this port and Liverpool, has returned to her old times of sailing for the season – viz Tuesdays and Thursdays."

The long awaited opening of the new hotel at Fisher's Cross, or Knox Cross (later Port Carlisle) was advertised in the Carlisle Journal (8 October 1831). The photograph shows the hotel today, it is now a private house called Solway House. This hotel was provided to provide accommodation en-route for travellers embarking or disembarking the Liverpool steamers and also for weekend visitors from Carlisle. Port Carlisle was seen as a fine place to escape from city life at the weekend; to take the salt air and to benefit from a bathe in salt water. This was the first step in making Port Carlisle into a spa-type resort for the local population. A couple of weeks later Mr Jeffery Peat, acting in the true spirit of free enterprise of the time, offered a rival mode of transport to the canal passage boat between Port Carlisle and Carlisle.

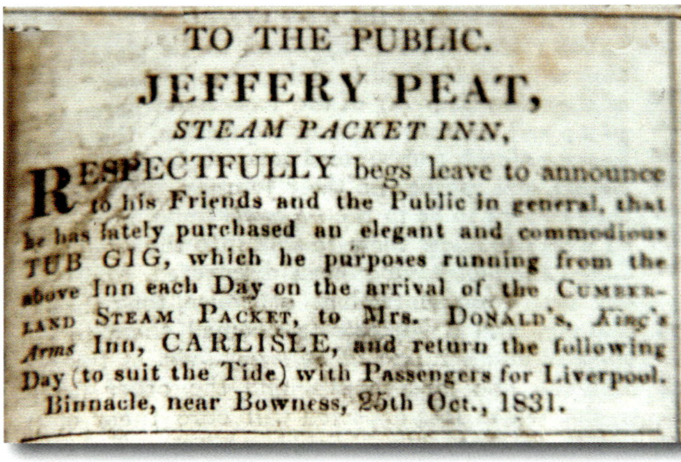

TO THE PUBLIC.

JEFFERY PEAT,

STEAM PACKET INN,

RESPECTFULLY begs leave to announce to his Friends and the Public in general, that he has lately purchased an elegant and commodious TUB GIG, which he purposes running from the above Inn each Day on the arrival of the CUMBERLAND STEAM PACKET, to Mrs. DONALD'S, *King's Arms* Inn, CARLISLE, and return the following Day (to suit the Tide) with Passengers for Liverpool.

Binnacle, near Bowness, 25th Oct., 1831.

In fact in 1819, before building of the canal commenced, there was very little at Fisher's Cross (or Knox Cross as it was also known) apart from the Custom House. The Georgian village of Port Carlisle developed very quickly with the arrival of the canal. that is what makes it so special. Almost all of the buildings date from the same era.

The building of a bonded warehouse came a step nearer in November 1831 after a meeting of the merchants and grocers of

Solway House Hotel.
Now a private residence.

Carlisle. Several took up shares and "arrangements were entered into for immediately commencing the work." The Journal commented that this was further proof of the rapidly increasing mercantile importance of Carlisle.

However, at a meeting with the Canal Committee on the 17 December the tradesmen were unable to come to agreement with the Committee on details such as the length of lease etc. and abandoned their plans to build their own bonded warehouse. All was not lost because the Canal Committee then went on to assure those present that they would build the warehouse themselves as soon as possible. Preparations went ahead and it was announced on the 11 February 1832 that building would commence immediately. The Carlisle Patriot explained in more detail:-

"A Bonding Warehouse is about to be erected by the Carlisle Canal Company, over their vaults, adjoining the Canal Basin. It is, we understand, to be but one storey, though of spacious dimensions. It is intended to appropriate the vaults also as stores for Bonded Goods. Such an establishment will enable the tradesmen of Carlisle to avail themselves of all the advantages to be derived from this being made a Bonding Port."

The Patriot continued with an item of news about the waterwheel:- "The engine employed for conveying a portion of the water of the Caldew to the Canal, is about being applied to the purpose of grinding bones for manure, in addition to its present use. A mill is to be erected above the engine house for that purpose."

The Journal of the same date reported on the weather which had been 'wet and boisterous' earlier in the week. The Eden and Caldew rivers had flooded the low areas around the city. The report went on:-

"In Caldewgate, the houses of a great number of poor persons were flooded to a considerable depth, and continued in that state the whole of Monday night. We are happy to state that these persons have been relieved by the Committee for the relief of the Poor, who have distributed coals among them to the amount of £l0."

So far the impression may have been given that everyone was happy with the service provided by the local carriers, which advertised so regularly in the press. A letter printed by the Journal (18 February 1832) shows that one person at least, who preferred to remain anonymous, was not satisfied with the service received.

London.

The Commissioners of Customs have, by an order of the 29th of last month, approved of premises at the Canal Basin in the port of Carlisle, for the deposit of tobacco under bond, for home consumption and shipment as stores. This measure will be a great accommodation, not only to the manufacturers of that article in Carlisle, but to those in the neighbouring towns of Penrith, Brampton, Hawick, Annan, &c.

TO THE EDITOR OF THE CARLISLE JOURNAL.

Sir, -- The Carlisle Steam Navigation Company cannot surely be aware of the unaccountable delay that invariably takes place in the delivery of goods they bring for Annan and the neighbourhood.The goods certainly go by steam when at sea; but may be said to lie dormant after arriving at the Binnacle. Whether the blame belongs to your side of the water or to ours is their "look-out;" but it is quite notorious that, when the steam-vessel arrives at Binnacle on Wednesday, we never get our goods delivered here till the following Monday afternooon, thus taking *five* days to come *four miles*.

By giving this insertion, you will oblige,

Sir, your obedient servant,

Annan, 2nd February, 1832. A CONSTANT READER.

On 5 May 1832 the Carlisle Canal Company was reported as intending to build a new Custom House at the Canal Basin; as the lease on the existing building had only twelve months to run. The new building was to be built adjoining the Bonding Warehouses currently under construction. The Journal commented on the proposal as follows:-

"Previous to the establishment of bonding warehouses, the receipts at our Custom

House- or rather we should say the money remitted by it to the Treasury- did not exceed £3000 a -year, while at present the receipts exceed £20,000 a- year! The system is yet in its infancy in Carlisle; but from this striking fact we may judge what are likely to be its effects, when brought into full operation."

The Carlisle Patriot, 22 June 1832, reported that a new steamer the "Elizabeth" was in an advanced state of construction and should be ready to make her first trip in a fortnight. The report continued in typical lyrical fashion:-

"We hear that numerous parties of pleasure are forming to avail themselves of her accommodation for an excursion to Mona's Isle." However, it was 4 August 1832 before the boat was launched from the building yard near the Canal Basin. The Carlisle Journal reported:- "We understand she will trade between the Canal Basin and the Isle of Man, and occasionally to Scotland, her paddles being so constructed, by being raised up, that she can easily pass through the locks and bridges upon the canal."

The same edition of the Journal reported on Welsh strike-breakers passing along the canal:-

"On Thursday evening, between l50 and 200 colliers and lead miners, from Wales, arrived at our Canal Basin from Bowness, where they had been landed from the St. Winifrid, steamer, on their way to Newcastle to supply the place of the refractory colliers who have struck work. The men were provided with bread and cheese, and a pint of ale each at Stanwix, and then proceeded towards Brampton, where it was intended they should remain all night, and march again this morning for Newcastle. They were followed out of Carlisle by a large crowd, who seemed much out of humour with the ancient Britons and their mission"

One week later Mr Lowry, the Carlisle Coroner, had a narrow escape from drowning when returning by the passage boat from Bowness. He "slipped his foot" when stepping on board and fell into the canal. A seaman threw him a rope, which he caught hold of, and was "drawn out, after being in the water some considerable time."

One cannot help feeling that the inclusion of this item of news in the weekly paper had more to do with the person involved than the actual seriousness of the event.

A much more serious accident occurred in the Canal Basin a few weeks later as reported by the Carlisle Journal, 8 September 1832:-

"On Saturday last, a man named Thomas Richardson, aged 51, a labourer in the habit of working about the Canal Basin met with his death in a sudden manner. He had been employed in assisting to unload a vessel, and while standing near the hold whilst a pack of wool was being heaved out, it swung against him, and he fell into the hold, a height of about 10ft. He was taken up insensible, and died in a very short time afterwards. An inquest was held on his body on the 3rd. inst. and a verdict of 'accidental death' returned. Richardson was a married man and had a wife and family."

Meanwhile preparations for the new Custom House were proceeding apace. The Carlisle Patriot, 29 September 1832 announced:-

"The foundation stone of the new Custom House for Carlisle was laid this day (Friday). The site is on the west side of the Canal Basin, near the swing bridge - a situation that will be found most convenient, being near to the bonded warehouses as well as adjacent to the intended Railway depot, and to the Canal warehouses. The building is to be of polished white stone and will consist of three offices on the ground floor and a large room for general purposes, with offices behind, on the second floor. It is to be of a plain, but neat style of architecture and will have a very respectable appearance."

The new Custom House just prior to it's demolition about 1981. The edge of the canal basin with steps leading down can be seen in the foreground and the 1974 building of the Cumberland Infirmary in the background. At this time the whole area had ceased to be a railway goods yard. About 1974 British Rail moved in on a Bank Holiday weekend and demolished the warehouse and other buildings and another piece of Carlisle's industrial history was lost. The site of the warehouse is now occupied by a doctor's surgery and pharmacy.

These pictures were taken during the demolition.

Meanwhile the building yard near the Canal Basin was still kept busy. On the 3 November 1832 it was reported that the keel for yet another vessel, intended for the 'Carlisle Shipping Trade' had been laid.

These were exciting times for the city. Quite apart from the improvements in transport and consequent boom in industrial development, more resources were being applied to public works, particularly public health. Only three weeks later on the 24 November 1832 the Carlisle Journal reported as follows:-

"CUMBERLAND INFIRMARY. - This building is now finished, and presents a most beautiful appearance on the outside. We have not had an opportunity of inspecting the accommodations inside, but we have received several letters complaining that they are by no means equal to the demand which may be expected in an infirmary of this kind. One thing, at all events, is certain, that the situation is most convenient to the medical men of the city. We hear that the apartments are to be furnished with as little delay as possible, and that the institution is expected to be ready for the reception of patients early in the ensuing spring." The Carlisle Patriot went into much more detail regarding the architecture and the construction of the building. They described the portico as:- "a tetra -style portico, of the Doric order, after the Choragic Monument of Thrasyllus and Thrisycles, at Athens - modified to meet the expenditure."

County Infirmary, Carlisle *W H Nutter*

One might wonder how many of the paper's readers would appreciate this description. The article went on to describe the extremely spacious and handsome vestibule, hall and staircase and the layout of the physicians' and committee rooms. The principal and end fonts of the building were described as:- "constructed of polished white stone, procured from the Chalk quarries near this city - with the exception of that for the massive fluted pillars of the portico, and the pillasters (sic), which are formed of huge blocks of Yorkshire stone, none of sufficient size being to be had in this county."

This last statement most likely illustrates one of the reasons for siting the Cumberland Infirmary so near to the Canal Basin. These large blocks of Yorkshire stone were transported to the Infirmary site via the Carlisle Canal. A report in the Patriot more than a year earlier (11 June 1831) bore witness to this fact and illustrated the problems associated with moving such large pieces of masonry with the relatively primitive equipment available at the time:-

"It is a remarkable circumstance, that plentifully as this county abounds with stone, it has yet been found necessary to procure a great portion of that required for the General Infirmary, now erecting near this city, from the neighbourhood of Leeds. This is owing to the large dimensions of which the specification for the building require each stone to be, - none of sufficient size and requisite quantity being wrought in this neighbourhood. The stone is conveyed by canal to Liverpool, and thence by sea to the Carlisle Canal - a distance of at least 200 miles.

Some men employed in unloading a ship-load of stone, in the Canal Basin, had a narrow escape from destruction a few days ago. Whilst a block of stone of an immense weight was being drawn up, the rope broke, and it was precipitated with great violence down the hatchway. Two or three were below at the time, but not the slightest injury was inflicted upon any of them."

The Patriot went on to explain that the Infirmary would normally have up to fifty two beds, but that more could be accommodated in an emergency. The rooms and passages had been cleaned out and painted, and workmen were presently laying out the walkways, gardens and shrubberies. The building had been completed on time and the only thing lacking was a permanent fund for its continued support. This, they hoped, would be attended to shortly and encouraged all, especially the wealthy, to contribute. According to the Directory of Cumberland (Mannix and Whellan, 1847) the infirmary was built for the princely sum of £8356-5s-1d. The whole of this money was raised by public subscription.

The original part of the infirmary as seen today.

Sometime during the last 180 years it acquired a third storey.

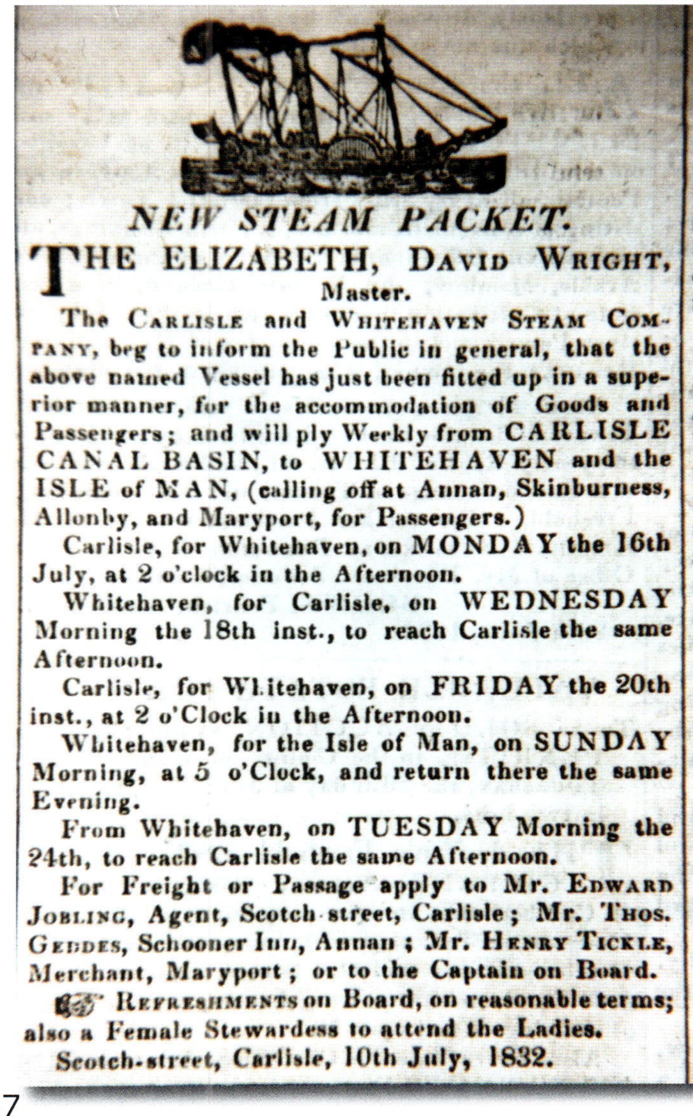

NEW STEAM PACKET.

THE ELIZABETH, DAVID WRIGHT, Master.

The CARLISLE and WHITEHAVEN STEAM COMPANY, beg to inform the Public in general, that the above named Vessel has just been fitted up in a superior manner, for the accommodation of Goods and Passengers; and will ply Weekly from CARLISLE CANAL BASIN, to WHITEHAVEN and the ISLE of MAN, (calling off at Annan, Skinburness, Allonby, and Maryport, for Passengers.)

Carlisle, for Whitehaven, on MONDAY the 16th July, at 2 o'clock in the Afternoon.

Whitehaven, for Carlisle, on WEDNESDAY Morning the 18th inst., to reach Carlisle the same Afternoon.

Carlisle, for Whitehaven, on FRIDAY the 20th inst., at 2 o'Clock in the Afternoon.

Whitehaven, for the Isle of Man, on SUNDAY Morning, at 5 o'Clock, and return there the same Evening.

From Whitehaven, on TUESDAY Morning the 24th, to reach Carlisle the same Afternoon.

For Freight or Passage apply to Mr. EDWARD JOBLING, Agent, Scotch-street, Carlisle; Mr. THOS. GEDDES, Schooner Inn, Annan; Mr. HENRY TICKLE, Merchant, Maryport; or to the Captain on Board.

REFRESHMENTS on Board, on reasonable terms; also a Female Stewardess to attend the Ladies.

Scotch-street, Carlisle, 10th July, 1832.

The only other item of interest in the local press concerning the canal in 1832 was a brief report in the Carlisle Journal, 1 December 1832:-

"On Tuesday evening last, Mr. Thompson, of the Canal Office, had a narrow escape while proceeding to Carlisle on horseback, near the new Caldewgate poor-house, where his bridle broke and the horse fell with great violence, but luckily neither received injury."

The Journal editor was obviously short of news items for that particular edition of the paper. However, the same edition mentioned that Messrs. Porter, Ironfounders, were presently exhibiting a 'Patent Pump' of "very extraordinary powers." This pump was described as being the greatest improvement in the art of raising water within the last 2000 years. This pump was to be put to use in the construction of the Canal Branch Railway.

Early in January 1833 a man named Beachy of Caldcoats was arrested on a charge of stealing a cask from the Canal Basin. A more important news item in the same edition of the Carlisle Journal recorded that the last stone had been laid in the archwork of the new Railway Bridge at the 'Mains'. The Mains, off London Road, was the site of the original Carlisle Passenger Railway Station. Goods were to be forwarded to the canal on the Canal Branch line, which was to be built between the 'Mains' station and the Canal Basin.

Burgh-by-Sands Church, Winter Morning *Sam Bough*

The canal is in the foreground

An interesting article in the Carlisle Journal, 29 March 1833, reported on a new style Pacquet Boat, due to be introduced on the Kendal and Lancaster Canal:-

"“EXPEDITIOUS CONVEYANCE - The Kendal and Lancaster Canal Company have in contemplation the commencement of an expeditious and superior mode of conveying passengers, &c., betwixt Kendal and Lancaster, by a pacquet—boat, built on a light construction, which is expected to sail at the astonishing rate of 10 miles per hour! The locks at Tewitt-field are now undergoing considerable alterations, on an entirely new and improved system - so as to admit the pacquet- boat going through them with much greater rapidity than has hitherto been the case [Would not the adoption of these newly invented boats prove serviceable to the proprietors of the Carlisle canal?]."

As we will see later, the Canal Company did indeed take up this suggestion with the introduction, just over a year later, of the new passage boat *The Arrow*.

Port Carlisle

Up to this time the place now known as 'Port Carlisle' had gone under a variety of names. The original 'Port Carlisle' had been the jetty at Sandsfield, mentioned at the beginning of this book, and the canal outlet was generally known as Fishers Cross, Knox Cross, or just Bowness. The building of the hotel 'Solway House' at the canal entrance provided the Carlisle Journal with the opportunity to write an article about this developing community and confirm its new identity as 'Port Carlisle:-

"PORT CARLISLE. - At the mouth of the Carlisle Canal, at a place formerly known by the name of the Binnacle, there has been recently erected one of the pleasantest and most commodious houses on the shores of the Solway; and it is kept by one of the kindest and most hospitable hostesses that ever gave welcome to a traveller; and as the tired citizen, after enjoying the refreshing sea breezes, throws himself into an armchair, before a blazing fire in her snug and tidy parlour, he may well exclaim with the poet:-

'Whoe'er has travelled life's dull round,

And been its busy mazes in,

Must sigh to think he's always found

His warmest welcome at an Inn.'

This place was hitherto been indifferently called Bowness, Binnacle, and the Canal Mouth, which has given rise to much confusion; and the Committee of the Canal Company, taking these premises into their consideration, have resolved upon giving to the place the name of PORT CARLISLE. This is a most appropriate CARLISLE. This is a most appropriate designation. Several miles along the coast are so called in the Custom House books; but as this is now the great outlet and inlet for the merchandise sent from and consumed in Carlisle, and has direct water communication with the city, it has a fair and legitimate title to the name by which it is henceforth to be designated. Besides the house which we have particularly named, several others have been erected, and others are projected, and the place will soon become a very pleasant and handsome little village."

The last stretch of canal approaching Port Carlisle is beneath the line of trees.
The stone dock can be seen opposite the sea lock.

Hadrian's Wall footpath follows the bank of the canal through the trees.

Here the canal trench still holds water.

In February 1834 two more residents of the area were found drowned in the canal. The Carlisle Journal, 15 February 1834 reported on two inquests as follows:-

"An inquest was held on Sunday last, before Richard Lowry Esq., coroner, upon the body of Joseph Carruthers, aged 44, a blacksmith, and also a keeper of a small public-house at the Raffles, near this city. It appears that for some time past the deceased had been in an unsettled state of mind; and on Saturday morning last, he left his house early, and proceeded towards the Canal. He took off his apron on arriving at the Basin, and then threw himself in. He was followed from home by some of his family, who traced him to the basin side, but arrived too late to save him. His body was got out about two hours afterwards. The jury returned a verdict of 'Found Drowned.'

Another inquest was taken at Easton, in the parish of Bowness, on Monday last, by the same gentleman, in view of the body of Joseph Norman, aged 36 years, many years a butcher in this city. He had been missing since the 30th January last, on which day he had been employed by Mr. John Graham, butcher, to drive a few beasts to Bowness, to be shipped from thence to Liverpool, per one of the steamers. He duly arrived at Bowness and embarked the cattle, but though he had received two sovereigns for the purpose of paying their freight, he refused to pay it, and set off on his way home. He called in at one or two public houses, and began to drink freely, and the last time he was seen alive was at a public-house at Easton, where he was engaged in a drunken broil, with his coat off to fight, and much intoxicated. Soon after this he seems to have left the house unobserved, and by some means fallen into the Canal, which is near the spot, and which at this place is particularly dangerous, the banks being steep and unprotected."

The article carried on to describe in detail the investigation leading to his body being found floating in the canal a week later at Easton. The coroner who heard these inquests is of course the same Mr Lowry who himself had a narrow escape from drowning in the canal only 18 months previously (Page 64).

On the 26th April 1834 the Carlisle Journal carried a long article on the new steam vessel *City of Carlisle* built at Liverpool for the new 'Carlisle and Annan Steam Navigation Company', otherwise known as the 'Carlisle Grocers Steam Navigation Company'. The vessel was due to arrive at Port Carlisle on the previous Wednesday and a "great concourse of people were attracted to Port Carlisle to witness the pleasing sight". As usual liberal refreshments were provided on board for the visitors. The vessel was described as:-

"built after a very beautiful model, with round stern, and formed expressly for quick sailing. She has a poop deck, and a very elegant female figurehead. She measures from stem to stem 132 feet, in breadth of beam 21 feet, and registers 181 tons. Her cabin is beautifully fitted up, with mahogany panels, and a very rich crimson paper, with a cornice of white and gold, which gives a rich and elegant appearance to the whole."

The report continued at length describing even more of the boat's attributes, as well as the wining, dining, and speech making, which by now had become traditional at such events. One undertaking that was toasted at this gathering was The Newcastle and Carlisle Railway; the success of which would greatly affect the profitability of the new steam navigation company.

These were exciting times in Carlisle. Industry was developing, trade was increasing and the canal was playing its part. The Carlisle Journal , 7 June 1834, reported:-

"Our Canal Basin presented, on Tuesday last, a scene of business and activity, strongly indicative of the rising importance of the place. There were no less than eight vessels in the basin, besides the lighters belonging to the steam pacquets, and all of them engaged in discharging their cargoes, which consisted principally of slate, iron, lead, &c.; and what makes the occurrence more remarkable is, that on the latter part of the previous week there was not a single sail, nor even a block of wood lying in the basin. The sight was highly gratifying as an evidence of the increasing commerce of our town, and the bustle and activity which was going on put one not a little in mind of some of the docks at Liverpool."

The Arrow Passage Boat

Perhaps the most important event of 1834 for the Canal Company was the arrival of the new iron-clad passage boat The *Arrow*, which can be seen on W. H. Nutter's watercolour below. The *Arrow*, which was built at Glasgow and hauled to Carlisle on a wagon using three horses, was a vast improvement on the previous passage boat; being very much faster and much more comfortable. The journey from Glasgow took five days and she was launched at the Canal Basin the morning after her arrival, 28 June 1834. She was described as 66 feet long and five feet eight inches broad:-

"There is no deck, but, with the exception of a few feet of open space at each end, she consists of two cabins, six feet six inches high inside, the roof being above the edge of the boat. The first cabin, which will hold 25 passengers or more, is very handsomely fitted up, with seats covered with hair cushions, the sides of blue damask; and the second cabin , which will contain perhaps 40 passengers, is very neatly, though more plainly furnished. On each side there is a row of windows, which pull down from the top and render the cabins extremely light and airy. The boat itself is made of wrought iron and the upper parts are composed of wood and painted canvas" (Carlisle Patriot, 5 July 1834).

Carlisle and Canal *W H Nutter 1842*

The Arrow passage boat pulled by ex- hunting horses is seen leaving the Canal Basin for Port Carlisle. In the background The Castle, Cathedral, Dixon's chimney, new Infirmary and Trinity Church can be seen. On the left is a passing place directly opposite the entrance to the timber dock.

Canal and Coal Staithes *Artist thought to be one of the Nutter family*

This painting depicts a view from a point west of that on the previous page. Interestingly it shows the coal staithes on the canal bank through the gap beween the ships. These can be seen on the map below which also shows the passing place and the patent slip in the timber dock where ships were built and repaired at Carlisle.

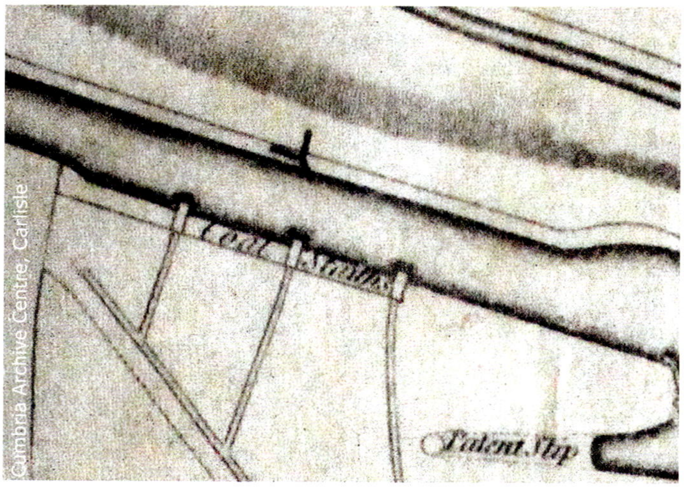

The *Arrow* attracted great interest, not least because of its great speed and its likeness to an Indian canoe. The boat was very soon 'tried out' on the canal. The Carlisle Journal, 5 July 1834, reported:-

"She was tried down the canal as far as the first lock, at Beaumont, on Saturday evening, with a numerous party of gentlemen on board. Her performance gave the greatest satisfaction, having run the distance at the rate of nearly 10 miles an hour. - She glides through the water with great ease and steadiness. The speed with which she moves through the water causes a considerable swell in her wake, though not to such an extent we hope as to cause any injury to the canal."

The *Arrow* accomplished the trip to Port Carlisle in one hour and forty minutes, compared with the old boat which took four to five hours. The Journal commented further:-

"We can scarcely over-estimate the advantages which the city is likely to derive from the plying of the new boat. For instance, we observe by the arrangements, she will go down to Port Carlisle, early tomorrow (Saturday) morning and return in time to convey all on the line to the market, in the evening she will start again for Port Carlisle at 5 o'clock, to carry back the market people, and afford an opportunity to tradesmen to go down to Bowness to spend the Sunday after the labours of the week, and return to Carlisle in time for business on Monday morning. We hear it is in contemplation to start an omnibus to bring passengers and luggage from the Canal Basin to the City."

Sir George Head in his book 'A Home Tour through the Manufacturing Districts of

England in the Summer of l835' describes his visit to the "Carlisle and Annan Navigational Canal" and, in particular, his encounter with the *Arrow* passage boat is vividly described:-

"A great degree of excitement was at first created by the novelty of the conveyance, as well as by the speed, which exceeded that of the old wooden boat previously on this canal, by just double. Nevertheless, though people were anxious to go on board her, she was, to all appearance, so cranky, - toppling and rolling from side to side so awfully when empty, that folks took a panic, and many declined on any account to venture. Certainly, were she to capsize, there would be little chance of escape, the passengers being all stowed away under an awning, and closed in on all sides, like sheep in a pen, very little, however, is to be apprehended on that score, for she is as buoyant as an Indian canoe, which latter vessel, as is well known, gets rid of a passenger now and then, like a kicking horse, pitching him out into the water, without herself approaching near the point of upsetting. A tolerable load on board brings the *Arrow* sufficiently low in the water, when all danger vanishes, and she is perfectly steady."

Sir George's return to Carlisle was not to be so trouble free and is worth recounting as it illustrates the physical problems of communication in those days before the invention of the radio and telephone.

"Having arrived in the *Arrow* with an intention of returning with the passengers of the *City of Carlisle*, it was some disappointment to find, not only that the vessel was later than usual, but to hear that some untoward event had taken place sufficient probably to prevent her arriving that day at all. From the extremity of the Jetty, as I perceived the smoke of two steamers instead of one gently ascending on the other shore of the Firth, it was evident that both vessels, the *Newcastle* and the *City of Carlisle*, were lying together at Annan Water-foot. By what accident, inasmuch as they plied in opposite directions, they could thus get together, I did not learn, not for want of taking pains to enquire, or receiving answers to interrogatories, assigning abundance of reasons, of these, the people on the spot, who by the way were all interested, were prodigal enough, though the real cause, whatever it might have been, they kept to themselves. In the meantime the two steamers showed no disposition to move either way, and as it was not the purpose of the commander of the *Arrow* to return to Carlisle without the Liverpool passengers, here we were under the necessity of remaining. After waiting a full hour the *City of Carlisle* got under way, and came safely alongside, barring a trifling casualty that happened to a heavy lighter she had taken in tow. The skipper of the latter, miscalculating the rate he was dragged through the water by the steamer, contrived to enliven the the spectators by running his vessel bump on the Jettyhead. The passengers all got out of the *City of Carlisle*, expecting immediately to proceed up the canal, - but no such thing. The passengers from the *Newcastle* also were expected to arrive, and till they came, he of the *Arrow* refused to budge. Another hour we were doomed to wait; all of which time the *Newcastle* continued to smoke at Annan Waterfoot.

Disinterested people were busily occupied in the solution of the same problem, namely, why, in the name of simplicity, the two vessels having remained so long together, the *City of Carlisle* had not brought over both sets of passengers, a heavy Dutch built vessel, capable, according to appearances, of stowing away all the inhabitants of the town of Annan! In the present case it was the lot of the passengers of the Newcastle to suffer on account of a misunderstanding, whatever it might have been, between the two captains, and thence doomed to an adventure by no means agreeable, namely to cross the Solway Firth in an open boat against wind and tide.

Two small skiffs were at last seen bobbing up and down, and making head slowly towards the Jetty. Both arrived quite full of people, passengers of the Newcastle, who landed in a highly discontented mood, and marched on board the *Arrow* with bags, boxes, and bundles, till there were as many as could obtain seats, and, over and above, more who were obliged to stand at the head and stern. With this ballast the *Arrow* glided up the canal as steady as a barge. Whenever it was necessary to detach the horses, recourse was had to a very neat expedient, which I have not seen adopted in other boats of the same class. By pressing on a bolt, the eye of the trace is instantaneously thrown off the hook, by a contrivance acting precisely like the trigger of a cross-bow."

By September 1834 work had started on the Canal Branch, the section of the Newcastle and Carlisle Railway between the railway station at the Mains on the London Road and the Canal Basin. The Carlisle Journal carried an extensive report on the works which described the good luck of Mr Grahamsley, the contractor. He had opened up a quarry at the well known Cuddock Pool, which was providing an excellent stone, suitable for building the bridge across the Caldew, near the Long Island. Apparently there was a traditional belief that Cuddock was originally a quarry, from which the stone for the Carlisle Cathedral was taken. Mr Grahamsley had taken a chance, dug and found excellent stone. This would be much less expensive than bringing stone from quarries further afield. The pool was filled and now lies under the Maryport and Carlisle Railway, the quarry providing much of the stone for the Canal Branch Railway. Then as now vandalism was a problem on any large contract. The Journal recorded that:-

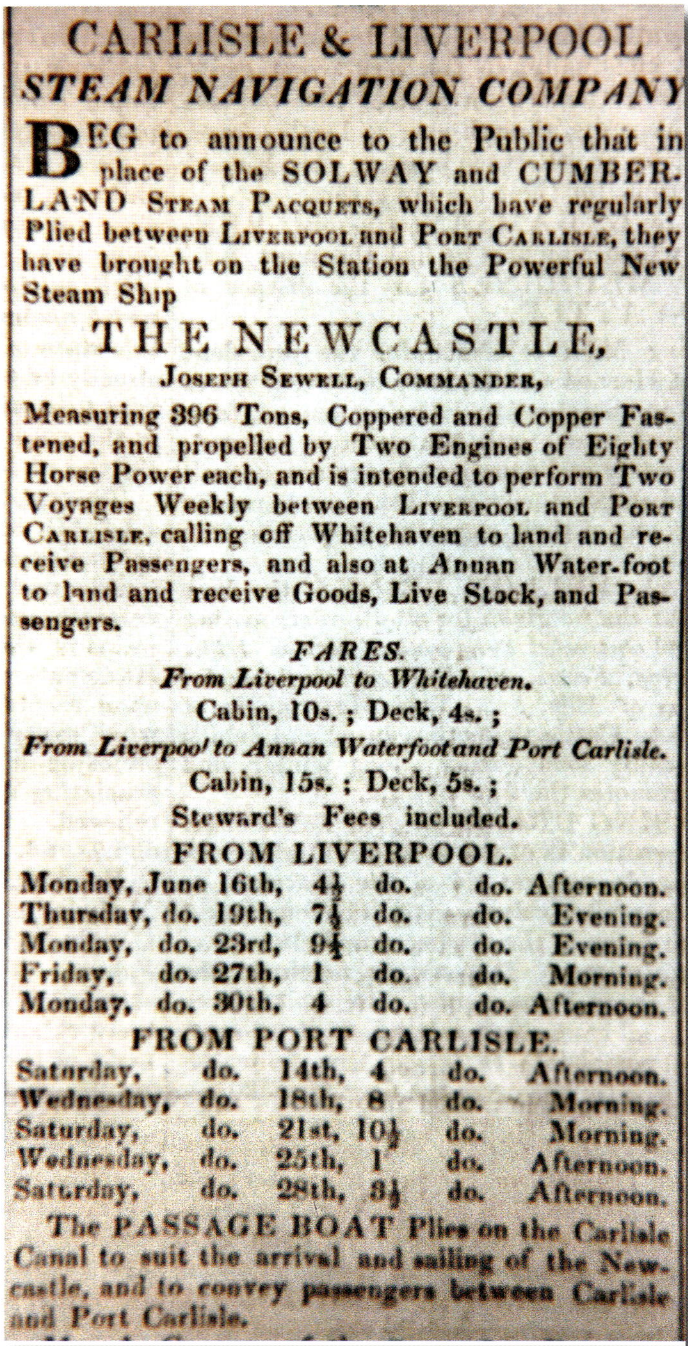
CARLISLE & LIVERPOOL
STEAM NAVIGATION COMPANY

BEG to announce to the Public that in place of the SOLWAY and CUMBERLAND STEAM PACQUETS, which have regularly Plied between LIVERPOOL and PORT CARLISLE, they have brought on the Station the Powerful New Steam Ship

THE NEWCASTLE,
JOSEPH SEWELL, COMMANDER,

Measuring 396 Tons, Coppered and Copper Fastened, and propelled by Two Engines of Eighty Horse Power each, and is intended to perform Two Voyages Weekly between LIVERPOOL and PORT CARLISLE, calling off Whitehaven to land and receive Passengers, and also at Annan Water-foot to land and receive Goods, Live Stock, and Passengers.

FARES.
From Liverpool to Whitehaven.
Cabin, 10s.; Deck, 4s.;
From Liverpool to Annan Waterfoot and Port Carlisle.
Cabin, 15s.; Deck, 5s.;
Steward's Fees included.

FROM LIVERPOOL.

Monday,	June 16th,	4½	do.	do.	Afternoon.
Thursday,	do. 19th,	7½	do.	do.	Evening.
Monday,	do. 23rd,	9½	do.	do.	Evening.
Friday,	do. 27th,	1	do.	do.	Morning.
Monday,	do. 30th,	4	do.	do.	Afternoon.

FROM PORT CARLISLE.

Saturday,	do.	14th,	4	do.	Afternoon.
Wednesday,	do.	18th,	8	do.	Morning.
Saturday,	do.	21st,	10½	do.	Morning.
Wednesday,	do.	25th,	1	do.	Afternoon.
Saturday,	do.	28th,	3½	do.	Afternoon.

The PASSAGE BOAT Plies on the Carlisle Canal to suit the arrival and sailing of the Newcastle, and to convey passengers between Carlisle and Port Carlisle.

"On Sunday night last some malicious scoundrel cut some of the leather pipes belonging to a patent pump used in draining water from the quarry"

Another problem encountered near St. Nicholas was the digging up of a skeleton. More such gruesome finds were expected as the place was realised to be the site of an ancient leper hospital, which would originally have been without the modern city.

The Carlisle Grocers Union, who had been running a fleet of sailing ships between Carlisle and Liverpool since the opening of the canal, had recently commissioned the steamer *City of Carlisle* and set up a new company, the *Carlisle and Annan Steam Navigation Company* - So, in March 1834, they published the notice on page 58, informing the public of their decision to withdraw their fleet of sailing ships from service.

The city leaders of this time were determined to improve conditions for the poor and needy amongst them. In the same edition of the Journal the following proposal to alleviate the periodic flooding of Caldewgate was reported:-

"We some time ago alluded to the propriety of entering into a subscription for the purpose of erecting a bank from the west side of the Caldew Bridge, down the river to below the Mill, at the bottom of Bridge Lane, and then running some little distance on the north side of the cut which conveys the water to the machinery for pumping water into the canal, for the purpose of preventing those inundations of water with which several parts of Caldewgate are afflicted during high floods. Leave for erecting such a bank has now, we understand, been obtained from the Corporation, the Old Brewery Company, and the Canal Company, but funds are still wanting to complete the work. One or two benevolent gentlemen have undertaken to collect subscriptions for this purpose and we trust they will find little difficulty in raising a sufficient sum to meet the expense of a work so well calculated to prevent the suffering endured by many poor families arising from the conjuncture of wet houses and cold and damp weather."

In late September came news of the construction of a small dock near the canal basin to receive the *Arrow* which had been in continuous use for nearly three months by this time. Problems with water supply were once more apparent. The level of water in the canal in September 1834 was so low that the only boats capable of passing along the canal were the *Arrow* and the lighters which serviced the Steam Pacquet Company. However, the new wheel for improving the water supply had been erected and the company were sure that, once the dock had been completed, the canal would be easily filled. This, as we shall see later, was not to be. More resources would have to be committed in the future to ensure that the canal did not run short of water. The Canal Company now had no further use for the old Passage boat and this was duly advertised for sale in October 1834.

MEMEL TIMBER ON SALE.

ARRIVED per the Galliot *Anna Margaretha*, H. H. SUHR, Master, at Port Carlisle, and now on Sale at the CANAL BASIN, CARLISLE, and at BURGH, a superior Cargo of MEMEL FIR TIMBER, CROWN PIPE STAVES, WAINSCOT LOG, DEALS, and LATH-WOOD.

Also a large STOCK of AMERICAN FIR TIMBER, BLACK BIRCH, MAHOGANY HEART and SAP LATHS, and an excellent Assortment of well seasoned DEAL BOARDS, of various Dimensions.

LANCASHIRE and WELCH SLATES.

Further particulars may be known on application to THOMAS WALKER & Co., Timber Merchants, Scotch-Street ; and to Mr. BENJAMIN TREMBLE, Agent, Burgh.

Carlisle, June 6, 1834.

PASSAGE BOAT FOR SALE.

To be SOLD, by PUBLIC AUCTION, at the CANAL BASIN, CARLISLE, on TUESDAY, the 28th Day of OCTOBER inst.

THE PASSAGE BOAT, "*Bailie Nicol Jarvie*," lately used upon the Carlisle Canal, and capable of being converted into a Lighter for the Conveyance of Goods, or a Floating Bath.

For further particulars apply to Mr. THOMPSON. Canal Office, Carlisle.

Not to be repeated.

Carlisle, 17th Oct. 1834.

Meanwhile plans for new docks at Port Carlisle were proceeding and by March 1835 the long muted petition re the surveying and buoying of the Solway Firth was finally presented to the Admiralty, who readily acceded to the request. By March 1835 the railway between Blaydon and Hexham was completed. However, due to problems with one particular landowner, locomotives were prevented from travelling over part of the line, and it was June 1835 before a bill was passed through parliament which overruled the objections to self-propelled steam locomotives being used.

At the end of July in 1835 a Regatta was held at Port Carlisle. The details of the race from the end of the steamer jetty, out to a boat moored near Burgh Marsh Point and back to the jetty, were described at length in the Carlisle Journal. The winner, a boat called the 'Rover' was manned by Capt. Scott, described as 'one of the best boatmen on the Solway'. This event illustrated the desire of the people to put Port Carlisle 'on the map' as an up and coming place for recreation and enjoyment, as well as a trading port. The same edition of the Journal, 8 August 1835, brought news of a further milestone towards the completion of the Newcastle & Carlisle Railway:-

"THE RAILWAY- We understand that the Railway Viaduct at Middle Gelt Bridge, close to the great cut at Cowran Hill, near Brampton, which has been upwards of two years in progress, is now nearly completed. This immense structure crosses two public roads and the River Gelt, at a height of 80 feet from the bed of the river, in an oblique direction, so as to prevent a bend in the railway; and contains three arches, each of 33 feet span. From the peculiarity and novelty of its structure, being built at an angle of 45 degrees, it has been an object of great curiosity and admiration of all mechanical men, who have seen it, there being no other in Great Britain built on the same principle, at all approaching it in magnitude. Erected by Mr M'Kay, of Unity, the contractor, - from the plan, and under the constant personal superintendence of Mr. Thomas Slack, mason of Langholm, on whose skill and talent it reflects the greatest credit."

NEWCASTLE & CARLISLE RAILWAY
TO BE LET,

THE MASONRY and EARTHEN-WORK, between the LONDON ROAD and the CANAL BASIN, Carlisle.

The Masonry consisting of Culverts, Walls, Bridges, and other. Work appertaining thereto.

Plan Sections and Specifications may be seen after Tuesday the 1st April next, at the Office of Mr. NANSON, Solicitor, 9, Castle Street, Carlisle, where Tenders must be delivered on or before Saturday the 12th of April next.

Railway Office, 20th March, 1834.

NEWCASTLE AND CARLISLE RAILWAY.

NOTICE is hereby given, that a further call of £10 per Share in the NEWCASTLE and CARLISLE RAILWAY COMPANY, was made by the Directors of the said Company, at a Meeting held this 18th day of MARCH, 1834, and the said Directors did direct and appoint that the Monies, payable under and by virtue of such call shall be paid to ROBERT BOYD, Esq., the Treasurer of the said Company, at the Bank of Sir MATTHEW W. RIDLEY, Bart. and Co. Newcastle-upon-Tyne, on the 15th day of APRIL next.

MATTHEW PLUMMER.
Chairman.

Newcastle-upon-Tyne, March 18, 1834.

Unfortunately accidents were bound to occur on such large projects. The Carlisle Journa1, 20 August 1835, reported the death of Joseph Law, a 46 year old workman, who was run over by two railway trucks near Gallows Hill whilst involved in the construction work. Just five weeks later a second inquest was held on another railway victim. The 'Carlisle Journa1' reported:-

"On Saturday last, an inquest was held before Wm. Carrick, Esq., coroner at Great Corby, in view of the body of John Hamilton, aged 16 years, who was killed on the day preceding by a train of Mr Grahamsley's wagons. It appeared from the evidence of a fellow-workman, that the deceased was riding upon the last of a train of six waggons, laden with stones, and propelled at the rate of six miles an hour by a stationary steam engine, when he imprudently attempted to step over to the adjoining wagon. There was at this time a space of upwards of three feet between the waggons, and in endeavouring to leap across this, his foot slipped, and he fell between them. His legs became entangled in the wheels of both waggons, and in this dreadful situation he was carried along a distance of 150 yards before the train was stopped. One of his legs was mangled in a most shocking manner, and he was otherwise so much injured that he survived the dreadful accident only two hours. The jury returned a verdict of 'Accidental Death,' and imposed a nominal deodand upon the waggons."

To continue on this melancholy note the Carlisle Journal carried the following news item on 7 November 1835:-

"SUPPOSED CASE OF SUICIDE - On Wednesday morning last, a man named William Richardson, who lived in Caldewgate, and who has lately been employed by Messrs. Dunn and Routledge, cabinet makers, Annetwell-street, in this city, left his home, and has not since been heard of. He appeared at the time to be very dejected, and on leaving the house kissed both his children (an unusual act with him on merely going to his work). Since then, his hat has been found upon the banks of the canal, near Carlisle, and little doubt remains that he has drowned himself. Persons have been employed all this day (Friday) in dragging the Canal for the body, but up to the time of our putting to press we had not heard that he had been discovered."

It was six weeks later when the paper reported the body found, `by the Rev. R. Graham, who was walking the canal bank near Newtown Bridge. The body was fully clothed as when the deceased had left home. It was removed to the Green Dragon public house, Newtown, where an inquest was held the next day. Verdict ' found drowned.'

A new dock at Port Carlisle

The need for more protected docking facilities at Port Carlisle was emphasised by a report of damage done to the *Brittania* of Port Carlisle, whilst berthed there during a gale at the end of November 1835. The *Brittania*, owned by Mr. Hewitt, timber merchant, Carlisle, was driven from her moorings and shortly after capsized, breaking her masts and suffering considerable other damage. The vessel had arrived from America the previous day with a cargo of timber.

The users of the facilities at Port Carlisle were most keen to see an improvement of the docking facilities at the port.

On Tuesday 10 November 1835 a meeting was held in the Town Hall, Carlisle, for the purpose of empowering the Canal Committee to give notice of an intention to apply to Parliament for an extension of the powers of the Carlisle Canal Act. A long report in the Carlisle Journal, 14 November 1835, described the business of the meeting. It was intended to construct a 'floating' dock at Port Carlisle, in which :-

"vessels of large burthen can enter at high water and ride in safety at all times. This will form the nucleus of a Harbour of any extent which the future necessities of our commerce may require. Nature has done

CARLISLE CANAL NAVIGATION.

NOTICE is hereby given, That a Special MEETING of the PROPRIETORS of the CARLISLE CANAL NAVIGATION, will be held at the Town Hall, CARLISLE, on Wednesday, the 24th Day of February next, at Twelve o'Clock at Noon, when the Draft of the proposed Bill, to enable the Carlisle Canal Company to make a Dock, or Docks, and other Works, at or near Port Carlisle, in the Townships of Bowness and Drumburgh, in the Parish of Bowness, in the County of Cumberland; and to place and maintain proper Buoys, Beacons, and Lights, in or near the Channel of the Solway Frith, and for otherwise improving the said Port; also for altering, amending, and enlarging the powers of an Act made and passed in the 59th year of the Reign of his late Majesty, King George the Third, entituled, "An Act for making and maintaining a Navigable Canal from or from near the City of Carlisle, to the Solway Frith, at or near Fisher's Cross, in the Parish of Bowness, in the County of Cumberland;" and also for Enlarging the said Canal, in the said Townships of Bowness and Drumburgh, and increasing and altering the Tolls, Rates, or Duties, by the said Act authorised to be taken; will be submitted to the Proprietors present at the said Meeting, for their approval. Dated the 20th Day of January, 1836.

W. NANSON, Solicitor.

TO EXCAVATORS.

TO BE LET,

THE EXCAVATION of a DOCK at PORT CARLISLE, near the Sea Lock of the CARLISLE CANAL. Plans and Specifications may be seen at the Canal Office, Carlisle; and Proposals will be received by Mr. THOMPSON, at the Canal Office, until THURSDAY the 6th MARCH, 1834.

everything for the situation chosen it requires but the application of art to raise it to a second Liverpool.- Extending northwards from the mouth of the Canal, and in immediate connection with it, there is 'ample room and verge enough,' and sufficient water for all commercial purposes which can ever be required."

The article went on to argue the benefits of Port Carlisle over Maryport as a harbour, having at least three feet more water at high tide than Maryport. A canal for sea-going ships only eleven miles long already linked Port Carlisle to Carlisle. The distance from Maryport to Carlisle was upwards of 30 miles and had not even been surveyed for a railway yet. The smoothness, speed and comfort of the new enclosed passage boat, the *Arrow*, was compared favourably with the lack of comfort and exposure on the railways of that time, for all but first class passengers. The argument continued:-

"The proposed Dock will put Carlisle upon a footing with almost any port, - at least will put us on a footing with Manchester; for we shall then be able to import West Indian produce direct, and will obtain facilities not only for the transaction of our present trade which we never before possessed, but for opening new channels of trade of which the most sanguine amongst us scarcely ever before dreamt. To show how clearly this is seen by others who have no local prejudices to warp their judgement, as well as by us, we may mention a fact easily proved, that within the last 3 or 4 years, shares in our Canal might have been bought, in almost any number at from £18 to £25 per share, whilst now they are as high as £40, and are most difficult to be obtained even at that price. Applications from Manchester for shares at that price have been made lately, and no sellers to be found. The same improvement has taken place in the Newcastle and Carlisle Railway shares: two years ago, it was difficult to obtain a price of any kind for them in the market, now the whole of the forfeited shares have been bought up at upwards of £90 each, and they are actually selling at par."

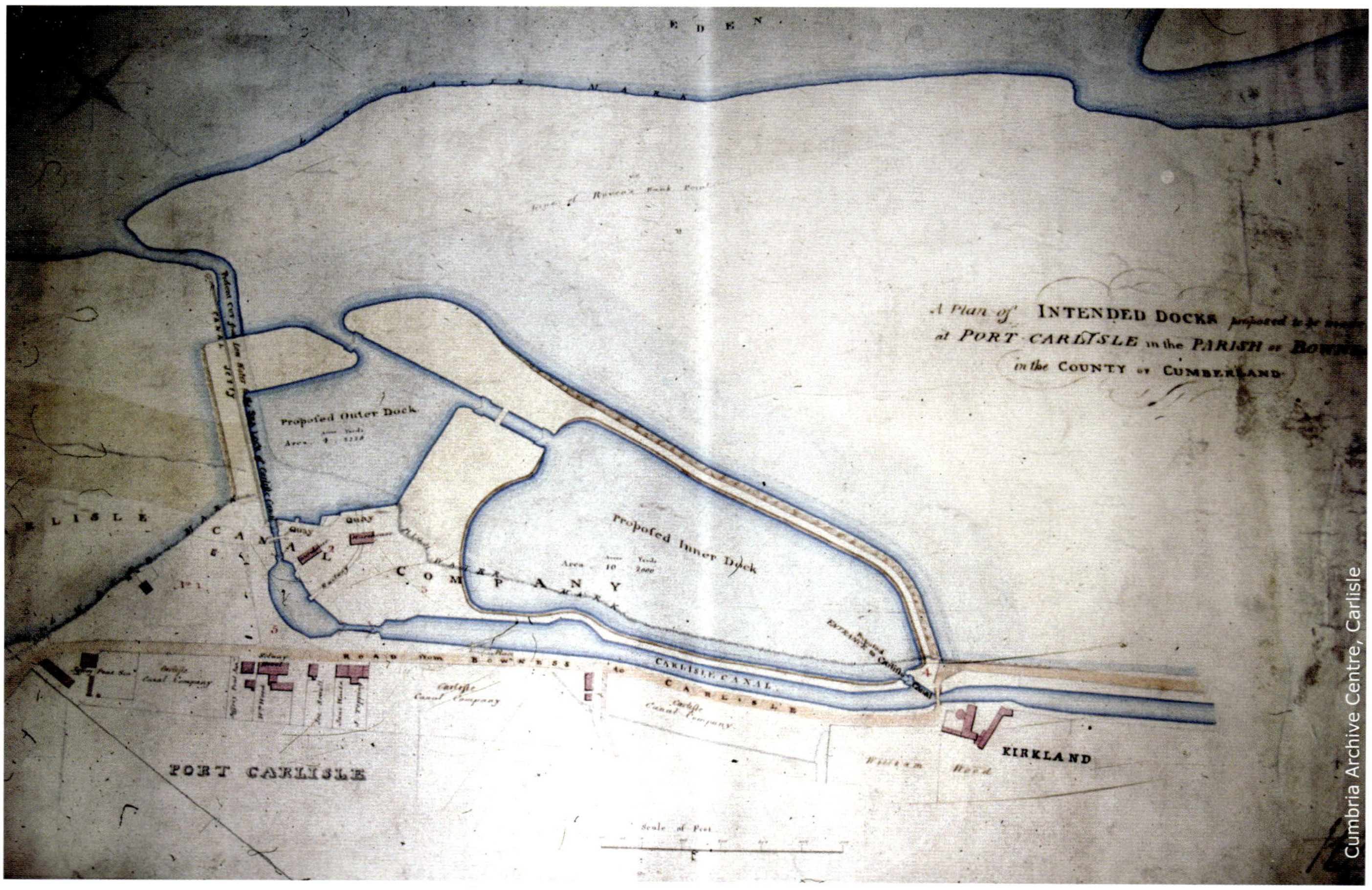

Cumbria Archive Centre, Carlisle

The projected docks at Port Carlisle

These arguments won the day and the meeting decided to go ahead with the application. This resulted in the notice on page 77 appearing in the Journal, 23 January 1836. The draft of the proposed bill was then agreed at the February meeting mentioned in the notice. At this meeting estimated costings were given for the proposals. The docks, with adjoining tide basin, would contain an area of 15 acres dock room and would cost £26,500. It was planned initially to carry out the work for the tide basin at £l5,600, leaving the additional work to be done according to trade demand. The floating dock was muted principally for the benefit of the Steam Navigation Company's vessels.

The Canal committee Annual General Meeting of July 1836 was a most interesting one. The Newcastle and Carlisle Railway was nearing completion, plans for docks at Port Carlisle and buoying and lighting of the Firth were going ahead and there was much information to impart to the shareholders. The Act for construction of the docks had received the royal assent on the 7 June and Mr Hartley, the engineer, had been asked to consider the "most eligible mode of executing the works."

The Committee reported that it had been decided to complete only the outer dock, in the first instance, as this would provide ample accommodation for a considerable time. Execution of the works could not proceed until the company had come to an arrangement with the Earl of Lonsdale, who was Lord of the Manor, and he had promised to give the matter his earliest attention.

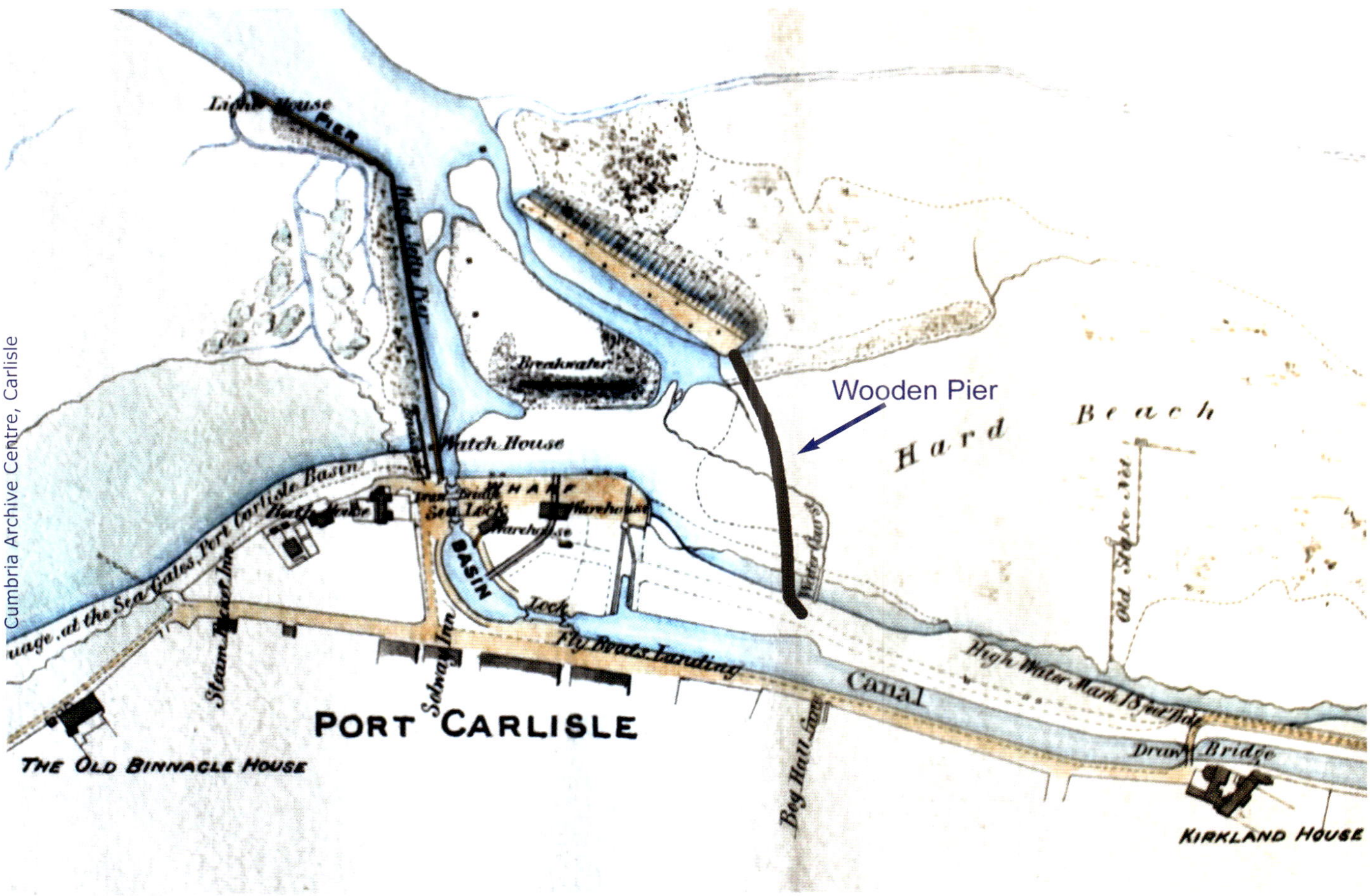

The docks as actually constructed without the inner floating dock. Strangely the wooden pier linking the stone dock with the shore is not shown on this map, possibly because it had not yet been constructed.

The line of this pier, which carried a horse-drawn railway line, is indicated by me on the map. It shows very clearly however the steamer pier extending out into the channel for about a quarter of a mile with a lighthouse at the end. This ensured that passengers could embark and disembark the steamers at times other than high tide. The warehouses, the canal basin, the linking paths, and the important buildings such as the Solway Inn are also shown.

Port Carlise - Ship 'The Robert Burns' *L B Norman*

The painting above is one of only two that I know of depicting Port Carlisle. It accurately depicts Port Carlisle in 1856. Here can clearly be seen, anticlockwise from the right, the steamer pier, the Port Carlisle bathhouse, the sea lock entrance to the canal, the Custom House, the engine shed, the Solway Hotel and the houses of the village. Behind the ship are the two warehouses, shown on the map on the previous page.

The *Robert Burns* is one of several ships of that name. This particular ship was used as an emigration ship. In 1851 the ship sailed from Port Carlisle to Quebec with 50 emigrants on board. She was towed out of the port by the *Prince of Wales* steamer, sailing under the command of Captain John Stewart.

The sea lock entrance in 2013. The two cottages were the original warehouses.

The wharf (seen in 2013) against which the 'Robert Burns' in the painting above was berthed

Top: *The stone dock in 2013. The other three photographs were taken in 1997 and show the remaining timber fenders, the steps up onto the dock and the view from the top looking across to Annan Waterfoot. At the top left of the last picture can be seen the remains of the wooden steamer pier.*

The stone dock is disintegrating year on year and will not be with us forever. It would be far too expensive to try and save it. However it may be possible, eventually, to remove the silt from the turning circle, seen below, and expose the dock walls to make a small marina.

Here the stumps of the wooden pier between the stone dock and the shore can still be seen.

The turning circle at high tide. the curved sandstone wharf (arrowed) can be seen.

Meanwhile the building of the Canal Branch Railway claimed a victim. One John Hodgson who, with another man, worked the windlass of the crane used in the construction of the bridge across the Caldew, was killed due to the crane collapsing. The Carlisle Journal, 20 February 1836 described the events leading up to his death:-
"The windlass is placed upon a platform 27 feet from the ground, and upon this the deceased was stationed when the accident took place. One of the posts fixed into the ground, and attached to guy ropes, supporting the crane, sprung, and the shock caused another of the posts to give way : the crane, now being unsupported on two sides, fell over against the arch of the bridge, and pitched the deceased and his companion to a considerable distance. The former fell upon his head, by which his skull was fractured, and he died immediately. The other man escaped with comparatively little injury. A strict enquiry was made upon the inquest, with a view to ascertain whether the posts had been sufficiently secured, and other proper precautions taken by the superintendent of the works, to prevent similar accidents; but nothing was elicited to cast blame upon Messrs. Grahamsley or their agent, and the jury therefore returned a verdict of accidental death, and imposed a nominal deodand of one shilling upon the crane."

This is the first inquest I have come across whilst researching this book where the possibility of fault on the part of the employer was even contemplated. It appears that just about every death at work was 'accidental' and any fines imposed were set against the inanimate machinery rather than the employer!

Tullie House Museum and Art Gallery Trust

Works at the new bridge across the River Caldew featuring the cranes, one of which collapsed.

W Carmichael 1836

The Carlisle Journal, 19 March 1836 contained a short report on a proposed railway across the Solway. The proposed 'Grand Caledonian Junction Railway' was to cross the Solway near the entrance to the canal. Apparently the scheme was not considered a very feasible one at the time. This was, however, foretelling the end of Port Carlisle as a trading port. Although the construction of the Solway Junction Railway did not begin until 1865, twelve years after the closure of the canal, the viaduct at Bowness effectively prevented sea-going ships from reaching Port Carlisle. As a result compensation was paid by the railway company to boat owners who were affected.

Jonathan Dodgson Carr

Early in June 1836 this advertisement appeared in the local press, showing that J. D. Carr was still in business at Castle Street five years after opening his bakery (see page 60). Just over six weeks later the advertisement below right was published, requesting tenders for J. D. Carr's proposed shop and factory on land adjacent to the canal. Jonathan Dodgson Carr had by this time become firmly established in the city and was looking to expanding his business. He had obviously bought up a large area of Caldewgate in preparation for this expansion because, at the end of the year, he put some of it back on the market.

WANTED IMMEDIATELY

TWO APPRENTICES - lads about the age of Fourteen Years - to the BREAD and BISCUIT BAKING Business.
Apply to J.D. CARR, 28 Castle Street.
N.B.-None need apply but those who can give respectable references.

Carlisle, 6 Mo. 2, 1836

TO MASONS AND BUILDERS

To be LET the BUILDING of a CORN MILL, WAREHOUSE, BAKEHOUSE, and other BUILDINGS in CALDEWGATE, CARLISLE. Plans and Specifications to be seen at J.D. CARR, Castle Street, after TUESDAY 26th July, where Tenders will be received until WEDNESDAY 3rd August, on which day the Contractor will be declared.

BUILDING GROUND

TO be SOLD by PRIVATE CONTRACT a valuable PIECE of freehold BUILDING GROUND, situated in CALDEWGATE, CARLISLE containing 2500 square Yards.

The Situation of the above Ground is very eligible, being within a few yards of the Newcastle and Carlisle Railway and the Carlisle Canal Basin.

For further Particulars apply to J. D. CARR, or Messrs. LAW and BENDLE, Solicitors, Carlisle.

Jonathan Dodgson Carr, who five years earlier, at the age of 25, had walked from Kendal and set up his shop in Castle Street had prospered in his trade. In May 1837 he opened his new shop, flour mill and bakery in Church Street, Caldewgate. In the window of this bakery he displayed the hand-made biscuits which were so good that, in 1841, he received a Royal Appointment from Queen Victoria.

Jonathan was a Quaker and a progressive employer. An old magazine of 1845 giving a visitor's impression of Carlisle and the Biscuit Works records the following:-

"Here is also an extensive biscuit factory belonging to Mr. J. D. Carr, the whole process from grinding the corn to finishing the biscuits, being performed on the premises. The quantity of fancy and other biscuits made annually is from 400 to 500 tons, and they find their way to all parts of the globe. A school-room, library and reading room are attached to the premises for the daily use of old an young in the establishment. Here is also a bath, 14 feet square, supplied by water from the steam engine at a temperature of 90 degrees, for the health and comfort of the workmen."

This establishment was to become the largest and probably the best known factory in the area and the canal would play an important part in its development, facilitating the import of raw materials and the export of, what were to become, Carr's world famous biscuits.

Jonathan Dodgson Carr
1806 -1884

An original Carr's letterhead showing the Caldewgate biscuit works which contains an interesting amount of detail.

On the drawing (shown enlarged here) can be seen the masts of ships in the canal basin, the large warehouse and an early freight train setting off on the Canal branch line towards London Road.

The canal was extremely important to Carr's. At a time when transport by road was slow and unreliable and railways were in their infancy raw materials such as corn, sugar and fats could be imported in bulk by ships direct to the factory. Likewise the finished product could be exported anywhere in the world.

In November 1846 the Carlisle Journal reported on the Government contracting Carr's to supply biscuits to alleviate the extreme poverty prevalent at that time in Western Scotland:-

"Carr's Biscuits.-Owing to the great scarcity of vegetables, and especially the potato, the destitution of the labouring poor in the West Highlands and Islands of Scotland, has been such that the Government have felt it their bounden duty to extend the same munificent charity towards the relief of the starving Highlanders that has already been bestowed on the inhabitants of the sister country Ireland. In the hope of doing this more effectually, the Government had in view to establish provision warehouses in the suffering localities, and to sell bread - now the staple food - at a low price, rather than give flour, which might not be so frugally used, or money which might not be so profitably expended. Mr Blamire, the chief Tithe Commissioner, being consulted by Government on this subject, directed their attention to the rye and maize bread manufactured by our townsmen, Mr Carr, as likely to be a great boon in the way of cheapness, and at the same time of the most wholesome character as food. We understand that the Lords of the Treasury communicated with Dr. Lonsdale relative to the maize and other varieties of bread made in Mr. Carr's establishment, and that he reported the maize bread to be at present the dearest bread, and whilst the coarse biscuits, known as 'sea biscuits,' made of the coarse flour of our best wheat, combined the qualities of cheapness and wholesomeness. We need not say that bread baked in Carlisle could not be eaten at Oban or Inverary, unless Highland stomachs are prepared to digest a fortnight's 'bake;' and, therefore, biscuits are the only prepared bread that could be conveyed great distances. The coarse biscuits of Mr Carr will keep for months, and such are the facilities at Mr. Carr's disposal that after the paste is prepared, his workmen can cut and prick no less than five stone per minute, or nearly two tons per hour. Were it as easy to bake them, a wonderfully large supply of biscuits could be obtained in a single day; but supposing Mr. C. furnishes the Government, which he will in all likelihood do, with *one* ton a day, and that we allow each grown up person four of the biscuits per day, (a good allowance along with other food), more than 3,000 people will be daily supplied form one establishment, the members of which only require to work an hour and a half. Lord John Russell had expressed himself much pleased with the biscuits; and on Friday last a package of them was sent down to Windsor, where the Cabinet Council met, so that it is more than probable her Majesty and dinner party would partake of the same."

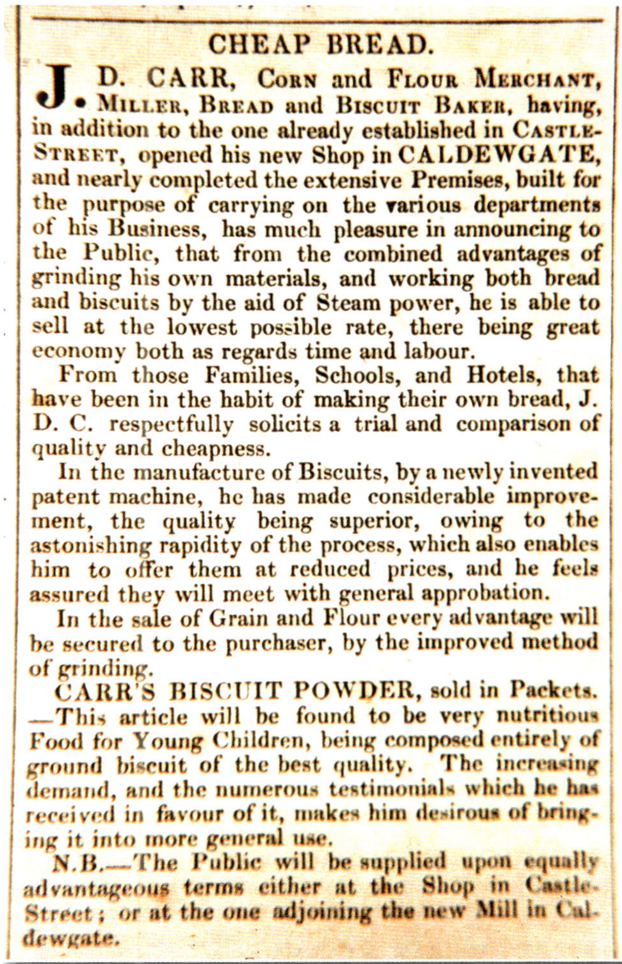

CHEAP BREAD.

J. D. CARR, Corn and Flour Merchant, Miller, Bread and Biscuit Baker, having, in addition to the one already established in Castle-Street, opened his new Shop in CALDEWGATE, and nearly completed the extensive Premises, built for the purpose of carrying on the various departments of his Business, has much pleasure in announcing to the Public, that from the combined advantages of grinding his own materials, and working both bread and biscuits by the aid of Steam power, he is able to sell at the lowest possible rate, there being great economy both as regards time and labour.

From those Families, Schools, and Hotels, that have been in the habit of making their own bread, J. D. C. respectfully solicits a trial and comparison of quality and cheapness.

In the manufacture of Biscuits, by a newly invented patent machine, he has made considerable improvement, the quality being superior, owing to the astonishing rapidity of the process, which also enables him to offer them at reduced prices, and he feels assured they will meet with general approbation.

In the sale of Grain and Flour every advantage will be secured to the purchaser, by the improved method of grinding.

CARR'S BISCUIT POWDER, sold in Packets.—This article will be found to be very nutritious Food for Young Children, being composed entirely of ground biscuit of the best quality. The increasing demand, and the numerous testimonials which he has received in favour of it, makes him desirous of bringing it into more general use.

N.B.—The Public will be supplied upon equally advantageous terms either at the Shop in Castle-Street; or at the one adjoining the new Mill in Caldewgate.

Land was needed on the west side of the Canal Basin to facilitate the transit of goods between Railway and Canal and the shareholders at the Annual General Meeting of July 1836 were informed that the Committee had purchased about eleven acres of land. Some land had already been allocated to businesses associated with the canal. Mr. Ellwood Brockbank had leased one acre of ground for a saw mill and timber yard, at the rent of £40 per annum. Messrs. Graham and Williams had also leased a small parcel of ground, near the village of Burgh, for the erection of alkali works.

A Mr John Marshall, of Hallsteads, obviously had faith in the future prosperity of the Canal Company. The Committee reported that this gentleman had proposed advancing the whole or any part of the borrowed capital of the company at the reduced interest rate of 4%. They had therefore notified their existing lenders that they could either have their capital repaid, as of 1 July 1836, or accept a lower interest rate of 4% from that date.

The report then alluded to the survey of the Firth which had been directed by the Board of Admiralty and continued:-

"This survey has been since commenced, and is now in progress, under the direction of Lieutenant Robinson, and your Committee cannot but anticipate incalculable advantages from it to the navigation, particularly as the company are empowered, by the new Act, to levy rates for buoying and lighting the Firth upon all vessels navigating it to the northward of Silloth Bay. This important provision, after receiving the sanction of Trinity House, to whom it was submitted, under the regulations of Parliament, passed without opposition, and an adequate fund is thus provided for the improvements of the navigation by proper buoys and lights"

The report then went on to discuss the revenue for the previous year. Canal dues came to £3,212 13s. 2d., an increase of £211 12s. 9d. on the previous year. Rents of land, warehouse dues, passage boat etc. brought in an extra £913 16s. 5d., making a gross revenue of £4,126 9s. 7d..

The expenditure had been more than usually heavy, mainly due to the need to improve the strength of the works at Port Carlisle as much larger steam vessels were now using the facilities. The expenditure account was as follows:-

Salaries and Wages	£370 - 2 - 0
Poor and County Rates	41 - 13 - 0
Incidental Expenses	164 - 17 - 0
Law Expenses	47 - 19 - 10
Rents and Damages, and Interest to landowners	96 - 14 - 0
Fencing	46 - 7 - 6
Jetties, Locks and Bridges	444 - 8 - 8
Earth Work	144 - 9 - 6
Sundry Repairs	153 - 12 - 6
Expenses of Waterwheel and Pumps	68 - 7 - 1
Buoyage and other Expenses in the Channel of the Solway Firth	120 - 0 - 8
Steam Vessel Berths	51 - 19 - 3
Bankers' Commission and Interest	13 - 7 - 7
In addition to the above have been incurred, during the year, the following items of Permanent Outlay:-	**£1,763-19 - 5**
Purchase of Land	45 - 0 - 0
New Water Wheel and Pumps, balance of Contract	748 - 7 - 3
Ice Boat	306 - 5 - 0
	£1,758 - 12 - 5

From these figures the nett income for the year ending 31 July 1836 was presumably about £600, after deduction of the above expenditure. The report concluded with the observation that the new Act of Parliament included a provision for the company to pay off its existing debts either by the issue of new shares or by apportioning the debt amongst the original shareholders. The expenditure on the ice boat is interesting. Six years earlier (see page 56) an ice boat was in use to keep the canal open during freezing weather. This was a replacement for that boat. Quite a lot of research went into deciding the construction of the boat, as can be seen from the following abstracts from The Canal Company Minutes:-

22 May 1835 - ordered - that information should be sought on the construction of ice-boats.

19 June 1835 - reported - that no information had yet been received on the ice-boats used on the Forth and Clyde Canal.

17 July 1835 - a communication from the Avon and Calder Navigation enclosing a report on the construction of ice-boats was produced and read - ordered - Mr Boyd to prepare a plan and estimate for an ice-boat.

14 August 1835 - A letter from the Forth and Clyde Canal Company on the subject of ice-boats was produced and read.

18 September 1835 - ordered - a new ice-boat be built and that previous to its construction Mr Boyd be directed to visit the Forth and Clyde Canal and inspect the ice-boat used there, as well as the mode of conveying loaded wagons along it.

2 October 1835 - ordered - that an estimate of expense of building a new ice-boat be prepared.

6 November 1835 - reported - that an estimate of the cost of building a new ice-boat was produced.

ordered - that the proposal of Messrs K. Wood and Sons to build an ice-boat for £300 be accepted. *(Kelsick Wood was a renowned Maryport shipbuilder).*

Meanwhile negotiations with Lord Lonsdale regarding the proposed docks at Port Carlisle were becoming rather protracted. Lord Lonsdale agreed to the site of the dock as shown in the plan but required two proposals to be satisfied. One of these was that there should be "a right of way between the canal and the intended docks, in case the said docks should be enclosed by a wall or bank". The other, more controversial proposal, was that he:- "expected a compensation by way of tonnage dues upon the trade which may frequent the docks or a percentage upon the receipts and profits of the same".

The Canal Company opposed this second proposal very strongly and raised the following arguments against it:-

I. Prior to the building of the canal, his Lordship's income from anchorage dues had been negligible.

2. Since his Lordship was a major shareholder in the Canal Company he would automatically profit from the new docks.

3. The land on which the docks stood was under water at high tide and therefore useless for any other purpose.

4. Experience had shown that land would be reclaimed to the west of the docks as a result of their construction and this land would automatically become Lord Lonsdale's property.

In spite of these arguments Lord Lonsdale persisted in his demands for compensation and he finally obtained a satisfactory agreement in the matter.

Almost fourteen years since the opening of the canal it was found necessary to close it for repairs. The repairs must have been quite major as the canal was closed for a period of sixteen days. The advertisement below left appeared in the Carlisle Journal. It gives the impression that the whole of the canal was to be closed to traffic.

CARLISLE CANAL NAVIGATION.

NOTICE is hereby given, that the CARLISLE CANAL will be CLOSED on SATURDAY, the Tenth day of JUNE next, (for the purpose of making repairs,) and will be OPENED again on MONDAY morning, the Twenty-sixth day of the same month.

By Order of the Committee of management,
GEORGE THOMPSON.

Dated, 27th April, 1837.

However, the Steam Pacquet Office included the notice (on the right) with their usual advertisement for the *Newcastle* steamer sailings. So the canal was still navigable on the long level section between Dikesfield, just beyond Burgh, and Port Carlisle. However the canal was effectively closed to heavy goods traffic to and from Carlisle.

NOTICE.

In consequence of the STOPPAGE of the CARLISLE CANAL from the 10th to the 26th of JUNE, the "CARLISLE and LIVERPOOL STEAM NAVIGATION COMPANY" hereby give NOTICE, that, during the time of the Stoppage, they will receive and deliver Goods at DIKESFIELD. Omnibuses will run between Carlisle and Dikesfield, and the Passage Boat will ply between Dikesfield and Port Carlisle, for the Conveyance of Passengers.

Passengers from Carlisle will be entered at the Company's Office.

JOHN CARRUTHERS, Agent.

Steam Pacquet Office, Carlisle,
May 31st, 1837.

Accidents continued to be a problem on the railway. On Thursday 4 May 1837 a serious accident occurred on the Canal Branch of the Newcastle and Carlisle Railway. The Carlisle Journal reported:-

"The Eden, locomotive engine, was taking a train of coal waggons from the Station to the Canal basin, about ll o'clock, in the forenoon, having her tender in front and the train following, when, after passing the bridge which crosses the Denton Holm road, she suddenly dashed off the rails. The tender was driven with such velocity against the flank wall as to make a considerable breach in it, the engine was thrown upon its side, and a number of laden waggons were all crushed up in a heap close upon it. The engine man was sitting in his seat, apparently dead; but his attendant had leaped off, and escaped without injury. Dr. Elliot was fortunately passing along the Dalston Road at the time, and immediately rendered his assistance to the engine man, whom he found suffering from the effects of a severe concussion. After a short time, the man was able to articulate, though quite insensible, and was then bled by Dr. Elliot, and we are happy to say is now in a fair way of recovery.

The engine was not so much injured as might have been expected, but several of the waggons were much broken, wheels wrenched off, axle-trees broken, and several of the wooden sleepers split in two. The immediate cause of the accident is unknown. It is said by some that a stone was upon the rails, and that the engine was going at a greater speed than is authorised, upon that part of the line, by the directors. Others say that the switches had been placed in the wrong direction, and this seems very probable, as the rails near the switches bear marks of wheels having gone off with great force. The engine however was lying some yards from the switches, and the marks may have been caused by some of the latter part of the train. If the accident had occurred ten yards more to the east the engine and train must have been precipitated down a steep bank."

STEAM COMMUNICATION BETWEEN PORT-CARLISLE AND BELFAST.

BY the rapid and Powerful NEW STEAMER.
MAID OF GALLOWAY.
J. D. HASWELL, Commander.

FROM BELFAST TO PORT CARLISLE, CALLING AT WHITEHAVEN.
Tuesday, 17th April, 10 o'Clock Evening.

FROM PORT CARLISLE TO BELFAST, CALLING AT WHITEHAVEN.
Thursday, 19th April, 6 o'Clock Morning.

FROM BELFAST TO WHITEHAVEN.
Tuesday, 10th April, 9 o'clock Evening
Tuesday, 24th April, 12 o'clock Noon.

FROM WHITEHAVEN TO BELFAST.
Thursday, 12th April, 10 o'clock Evening.
Thursday, 26th April, 9 o'clock Evening.

Further particulars may be known by applying to
JOSEPH ROBINSON, & Co., English Street, Carlisle.
ROBERT HENDERSON, Donegal Quay, Belfast.
ABRAHAM CAMPBELL, Stranraer.
FISHER & STEWARD, Whitehaven.
CLARKE and DUNN, Quay Side, Newcastle.

Steamship Competition

The steamer trade between Carlisle, Port Carlisle, Annan Waterfoot, Whitehaven, the Isle of Man and Liverpool was obviously flourishing at this time. Every week large advertisements for the rival companies appeared in the local press, advertising the sailings, together with fares and arrangements for conveying passengers to inland destinations. The Carlisle and Liverpool Steam Navigation Company had commenced operations about 1826 with the *Solway* steamer (see passage boat advert P.45) followed by the *Cumberland* steamer in 1827 (advert P.52). These two vessels plied between Port Carlisle and Liverpool. Then, in 1832, the Carlisle and Whitehaven Steam Company commenced operations with their boat, the *Elizabeth*, direct from the Canal Basin (see P.67), sailing to Whitehaven and the Isle of Man. This was a smaller vessel than the *Cumberland*, with paddles which could be raised to pass through the locks of the canal. In 1833, presumably to cope with the increased traffic, twice weekly services were started between Carlisle and Liverpool using both the *Solway* and the *Cumberland* steamers (P.59). In 1834 a new company appeared on the scene. The Carlisle and Annan Steam Navigation Company introduced a service to Liverpool with their new steam pacquet the 181 ton, *City of Carlisle* (P.58). In 1835 the Carlisle and Liverpool Steam Navigation Company responded by replacing the *Solway* and the *Cumberland* with the larger and more powerful steam pacquet the 396 ton *Newcastle* (P.74). Not to be outdone the Carlisle, Annan and Liverpool Steam Pacquet Company (now re-named), introduced their new 448 ton steamship, *Royal Victoria* to the Liverpool route in 1837. In addition a new steam service was started between Port Carlisle and Belfast by the owners of the *Maid of Galloway*. A few weeks after the introduction of the *Royal Victoria* the company's press advertisement was increased to two columns in width. Not to be outdone, the original Carlisle and Liverpool Steam Navigation Company followed suit, a couple of weeks later, with a similar sized advertisement advertising both of their ships. This rivalry continued for a further 13 years, until 1850, when the Carlisle, Annan and Liverpool Steam Pacquet Company withdrew its service and the company was wound up.

The introduction of the new steam ship, the *Royal Victoria* was a major maritime event in 1837. At 448 tons she was the largest steamer yet on the Carlisle to Liverpool run. She carried a carved figurehead representing the young Queen Victoria and arrived at Annan Waterfoot to a tumultuous reception. An hour later she arrived at Port Carlisle to a similar ovation. The *Royal Victoria* would be a state of the art vessel for her time. She was powered by two steam engines, each of 100 horse power, manufactured by Messrs. W. and T. Wilson, of Liverpool.

STEAM TO LIVERPOOL AND BELFAST.

THE CARLISLE and LIVERPOOL STEAM NAVIGATION COMPANY'S large and powerful STEAMER, the

NEWCASTLE,

Captain JOSEPH SEWELL,

Sails between PORT CARLISLE and LIVERPOOL, calling at ANNAN and WHITEHAVEN (Weather permitting), at the following times:—

FROM PORT CARLISLE.	FROM LIVERPOOL.
Wednesday, April 18, at 5 o'Clock Morning	Tuesday, April 17, at 1 o'Clock Morning
Saturday, April 21, at 8½ o'Clock Morning	Thursday, April 19, at 5 o'Clock Evening
Friday, April 27, at 12½ o'Clock Noon	Tuesday, April 24, at 9 o'Clock Night

THE SOLWAY,

Captain THOMAS BURTON,

Sails between PORT CARLISLE and BELFAST, calling at Annan, Whitehaven, and Ramsey (Isle of Man), leaving PORT CARLISLE every Friday, and BELFAST every Tuesday, two hours before high water.

The Canal Company's Boat plies on the Canal to suit the Arrivals and Sailings of the above Vessels: she leaves the Caual Basin, Carlisle, two hours before the above times of Sailing from Port Carlisle.

The Lighter leaves the Canal Basin with Goods that are intended for LIVERPOOL or BELFAST, the day previous to the Vessels sailing from Port Carlisle.

These Vessels are large and powerful, in all ordinary weather performing the passage in ONE TIDE. The Cabins are fitted up with due regard to the comfort of Passengers, and attended by a Steward and Stewardess, from whom Refreshments of every kind may be had on the most reasonable terms.

The Fares and Freight are moderate, and all Goods are forwarded free of commission by the Company's Agents, of whom further Particulars may be known.

Mr. J. CARRUTHERS, Steam Packet Office, Carlisle.
Mr. DAVID BAXTER, Annan.
Mr. JAS. GRAHAM, 99, Scotch Street, Whitehaven.
Mr. HENRY HALTON, 21, Water Street, Liverpool.
At Dumfries, information as to Passage, &c., may be obtained at the George and Commercial Inns.

Mr. JOHN WALKER, Cromford's Court, Market-street, Manchester.
Mr. ROBERT STORY, Fenwick's Entry, Newcastle-upon-Tyne.
Mr. JOHN PIM, jun., 20, Waring Street, Belfast.

Her dimensions were 150 feet by 25 feet and depth 15 feet. A newspaper report about the ship described the passenger facilities as follows:-

"Her main cabin, which is very commodious, is fitted up in a style of great elegance; with painted panels of satin-wood with rose-wood styles. A remarkably elegant Mahogany side-board, well furnished with massy plate graces one side of the cabin, having a large mirror above it, supported by two marble pillars. The cabin would dine about forty people very comfortably. - The sleeping apartments exceed anything of the kind we have seen for elegance, comfort and convenience- being handsomely fitted up with silk curtains, and the beds are roomy and well provided with every necessary. About 43 sleeping births (sic) can be fitted up. There are also two small sleeping cabins, intended for the use of private families, who wish to be kept together. The Ladies apartments are remarkably neat and tasteful; and, indeed, the whole of the fittings up of the cabins, reflect the greatest on the taste and ingenuity of Messrs. Stretch and Rainford, upholsterers, of Liverpool, and the spirit and liberality of the owners. *The Royal Victoria* was heavily laden, having brought the heaviest cargo ever imported into Port Carlisle by one vessel. ------—-- .The landing of such a vessel as the *Royal Victoria* says much for the spirit and enterprise of our townsmen. She is the fifth steamer now belonging to the Port, and the third regularly trading between this City and Liverpool. A very few years ago, there were only two small sailing vessels employed in the trade - seldom sailing oftener than once a fortnight, - indeed, not unfrequently occupying a whole month in the voyage. We have now three steamers of the largest class, and fitted up in the first style, sailing three times a fortnight, and performing the voyage in 12 hours. The *City of Carlisle* which belongs to the same company; and the *Newcastle*, belonging to the Carlisle and Liverpool Steam Navigation Company, are also capital vessels, of great capacity and power; yet our merchants and tradesmen have not hesitated to expend nearly £20,000 in building a new vessel to supply the increasing demands of our trade. The spirited inhabitants of Annan deserve a full share of this praise, for they have entered cordially and lilberally into the undertaking."

So, by 1837 the canal was, at last, beginning to prosper from the combined effects of the increase in trade through the Solway, which it had initiated way back in 1823, and the coming of the railway to the Canal Basin.

The Carlisle Canal was by now beginning to show some small return on the monies invested in it over the years, but this was never likely to match the level of returns which shares in the new railway companies were realising, and that was to be its undoing in the long term. The performance of the railways and the ever more sophisticated locomotive engines that were being developed continued to astonish the general public.

The Final Years - Death and Resurrection as a Railway

Reports like the one below from the Carlisle Journal, 8 July 1837, were becoming ever more commonplace:-

"GIGANTIC TRAIN - On Monday week the 'Atlas' Engine John Barnes, Engineer, brought down on the Newcastle and Carlisle Railway, from Milton to Carlisle, a Train of 100 waggons of coals, lime and coke, the weights of which would not be less than 450 tons and the length nearly a quarter of a mile - The distance, $10^{1}/_{4}$ miles, was accomplished in three quarters of an hour. This is, we believe, the greatest mass ever moved by a locomotive engine over the same space in so short a time."

Meanwhile the canal continued to claim the occasional life by drowning. An inquest at Beaumont on 2 September 1837 recorded an accident to a 10 year old boy, William Potts, who had drowned the previous day in the canal at Burgh. In the words of the Carlisle Journal:-

"The deceased was employed at the Chemical Works at the- latter place by Mr Williams, the proprietor, and whilst engaged in cleaning casks in shallow water between the fender, adjoining one of the bridges, had incautiously, in the absence of another workman, ventured to the extremity of the framework, and then fallen into the middle of the channel. He was not missed for four hours, and when found was of course quite dead."

In the summer of 1837 the lease of the Solway Hotel came up for renewal and was advertised in the local press. Port Carlisle was becoming known, not only for its steamer trade, but also as a weekend retreat from the city for the tired business men with its salt water baths. '

An advertisement in the Carlisle Journal, 14 October 1837, requested tenders for work to improve the buoying of the Solway Firth. In its news column the same paper, referring to the advertisement, expressed the hope that some steps would also soon be taken to erect a light-house as recommended by Lieut. Robinson (P.93).

References to the canal in the local press became less frequent over the ensuing months, apart from the occasional advertisement. Railways were much more newsworthy, particularly when accidents occurred.

On Friday 17 November 1837 an accident occurred with the engine Samson, travelling between Greenhead and the Canal Basin with a train of empty wagons. The Carlisle Journal reported the details:-

SOLWAY HOTEL.

TO be LET, and Entered upon at Candlemas next, for such a Term of Years as may be agreed upon, all that excellent and well-accustomed INN and BATHING HOUSE, situate at PORT CARLISLE, now in the occupation of Mrs. Waite.

The Premises are close to the place where the Steam Packets almost Daily take in and discharge Passengers from Carlisle, Liverpool, &c.

The above Concern is well worthy the attention of any enterprising Person.

The present Tenant will show the Premises, and further Particulars may be had from the Owner, Mr. Wood, of Kirklands.

Kirklands, Bowness, 24th August, 1837.

" --- it (the train) stopped at the London Road Station for the purpose of having attached to it three waggons (sic) loaded with stone, to be left at the Dalston Road Station; when about two hundred yards from the place where the loaded waggons were destined to stop, the breaksman, David Colhoun, to save time, detached them from the train of empty waggons, on one of which he was sitting at the time, but unfortunately fell immediately the trains were separated, and the three loaded waggons passed over both his legs a little below the knees. Medical aid was instantly procured, when it was found necessary to amputate both legs, above the knees, which was accordingly done that evening, we are happy, however, to learn that the poor man is in a fair way of recovery, and hope that some provision will be made for his future maintenance. It is but proper to observe, that the act which has *cost him so dearly* was entirely his own. He had no orders to do what he did; on the contrary, the engine was ordered to stop to detach the waggons."

One month later in June 1838 came the announcement of the official opening of the Newcastle and Carlisle Railway over the whole of its length. The railway had been operating in sections since February 1835, but the full route of 60 miles, from Newcastle to Carlisle had only just been completed. The advertisement on the right described the opening event, to be held on Monday 18 June 1838, and advertised tickets for sale at 10s. (50p.) each for places on the inaugural train. The Canal Branch Railway was not included as it was for goods only.

In spite of the lack of publicity for the canal at this time it was still considered a reasonably secure investment

NEWCASTLE-UPON-TYNE & CARLISLE RAILWAY.

THE DIRECTORS HEBEBY GIVE NOTICE, that MONDAY, the 18th instant, having been fixed for OPENING the LINE throughout, the Ordinary Business of the Railway will be suspended for that day, and that the Completion of the Communication between Newcastle and Carlisle, a distance of 60 Miles, will be celebrated by a Procession of Railway Trains, the arrangements for which will be as follows :—

The PROCESSION will leave the Company's Station, at Redheugh, Newcastle, at 11 o'clock in the Morning, *precisely*, (stopping on their rout at Blaydon, Stocksfield, Hexham, Haydon Bridge, Greenhead, and Milton,) for the Company's Station, at the Canal Basin, Carlisle, where it will arrive about 3 o'clock, and after giving time for refreshment at Carlisle, will leave the Company's Station at the London Road, Carlisle, precisely at 5 o'clock for Newcastle, stopping at the same places as in going. And for the accommodation of the friends of this important undertaking, and the Public resident at Carlisle and its vicinity, who may be desirous of Joining the Procession at Newcastle, a Train will leave the London Road Station at 6 o'clock in the Morning for that place, calling at the various Stations above-mentioned.

Tickets for the Opening day only, may be purchased for 10s. each, at the Railway Stations; at the Close, Newcastle; London Road, Carlisle; Blaydon, Hexham, Haydon Bridge, Greenhead, and Milton.

By Order,
JOHN ADAMSON, Secretary.
Railway Office, Close, Newcastle-upon-Tyne, 5th June, 1838.

London Road Station

Canal Terminus, Carlisle

J W Carmichael 1835

Tullie House Museum adn Art Gallery Trust

Better known as London Road Station this engineering drawing shows the Ticket Office and the station canopy. The horse drawn omnibus was needed to carry passengers into the city centre or to the canal basin, as the line to the basin, the canal branch, was designated for goods only.

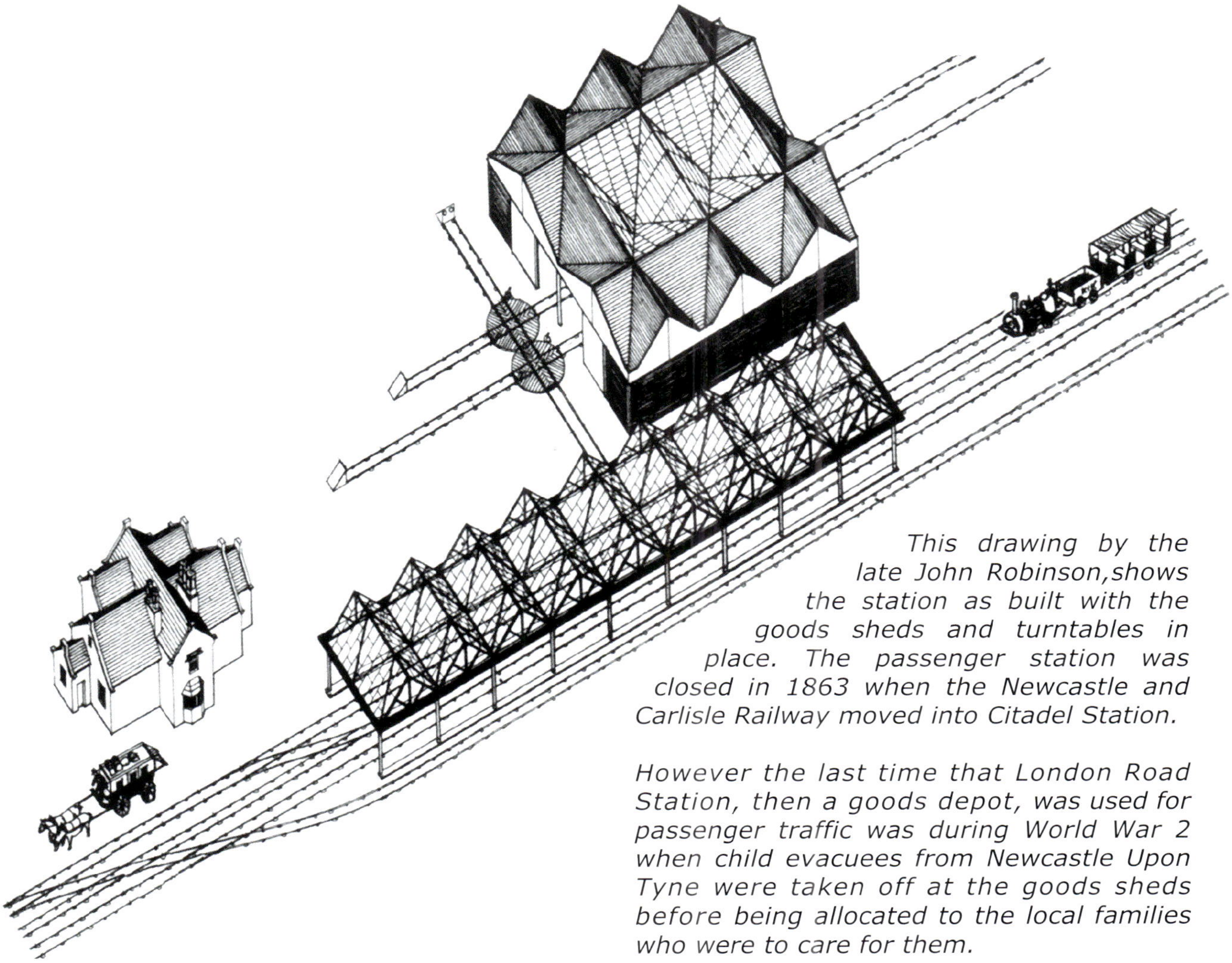

This drawing by the late John Robinson,shows the station as built with the goods sheds and turntables in place. The passenger station was closed in 1863 when the Newcastle and Carlisle Railway moved into Citadel Station.

However the last time that London Road Station, then a goods depot, was used for passenger traffic was during World War 2 when child evacuees from Newcastle Upon Tyne were taken off at the goods sheds before being allocated to the local families who were to care for them.

Below:
The Railway Inn - opposite the site of the London Road Station - seen in 1997
(now unfortunately closed)

Below:
Evacuees from
Newcaste Upon Tyne
arriving at London Road Station in 1940

and the Canal Company shares were in demand, as illustrated by the adjacent advertisement.

ON SALE,
SHARES in the Maryport and Carlisle Railway.
Do. in the Newcastle and Carlisle Railway.
Do. in the Carlisle, Annan, and Liverpool Steam Navigation Company.
Do. in the Carlisle Gas and Coke Company.
WANTED,
SHARES in the Carlisle Canal Company.
Do. in Carlisle and Cumberland Joint Stock Bank.
Do. in Carlisle City and District Bank.
J. and R. HOPE,
Share Brokers, Carlisle.
28th October, 1837.

A cautionary note here however. In the same advertisement shares in the Maryport and Carlisle Railway were advertised, a company that was to be a strong business rival to the canal.

The next newsworthy event regarding the canal appeared in the Carlisle Journal, 26 May 1838. The item read as follows:-

"THE ARROW - The Canal Company, we understand, intend to run their iron passage boat the *Arrow*, between this city and Port Carlisle every day in future during the season. On the Thursdays she will leave our Canal basin in the morning, and return in the evening, thus affording to parties of pleasure the opportunity of spending the day at Bowness." Previously the boat had only run three times a week during the summer to fit in with the steamer sailings. The company were now making provision for day trippers, which would further enhance the popularity of Port Carlisle as a coastal resort.

The *Arrow* (described in detail on pages 72 - 73) had proved to be a popular means of transport between Carlisle and Port Carlisle and was often overloaded because of the demand. The Canal Company therefore commissioned a new boat called the *Swallow* which was delivered in July 1838. The Carlisle Journal, 14 July 1838, reported the event:-

" The CANAL.- A new iron passage boat called the *Swallow*, was placed on our Canal on Saturday last, for the conveyance of passengers to Port Carlisle - the *Arrow* having been found too small for the increasing traffic of the city. It is a beautiful boat of its kind- 70 feet in length and seven and a half feet in breadth. It was built by Messrs. Hannay and Reid, of Paisley, and fitted up by Mr. Walker, of the same place. The cabins are elegant and commodious, affording room for nearly 100 passengers and their luggage. We saw her start on Wednesday with 80 passengers, and an immense quantity of luggage; yet with this loading, she only drew 16 inches of water, and made the passage in less than two hours, including all stoppages. What with the Canal and the Railway, there are now four large omnibuses, in almost constant employment, taking out and bringing in passengers."

This latter statement is a reference to the horse drawn omnibuses which were used to ferry passengers between the London Road Station, the town and the Canal Basin.

According to the Canal Company Minutes of May 1838, the buoying of the Firth, according to Mr Robinson's plan, had been completed. As a result a charge of 3 farthings (3/4d) a ton was to be placed on the steam companies for every vessel passing the buoys from Port Carlisle, Silloth Bay or any port or place north of Silloth Bay. This charge was allowed by the Admiralty to pay for the upkeep of the Buoys.

The large steamers often had problems transferring between berths at Annan Waterfoot and Port Carlisle. In order to alleviate this problem a new steam tug, the *Clarence*, was purchased to act as a tender to the Carlisle steam vessels and to be employed generally between Port Carlisle and Annan Waterfoot. Details of the *Clarence* and her purpose were published in the Carlisle Journal, l2 June 1838 as follows:-

" IMPORTANT T0 THE PORT OF CARLISLE - We are glad to notice that the suggestions we made some time ago, respecting a steam tug and ferry boat for Port Carlisle, is now about being carried into effect by the Canal Company, and the two Steam Companies, they having purchased a steamer called *Clarence*, from Robert Napier, Esq., of Glasgow. She is 96 feet long, 16 feet beam, and 8 feet depth of hold, and her draught of water is only four feet six inches. She has an engine of 45 horse power on board, and is now receiving a new boiler, and a complete overhaul. We believe during the summer season she will ply daily at tide time between Port Carlisle and Annan Water-Foot, and the canal passage boat will take passengers from here, so as to suit the time of her sailing from Port Carlisle, and leave again on her retum from Annan Water-Foot. This will afford great facility to passengers to and from Annan, and the charge will only be one-half the present coach fare. The *Clarence* we learn has very handsome cabins, being fitted up entirely for passengers. When an occasional low tide occurs, she will take passengers to and from the Liverpool and Belfast Steamers, tow Lighters with goods to and from Annan, and thus do away with the present detention, caused by taking goods on board the Liverpool Steamers, on their calling at Annan Water-Foot to land and receive passengers. In short we are quite certain it will highly benefit the interests of this port, both in, goods and passengers, more especially the latter, as matters will now be conducted with comfort and safety, and combine greater expedition. The *Clarence* is expected in two or three weeks."

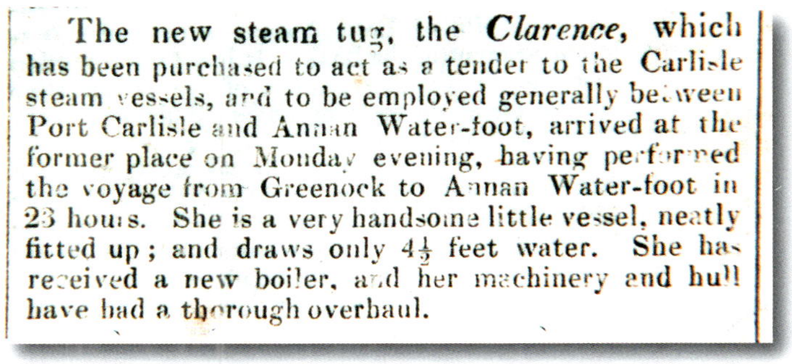

The new steam tug, the **Clarence**, which has been purchased to act as a tender to the Carlisle steam vessels, and to be employed generally between Port Carlisle and Annan Water-foot, arrived at the former place on Monday evening, having performed the voyage from Greenock to Annan Water-foot in 23 hours. She is a very handsome little vessel, neatly fitted up; and draws only 4½ feet water. She has received a new boiler, and her machinery and hull have had a thorough overhaul.

One of the continuing problems throughout the life of the Carlisle Canal had been water supply. It had been thought that the second, new waterwheel constructed in 1834, would solve the problem once and for all, but experience had proved otherwise. As the canal aged it leaked more and more and the increased traffic demanded even more water, because of the more frequent use of the locks. By 1839 the Canal Company were compelled to dig deeper into their pockets when they installed, what they hoped would be, the final solution to this problem. The Carlisle Journal, l June 1839 takes up the story:-

"Cornish High-Pressure, Expansive Condensing Steam Engine, At Carlisle. - On Saturday, the 25th inst., the steam engine, manufactured in Cornwall, by Messrs. Harvey and Co. of Hayle, from the specifications and plans of that eminent practical engineer, William West, Esq., for the Carlisle Canal Company, commenced working. The Directors assembled at twelve o'clock, and in a few minutes after the engine was started by Mr. Halton, the chairman of the Company, and Mr. West the engineer, who had arrived from Cornwall for that purpose. The volume of water sent forth excited universal surprise, and was in the highest degree gratifying to the Directors of the Canal Company, and many gentlemen and artisans from the city, whom curiosity had drawn to the spot. This engine will supply the canal with water from the river Eden. The height of the lift is about 50 feet. The steam cylinder is 60 inches in diameter, that of the pump 45; (the largest pump known to our correspondent in the kingdom;) 'length of engine stroke, l0 feet. In less than three minutes, nine loud huzzas announced that the water had been lifted to the pump head, whence it was poured forth in a continuous and rapid stream, at the rate of 6,624 gallons a minute. The engine working at twelve strokes - in twelve hours there will consequently be delivered into the canal 4,769,280 imperial gallons of water, equal to about 763,200 cubic feet, at an expense of coal under five shillings.

The canal, from Carlisle to the Solway Firth, is in length about twelve miles. There are six locks, each about 67 feet long, 22 feet wide, and $8^1/_2$ feet deep, and when required, such is the power of this effective machine, that the quantity of water contained in each lock, can be replace in less than 10 minutes, i.e. nearly as quickly as a vessel can be passed through.

In the course of a month Harvey and West's new patent valves, will be substituted for those now at work, when the friction will be much diminished, and the heavy blow, and injurious vibration (general with the common pumping engine valves) will be entirely overcome."

Pages 35 and 39 tell more about the water supply problems to the canal. Here at last those problems had been solved for good. The article went on to describe other engines built by the same engineer and to extol the virtues of the power and the economy of Mr. West's engines, and of the patent valves used. According to the Canal Company Minutes, the steam engine was purchased for £3700 and half an acre of ground was purchased at a cost of £100, from Mr Fawcett, for the steam engine house. When water was in plentiful supply the engine was put to use grinding bone meal (see advert below).

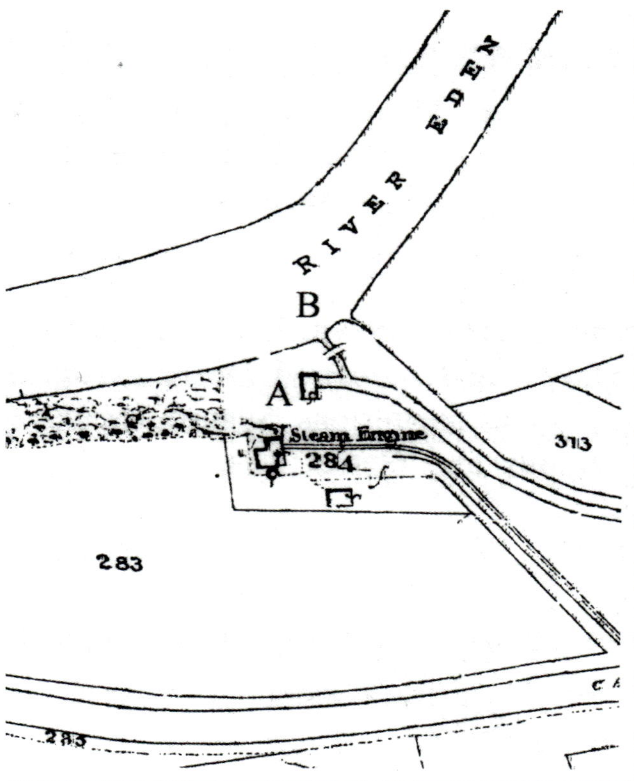

A dividend of 4% was declared in July 1839 in spite of the fact that the Canal Company had been persuaded by the Railway Company to reduce the charge for carrying coal by $12^1/_2$%. For this concession the Canal Company were guaranteed at least the same amount of business, with a possible improvement, instead of a continuing decline. This was because the Newcastle and Carlisle Railway company now had the option of exporting coal via Maryport, using the newly opened Maryport and Carlisle Railway.

In July 1839 the Newcastle and Carlisle Railway was once more in the news. The increase in traffic on the line was "truly astonishing" in the words of one reporter. Receipts for the week ending June 29 were £1934, and for the week ending July 6, £1936. This was an increase of £500 on the corresponding weeks in the previous year. It was also commented that, previous to the opening of the railway, it was difficult to support one coach on the road for passengers. On the freight side, half a dozen carriers carts, travelling once a week were able to conduct all the traffic. This fact alone illustrates the immense impact the coming of the railways and the steam package boats had on the lives of ordinary people. Travelling had suddenly become much less time consuming and also much less expensive.

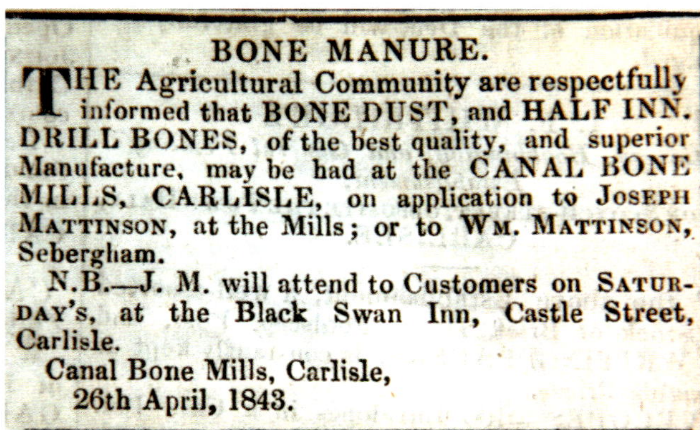

In July 1839 at the Annual General Meeting of the Canal Company a dividend of 4% on the Canal Company Shares was declared and the comment was made :-

"The increase of traffic upon the canal, during the last 12 months has exceeded the most sanguine expectations of its supporters."

About the same time the Carlisle Journal, 13 July 1839, reported that the steamer *City of Carlisle* was to make a pleasure trip to the Isle of Man on Monday week to return on the following Wednesday. A large party of citizens, ladies as well as gentlemen, had already engaged berths. This must have been one of the first Package Holidays on record. The pastime of cruising for pleasure and visiting exotic places had begun!

Seventeen Years after the opening of the canal a new Ship-building Company had been founded at the Canal Basin and or Thursday l6 January 1840 they launched their first vessel. The Carlisle Journal described the scene thus:-

"On Thursday last a beautiful new vessel was launched from the building yard of the Carlisle Shipbuilding Company and named the *Corby Castle*. Having been laid down alongside the canal she glided down the ways broadside into the water, amid the cheers of the multitude of spectators, in the most gallant style. The *Corby Castle* is intended to be schooner rigged, and will carry about 100 tons, she is a beautiful specimen of naval architecture, and reflects great credit on the builder, Mr P Nelson. This the first vessel built by the company, which was formed only about six months ago, and preparations are already in a state of forwardness for laying down another. The owners afterwards dined together, and spent a very pleasant evening."

So, even in this age of ever larger steamships there was obviously still a market for the smaller traditional sailing craft.

According to the Canal Company Minutes of 5 February, 1840, a light was finally to be placed at the end of the steamer jetty at Port Carlisle, with accommodation for a person to attend it.

This was followed at the end of that year with the launching of a new lightship for the Solway, built at Carlisle by Mr William Bell. William Carruthers was engaged, shortly after, as the master of the lightship at

MISS DOUGLAS.

FOR SALE, by AUCTION, on FRIDAY, the 11th of AUGUST, 1837, at Six o'Clock in the Evening, at Mr. THOMAS WALKER's, *the Gleaner*, in the Old Grapes' Lane, CARLISLE, the Superior SCHOONER, MISS DOUGLAS, (now lying in the Canal Basin) burthen, per Register, 55[illegible] Tons, new measurement, and 75 Tons, old measurement. Her dimensions are, Length 54 feet Breadth 16 feet, and Depth, 7½ feet.

This fine, fast-sailing Schooner was built at Bowness, and nearly re-built at Carlisle, under particular inspection, and of first-rate materials, in 1835. She was originally built for the Slate Trade, and has latterly been employed as a Regular Trader between Carlisle and Liverpool. She is amply supplied with Stores of the best quality, is in every respect adapted to the Trade for which she was or g nally built, and will be found well worthy the attention of Purchasers.

The Schooner and all her Stores to be taken with all faults, as they now are, without any allowance for weight, length, quality, or defect whatsoever.

Terms of Payment, 10 per cent. deposit. The remainder of the purchase-money to be paid, one half at 3 months, the other at 6 Months, with approved Security.

For further particulars apply to:—

JOS. ALLISON, } Assignees to
JOS. ADDISON, } WM. S. DENTON.
THOS. WALKER }

PROPERTY AT CALDCOATS.

TO be SOLD, in PUBLIC AUCTION, at the House of Mrs. REED, *White Lion*, ENGLISH STREET, CARLISLE, on THURSDAY, the 25th JULY, 1839, at Seven o'Clock in the Evening; all that Freehold DWELLING HOUSE, Five Four-Loom WEAVING SHOPS, and Rooms above; with a Byer, Stable, and other Conveniences, situate at CALDCOATS, in the Parish of Saint Mary, Carlisle.

The above Premises are only a few yards from the Carlisle Canal Basin, and the Newcastle and Carlisle Railway, and may be seen on application to JANE and MARY BOUSTEAD, of Caldcoats, the Owners.

Further Particulars may be had of Messrs. LAW and BENDLE, Solicitors, Carlisle.

BROWNE, Auctioneer.

The Solway Lightship

a salary of £6 per month. He was also allowed 8 shillings a week for "the victualling of two men."

The photograph shows the lightship in Silloth Harbour around 1890.The lightship was anchored off Allonby to guide shipping into the Solway. It was manned by crews who lived on board for days on a rota basis. The lightship on a number of occasions, found herself ashore after stormy seas broke the anchoring, sending her off to various parts of the Solway.

in 1920 the ageing boat was decommisioned and, for a while, lay in the dock at Silloth, but her life was not over yet. Local plumber and gas fitter, William Ferguson (father of entertainer A. C. Astor of Her Majesty's Theatre, Carlisle fame) purchased the boat and had it towed up the coast by tug on a high tide so it could be beached near Skinburness. It was then used as a teashop and visitor attraction. A set of steps up to the main deck allowed tourists walking to and from Skinburness to call in, explore ths ship and buy refreshments. In 1926 it was put up for sale but, as no buyer could be found, the ship was finally broken up for scrap in 1929. The very large Trinity House bell from the ship was salvaged and used as a signal bell on the first green at Silloth golf course. John Proudlock, of Silloth Golf course, explained that this is a hidden green and the bell was used to signal following golfers that the green was free. Unfortunately the bell was stolen about 30 years ago when scrap metal was fetching a very high value.

The docks at Port Carlisle were nearing completion at this time and the rates to be charged for vessels using the facilities were decided and published. The rates and duties levied on vessels navigating the canal were recorded in "A List of the Cumberland Shipping, William Sawyers," published in 1840.

The Trinity House bell on board the ship.

The bell on the first green at Silloth in 1933.

These three images show the lightship beached as a visitor attraction between Silloth and Skinburness.

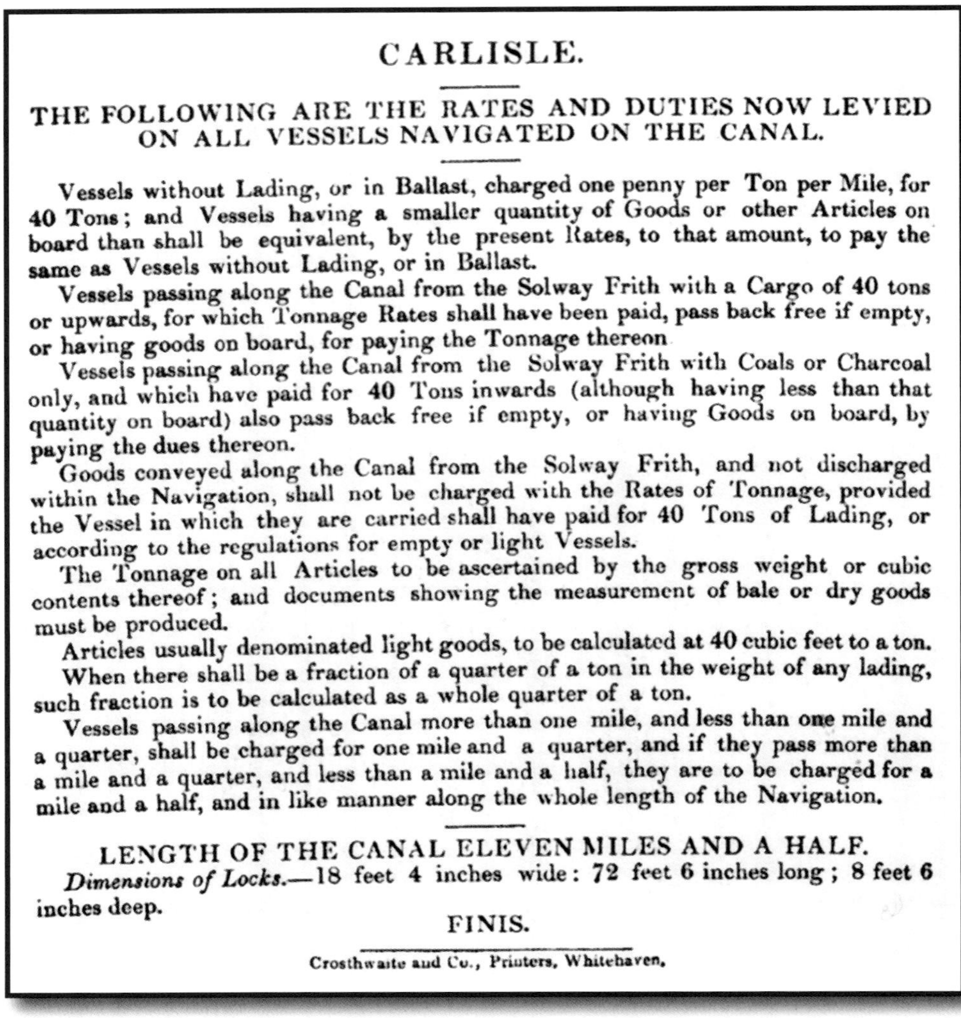

CARLISLE.

THE FOLLOWING ARE THE RATES AND DUTIES NOW LEVIED ON ALL VESSELS NAVIGATED ON THE CANAL.

Vessels without Lading, or in Ballast, charged one penny per Ton per Mile, for 40 Tons; and Vessels having a smaller quantity of Goods or other Articles on board than shall be equivalent, by the present Rates, to that amount, to pay the same as Vessels without Lading, or in Ballast.

Vessels passing along the Canal from the Solway Frith with a Cargo of 40 tons or upwards, for which Tonnage Rates shall have been paid, pass back free if empty, or having goods on board, for paying the Tonnage thereon

Vessels passing along the Canal from the Solway Frith with Coals or Charcoal only, and which have paid for 40 Tons inwards (although having less than that quantity on board) also pass back free if empty, or having Goods on board, by paying the dues thereon.

Goods conveyed along the Canal from the Solway Frith, and not discharged within the Navigation, shall not be charged with the Rates of Tonnage, provided the Vessel in which they are carried shall have paid for 40 Tons of Lading, or according to the regulations for empty or light Vessels.

The Tonnage on all Articles to be ascertained by the gross weight or cubic contents thereof; and documents showing the measurement of bale or dry goods must be produced.

Articles usually denominated light goods, to be calculated at 40 cubic feet to a ton.

When there shall be a fraction of a quarter of a ton in the weight of any lading, such fraction is to be calculated as a whole quarter of a ton.

Vessels passing along the Canal more than one mile, and less than one mile and a quarter, shall be charged for one mile and a quarter, and if they pass more than a mile and a quarter, and less than a mile and a half, they are to be charged for a mile and a half, and in like manner along the whole length of the Navigation.

LENGTH OF THE CANAL ELEVEN MILES AND A HALF.

Dimensions of Locks.—18 feet 4 inches wide: 72 feet 6 inches long; 8 feet 6 inches deep.

FINIS.

Crosthwaite and Co., Printers, Whitehaven.

On Saturday evening the 16 March 1840 there was a fatal accident at the canal basin. One Peter Henderson and another person were unloading a timber wagon when a piece of sycamore rolled from the wagon and knocked Henderson down, having given him a severe blow on the head. He was instantly lifted up and placed in a sitting position, but died immediately. An inquest was held the following day before the coroner, Mr Carrick, and a verdict of accidental death was returned, with a deodand of one shilling on the timber.

As mentioned before this imposition of a fine on an inanimate object was quite common in the 19th century. Such accidents were rarely attributed to the negligence of the employer. For those interested the dictionary definition of 'deodand' is as follows:- .

"Formerly in English Law, an object which caused the death of a person, either accidentally or intentionally, and which was then confiscated by the Crown to be used for charitable purposes."

Presumably the owner of the piece of sycamore had to pay one shilling or have it confiscated for the court to sell.

The first recorded accident at Port Carlisle since the completion of the new stone dock occurred on the 19 August 1840. The newspaper report, 5 September 1840, described how a seaman, called Jordan, died. He was the mate of a small vessel the *Janus* of Maryport, which had discharged its cargo at Port Carlisle :-

" -- on the 19th of last month deceased left "Miss Waller's" about nine o - clock in the evening, to proceed, as was supposed, to his vessel lying at the new pier. On his way he had to pass over the canal, by the lock gates, the footpath along which is exceedingly narrow, and without the protection of a handrail. He was not seen or heard of until the day on which his body was found, as before stated, by Mr Dodd, the superintendent of the works in the upper lock, his vessel having in the meantime sailed. His friends from Maryport, of which town he was a native, attended the inquest and identified the body. - Verdict, --- 'found drowned' ——--- "

In September 1840 the Newcastle and Carlisle Railway was five years and five months old since its partial opening in 1835. According to the Railway Magazine, 1,028,946 persons had been carried a distance of 16,641,869 miles, with no fatal accidents to passengers. There had been three slight accidents, and a sailor broke his thigh in jumping off the train. The accidents and deaths to employees, during the construction and running of the line, some of which have been reported earlier in this book, were not reported!

The *Solway* Steamer, being the first steamer to have operated out of Port Carlisle, underwent an extensive refit in 1841, receiving new boilers and thorough repairs to her hull and machinery. She returned on station to the Port Carlisle, Belfast run in May 1841. Unfortunately only three months later she grounded in the Solway. The Carlisle Journal, 28 August 1841, reported:-

"ACCIDENT TO THE SOLWAY STEAMER. ----- We regret to have to announce that on Tuesday last the *Solway* steamer while on its way from Belfast to Carlisle, laden with two hundred passengers and as many cattle, got out of the channel, owing to the darkness of the night, and struck upon Dumruff-Bank, at the entrance to the Scotch channel of the Solway Firth. She beat violently over the bank and made water so rapidly that the Captain, in order to save the passengers, was obliged to run her ashore, near the mouth of the Nith. One hundred and fifty six cattle were thrown overboard, and the passengers were, after some difficulty, safely landed in the boats. The vessel has sustained considerable damage, and though she still remains on the bank, hopes are entertained that, should the weather continue favourable, she may be got off and be prevented from becoming a total wreck. ---"

This was not a good time for shipping in the Solway. Only the previous week the *Solway* steamer had been involved in a rescue, when the Brig, *Samuel*, laden with timber from Quebec, had capsized alter hitting the Red Sands, near Bowness. The crew had taken to the jolly boat, were picked up by the *Solway* steamer and were then carried safely to Port Carlisle. The brig righted on the evening tide and was towed up to the new stone dock by the steam tug *Clarence*.

The incident caused great excitement in the village and nearly caused a tragedy. The Journal reported as follows:- " ---no sooner had the schoolmaster dismissed his numerous train of pupils than off they hurried to the ill-fated vessel, eager to ascertain whether or not she would prove a total wreck. One little urchin, named James Allen, more anxious than the rest, had incautiously approached beyond his depth, and would have been carried out with the ebb tide and drowned, had not a shout From some person near; attracted the attention of Mr. Irwin of Her Majesty's Customs, at Port Carlisle, who instantly leaped into the water, and after swimming some distance, rescued the child from a watery grave."

The Solway Firth was a treacherous waterway, especially for sailors who did not know the area. The Canal Committee minutes of 13 April 1843 illustrated this fact quite well. The Canal Committee were concerned at the number of troop ships which came into Port Carlisle, but did not make use of the services of the local pilot. The Committee ordered that a letter be sent to the Secretary of War about the dangers of conveying troops up the Solway Firth, in strange ships, without a pilot.

In October 1842 a rather controversial accident occurred near the Brick Lock at Burgh by Sands. A 15 year old girl, Mary Lowe, accidentally fell in to the canal at the west end bridge. At the time the pacquet boat was expected from Carlisle, but had not yet arrived and a flat (a boat with a flat bottom and square ends), called the *Gammon*, was in the

An aerial view of part of Brough. The line of the canal is shown. Five of the eight locks on the canal were within a two mile stretch through the village of Burgh by Sands.

lock above the point where the girl fell in. Margaret Norman, who was opening the upper gate of the Brick Lock, heard Mary call, and saw her fall into the water. Margaret rushed to the bridge and, on seeing part of the girl's dress above the water, she ran 50 yards to Mr Liddell's house. Mrs. Liddell and William Norman came in about five minutes, and obtained a drag to help locate the girl. The report in the Carlisle Journal, 8 October 1842, continued thus:-

"The *Gammon* flat was seen coming down the canal beyond the bridge, at the chemical works, and Mrs. Liddell ran forwards and met the driver on the towing path, with two horses near a gate, about 70 yards from the bridge, under which Mary Lowe was lying in the canal, and after informing him of the fact, desired him to stop the horses, which he did, On this, the driver called to the captain of the flat, who ordered him to drive on. He did so, the bridge was lifted, and the flat passed through and over the spot where the unfortunate girl had been seen to drop into the water, and it was not until the vessel had reached and passed through the bridge that the drag could be used, and the body of the girl, at the second attempt, in a few moments, recovered from its watery bed. The body, after remaining on the bank awhile, was removed to the house of her mistress, where a zealous effort was made by Mr. Spence, of the chemical works, to resuscitate the poor girl, but from the space of time which had elapsed before that gentleman had arrived and the previous delay occasioned by the vessel, unhappily without success. The jury gave their verdict 'accidentally drowned;' and having carefully weighed all the circumstances, agreed in pronouncing a censure upon the master of the 'Gammon,' as the delay caused by his persisting in going forward extinguished the last hope of restoring or preserving the life of this poor orphan girl.

The jury, through their foreman, the Rev. J. Lowry, strongly recommended to the coroner, W. Carrick, Esq., to lay the unhappy case before the Canal Company, that they might furnish the rules of the Humane Society and the proper instruments requisite for the future under such a melancholy catastrophe."

Many of the deaths due to drowning in the canal were drink related. Caldewgate in particular had been noted for the riotous and drunken behaviour of many of its inhabitants ever since the arrival of the first canal workers in 1821. In September 1843 an inquest was held on one, James Watson, a potter, aged 29, who had been found drowned in the canal near Grinsdale. The Carlisle Journal reported:-

" It appears that on the evening of Saturday, the 7th inst., the deceased was very drunk, and had been quarrelling and lighting in Caldewgate with several companions; that he was afterwards turned out of one or two public houses: and then proceeded on his way to a camp, where his party were passing the night, near Grinsdale to reach this place he would have to cross the canal bridge; and it is supposed he had missed his footing and fallen into the canal. Verdict; -- Found Drowned."

November 1843 saw further loss of life in the Solway. Timber was often ferried along the Solway by tying it together in large rafts. In this particular instance a raft of timber had broken adrift at Rockcliffe and was observed as it passed the harbour mouth at Port Carlisle. The Carlisle Journal report described what happened next:-

The harbour mouth at Port Carlisle from the top of the stone pier.

"Four local men William Carlton, innkeeper; John Carlton, his son, mariner; Matthew Sharp, mariner; and Robert Nicholson, eldest son of Mr. William Nicholson, late of Wetheral Abbey, all of Port Carlisle-- put off in pursuit of the timber in an open boat, the property of the Royal Victoria Steam Navigation Company. Although the steersman was cautioned not to use the boat on any account, and more particularly as she was not sufficiently ballasted for such tempestuous weather, he could not be entreated to return; and when opposite Battle-hill, the boat unfortunately capsized, when the whole of the persons named were precipitated into the furious element. In a short time after she upset, two of the crew were observed clinging to the side of the boat, but her anchor having caught hold of the ground, instantly brought her under water, thereby cutting off every chance of escape. None of the bodies have yet been found."

Until this time steam vessels had generally been propelled by paddle wheels. In 1844, however, a new steamboat was tried on the Carlisle canal which was driven by a propellor. The innovation caused great interest and excitement and was duly described in the Carlisle Journal, 24 February 1844:-

" STEAM BOATS ON CANALS' - A small steam boat of about six tons burthen, with an engine of six horsepower, and fitted up on a principle somewhat similar to the Archimedean screw, has this week been tried upon our canal, and has excited much interest among our scientific and mercantile men. The motion of the vessel through the water is extremely steady —- the vibrations of the engine are scarcely felt by those on board – and what is of the greatest importance of all, it causes no 'wash' at the sides of the canal, whereby the banks can be in any way injured more than by the common track-boat. The experiments tried during the week have given the greatest satisfaction to all who have witnessed them. The present boat was brought to the canal merely to show those interested the advantages of the 'screw principle,' but we believe it will be the forerunner of a class of iron steamers, built upon the same principle, to run between the canal basin and Liverpool, and intended to meet the change of traffic which must follow the opening of the Railway to Lancaster. This is a much better way of meeting difficulties, and entering upon competition, than lying down and 'blubbering' for protection.

STEAM TO DUBLIN.--- We are glad to hear that the Dublin Steam Navigation Company are about to run one of their splendid vessels weekly between Port Carlisle and Dublin, calling at Fleetwood. This will be a great accommodation to the public, and we have no doubt it will meet with every encouragement?"

As mentioned previously the people of Carlisle were well catered for in the provision of public houses. In 1844 one more was added to the list with the opening of the 'Sailor' at 34 Caldcotes, now part of Carr's Biscuit Works. The position of the original pub can be seen on the map on the next page.

The name of the pub was changed to the 'Jovial Sailor' in about 1850 and the picture below left is from a turn of the century photograph, just before the pub was rebuilt in its present position at the entrance to the canal yard. The present building dates from 1904.

An interesting little story about the pub

The Jovial Sailor Public House

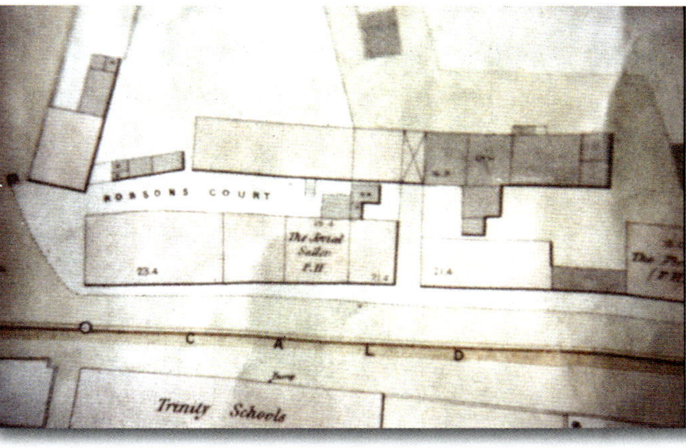

Cumbria Archive Centre, Carlisle

The photograph of the original Jovial Sailor on the previous page is reproduced from a newspaper cutting and shows the proprietor Mr John Nichols and his dog.

The photograph of the modern Jovial Sailor above was taken in 1997. Unfortunately at the time of writing the pub is empty and looking for a landlord.

The canal gatehouse to the left of the pub is the only remaining original canal building and is identical, except for the recently added dormer windows, to the Victoria Baths at Port Carlisle.

relates to the narrowness of the door to the gents toilet. A framed rhyme on the wall explains. The only problem with this quaint little tale is that the canal closed almost 50 years before the modern 'Jovial Sailor' was built.

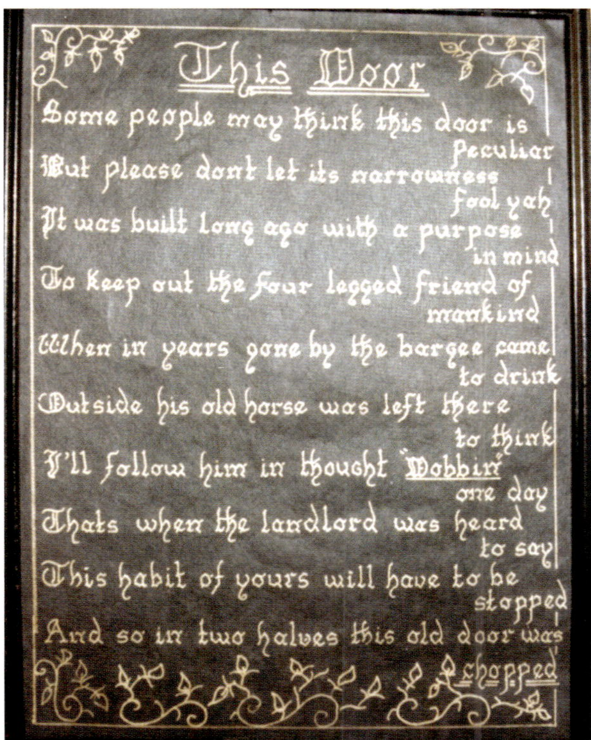

The Victoria Baths at Port Carlisle

The advertisement below heralded the completion of the Victoria Baths at Port Carlisle. This further enhanced the resort image of the village, which could be visited to partake of the sea air and healthy salt water baths. The Carlisle Journal carried the following report:-

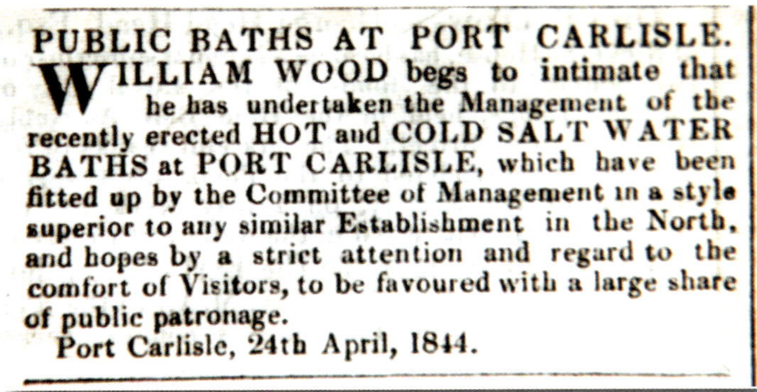

PUBLIC BATHS AT PORT CARLISLE.

WILLIAM WOOD begs to intimate that he has undertaken the Management of the recently erected HOT and COLD SALT WATER BATHS at PORT CARLISLE, which have been fitted up by the Committee of Management in a style superior to any similar Establishment in the North, and hopes by a strict attention and regard to the comfort of Visitors, to be favoured with a large share of public patronage.

Port Carlisle, 24th April, 1844.

"BATHS AT PORT CARLISLE --The excellent salt water hot and cold baths, recently erected at Port Carlisle by a Joint Stock Company, are now in full operation, and will be found a great accommodation to the public, and a source of general attraction to the port - see advt.."

The Victoria Baths building, was constructed using money raised from the issue of five hundred £1 shares in 1844. Apparently inflation did not have much effect on its value over the years, because the father of the present owner, Roger Brough, bought the building for £540 in 1944;one hundred years after its construction.

Port Carlisle Bathhouse - front and rear views.

The large metal object that the gentleman is inspecting is the replacement boiler mentioned in the advert opposite and pictured below left.

It was recently removed during building renovations.

A handpump was used to pump filtered sea water direct from the Solway through a pipe under the road into the building.

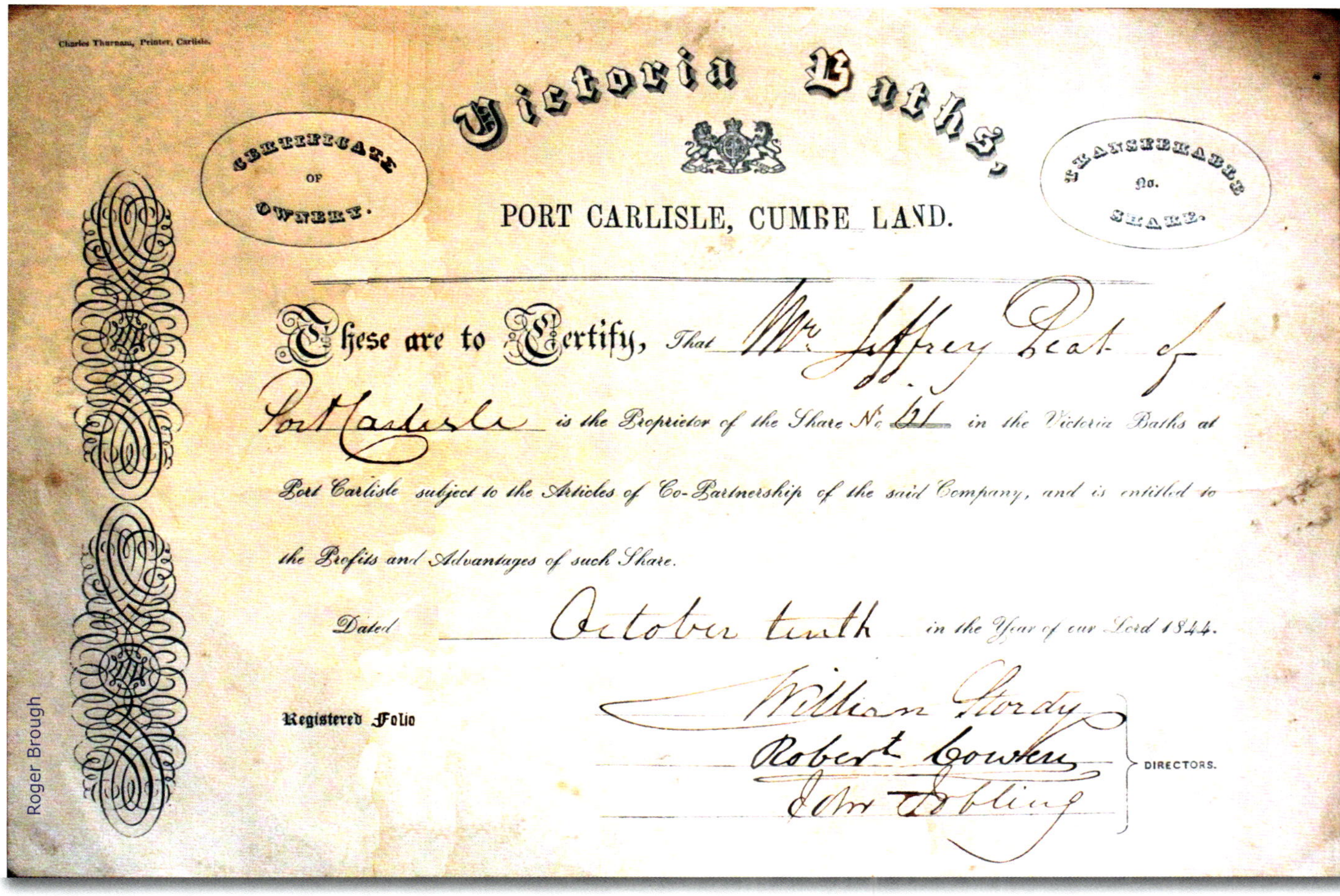

Charles Thurnam, Printer, Carlisle.

Victoria Baths,

Certificate of Ownery.

Transferable No. Share.

PORT CARLISLE, CUMBE LAND.

These are to Certify, That Mr Jeffrey Peat of Port Carlisle is the Proprietor of the Share No 61 in the Victoria Baths at Port Carlisle subject to the Articles of Co-Partnership of the said Company, and is entitled to the Profits and Advantages of such Share.

Dated October tenth in the Year of our Lord 1844.

Registered Folio

William Stordy
Robert Cowen
John Dobling
DIRECTORS.

Roger Brough

Roger Brough

Mrs Mary J Irving owner of the Port Carlisle Baths in the late 19th and early 20th century, pictured in the boiler room

Baths at Port Carlisle.—As the season for the sea side advances the visitors to the baths at Port Carlisle increase in number. A new boiler has recently been erected, and answers admirably, whilst the pipes and filtering apparatus by which salt water is introduced, for either hot or shower baths, work so effectively as to ensure at all times a clear supply. The arrangements, under the attentive superintendence of Mrs. Murray, are unexceptionable, and a delightful hot dip may be obtained at a few minutes' notice.

VICTORIA BATHS, PORT CARLISLE.

GREAT REDUCTION IN PRICES.

THE Public are respectfully informed that the above BATHS have just been put in good order; and either Hot, Cold, or Shower Baths, may be had on giving a few minutes' notice.

RATES.

HOT BATHS:
Single Bath, 1s. 6d.; Four Baths, 5s.; Upwards, 1s. 3d. each.

COLD BATHS:
Single Bath, 9d.; Five Baths, 2s. 6d.; Upwards, 6d. each.

SHOWER BATHS:
Each Bath 6d.

Apply to Mrs. Murray, Canal Cottage, adjoining Baths.

WELSH SLATES.

ON SALE, at the CANAL BASIN, a large quantity of Bangor and Port Madoc SLATES, at very low Prices.—Apply to Wm. Black, Slate Merchant, 8, Botchergate, Carlisle.
Carlisle, June 12th, 1850.

In July 1844 the first sign of future problems with the harbour at Port Carlisle were becoming apparent. The Carlisle Journal, 13 July 1844, described the problem and offered some interesting solutions:-

"Navigation at Port Carlisle.

We are sorry to hear that the bar leading from the canal to the Jetty end, at Port Carlisle, has latterly very much increased, and that the Liverpool and Irish Steamers very seldom get further than Annan Water Foot, as they dare not attempt coming to Port Carlisle, excepting in a fourteen feet tide, or upwards. It appears therefore most desirable that the canal Directors should bestir themselves, and use some effective means to improve the navigation, either by lengthening the Jetty, bringing the rivers Wampool and Waver by a cut to Port Carlisle, to clear away the obstruction, or by extending the navigation to Bowness. If something of the kind be not done the trade may be driven to some other port in the Firth, which might be very prejudicial not only to the interests of the Canal Company, but to the inhabitants of Carlisle generally.-- "

The second suggestion is quite interesting. If put into practice it would have meant cutting a channel across Glasson Moss - so Anthorn would really have become an Island. As locals know this area is commonly referred to as 'The Island'. One of the reasons for this silting up of the dock area was to be found not very far to the east. Here, at the point where the back drain discharged into the Solway, a jetty was being constructed; which was to become known as Ravenbank Jetty.

On 3l August 1844 the Journal reported that, a few days before, Lord Lonsdale had visited Burgh to inspect the large embankment he was having built, to prevent the loss of soil from part of 2,000 acres of marsh land. Part of this scheme to reclaim land east of Port Carlisle was the building of the Ravenbank Jetty. However, as the passage of time was to show, the effect of the jetty was just the opposite of that intended.

In spite of the sand bar problems, the Carlisle and Liverpool Steam Navigation Company were doing quite well. At their half-yearly meeting, held at the Solway Inn, Port Carlisle, a "very satisfactory balance sheet was submitted," and a dividend of £5 per cent. upon the half year was declared and paid.

A month later news came of the approval, by the Commissioners for Customs, of premises in the canal basin, to be used as a tobacco bond. This facility had been requested for a long time and was welcomed as "a great accommodation, not only to the manufacturers of that article in Carlisle, but to those in the neighbouring towns of Penrith, Brampton, Hawick, Annan, &c."

The great railway revolution was in full swing at this time and the canal company felt increasingly threatened by this new mode of cheap transport. In September 1845 the Canal Committee put forward a resolution to oppose the Parliamentary Bill for the Glasgow, Carlisle Railway via Dumfries. Their reason for opposing the Bill was that it would be injurious to the canal. Prior to the construction of a railway between Dumfries and Carlisle almost all of the passenger and goods traffic came via Annan Water Foot and the Carlisle canal.

One of the main reasons for the lack of profitability of the Carlisle canal was that only about half of the original cost was raised through share income. Throughout most of the life of the canal the Company had to service a loan which eventually reached about £78,000. At the end of 1844 a special general meeting was held to deal with this problem.

The total debt of £77,437 was apportioned across the existing shares at £52 - 10s (£52.50) per original £50 share. Shareholders were then to be charged interest on this apportioned debt annually at £4 - 10s. per cent (£4.50). This interest was deducted from the dividend declared each year. This made the books look better but was not much consolation to the individual shareholders. For example, in July 1846 a dividend of £3 - 13s - 6d (£3.68) was declared per original £50 share (i.e. about 7%). However interest at 4 1/2 % on £52 – 10s (i.e. about £2 - 7s - 3d) would be deducted, leaving a paltry £1 - 6s - 3d (£1.32) effective dividend per share.

In April 1846 there was a disruption to the Canal Branch Railway when the bridge over the Caldew at Long Island sank nearly two feet. The bridge had been piled and it was thought that it had probably not been driven 'home' to the bedrock. The bridge had to be taken down, but disruption to the rail traffic, to and from the canal basin, was minimised by using a "temporary railway fixed upon planks."

Four months later the bridge repair had commenced, but further problems developed, as reported by the Carlisle Journal, 1 August 1846:-

"It will be remembered that early in the spring the bridge upon which the Newcastle and Carlisle Railway crosses the Caldew in the Denton Holme sunk, and that since that time temporary rails have been laid upon wooden piles, until the old erection could be renovated. Mr Tate, the engineer, has lately been directing the operations for this purpose, and on Wednesday last two of the arches requiring rebuilding were blasted - the keystones being removed, and the remainder falling into the river and to some extent choking its bed. Preparations were completed on Wednesday evening for throwing down the third and last arch on Thursday morning. But the flood anticipated the workmen: it swept the arch down, and this, added to the material already deposited there, formed a very serious obstruction to the flow of the rising waters, which rushed down with that velocity and force for which the Caldew is remarkable. The effect was most disastrous.

Finding itself opposed, the torrent 'backed' into the Denton Holme, coursed along the base of the railway embankment, throwing down the hedge of a potato field of Mr. R. Simpson, builder, and utterly destroying his crop, and it swept away the greater portion of 130,000 bricks which were set ready for drying in the kiln of Mr. T. Nelson.--." The report continued at some length, detailing further damage.

The same newspaper reported another shipwreck in the Solway. This time, luckily, the crew took to the boats and escaped, with even their clothes chests. The barque *Eliza Arm* of Whitehaven, about 400 tons, foundered on the Robin Rigg sandbank and broke up. Her cargo of timber from Quebec

CANAL BONE MILLS.

April 15th, 1846.

WE, the undersigned, WILLIAM and JOSEPH MATTINSON, do hereby certify that the Co-partnership hitherto existing between us, as Bone-dust Manufacturers, has this day been dissolved by mutual consent.

WM. MATTINSON.
JOS. MATTINSON.

Witness—Wm. Wright.

Messrs. JOS. MATTINSON, and Co. beg to inform the Public, that the Canal Bone Mills will in future be conducted under the above firm, where Bone Dust may be had on the most reasonable terms.

Canal Bone Mills,
April 15th, 1846.

The canal bone mill was still in operation although the partners had decided to go their separate ways.

VESSEL FOR SALE.

TO be SOLD, by PUBLIC SALE, on TUESDAY, the Fifth of November, 1844, at the house of Mrs BESWICK, Queen's Head Inn, Caldewgate, CAFSISLE, the whole of that strong Oak-Built SLOOP or VESSEL, called the *ISABELLA OF ANNAN*, Port Dumfries; Burden per Register, 43 Tons; now lying at the Canal Basin, Carlisle.

For further particulars apply to Mr. JOHN JOHNSTON, Annan, or to Mr. JOSEPH NANSON, 9, Irish-Gate Brow, Carlisle.

was scattered all round the Solway coast, but most of it was expected to be salvaged.

In January 1847 the possibility of converting the canal into a railway was raised for the first time. Plans and estimates had been prepared by the canal company and the local papers had "every reason to believe that the project will be carried into effect at no distant day."

Another Carlisle boat, the schooner *Robert*, Capt. Tristram Rome, 80 tons, was reported lost at sea in January 1847, travelling in ballast, for Bangor. The crew of three comprising the captain (and owner), the mate and another seaman were presumed drowned.

The plan to convert the canal into a railway received a further boost when several of the directors of the Newcastle and Carlisle Railway came to survey the canal between Carlisle and Port Carlisle. They were unanimous in agreeing that the plan was practicable and indeed very desirable from their point of view. They found that the depth of water at high tide at Port Carlisle was 18 feet 6 inches, whereas at Liverpool it was only 17 feet, showing that the largest vessels could dock at Port Carlisle.

In March 1847 another sad death occurred at Port Carlisle. The Carlisle Journal, 12 March 1847, reported:- "On Wednesday evening, a little girl, daughter of Mr W. Robinson, butcher, was sent for some milk to Kirkland, and on her retum is supposed to have been playing at ball and to have fallen into the canal. The water was dragged during the night, and the body was found on Thursday morning."

In July 1847 the Canal Committee finally approved the plan to convert the canal into a railway. This decision did not satisfy everyone. Several local traders thought the canal could make money if it was run in a different manner and so they went away to devise an alternative scheme, which we will hear about later.

Meanwhile the Carlisle and Liverpool Steamship Company were still doing very well, so well that, in October 1847, they launched a new vessel the *Cumberland* to replace the 'Newcastle.' Steamships were getting bigger. The new *Cumberland* was 600 tons and was propelled by two oscillating engines of 280 HP. She was commissioned for use between Port Carlisle, Annan and Liverpool.

E. Brockbank, proprietor of the Canal Saw Mills, came into dispute with the canal company in December 1850. He had apparently given notice to quit and then refused to remove his stock of wood and machinery from the land.

A letterhead for the canal sawmills.
The masts of the ships in the basin can be seen in the background.

The canal company wrote to him several times on this matter over a four month period. The company eventually offered him £80 for the steam engine and other machinery. This Mr. Brockbank refused and so the company said that he could remove the same, under the supervision of the canal engineer, Mr Boyd, otherwise the equipment would be sold for whatever it would bring.

In July 1848 the Canal Committee received an offer from Peter Dixon, acting for J. D. Carr and Co., to lease out the canal as an alternative to converting it into a railway. The conditions under which this would be done were then presented to a Special General Meeting of the canal company in September 1848. The conditions were as follows :-

1. that they could secure $4^1/_2$ % interest upon the debt of £72015 and, after paying the expenses of the buoys and lights to pay £200 annually. `

2. in the event of a surplus after all expenses of management and keeping the canal in order are paid then such surplus to be divided between the shareholders and the lessees.

3. in case Mr Hudson should take the Maryport Railway the canal company should do all in their power to prevent him imposing differential dues on articles carried by the canal in favour of those carried by the Maryport Railway.

4. a survey to be taken by two competent persons, appointed by the Canal Committee, and the Lessees to ascertain the present state of the canal with the view of its being kept in like order during the lease.

5. that the Lessees in the event of being able to provide money at an easier rate than $4^1/_2$ % have the option of paying off the debt in all or in part.

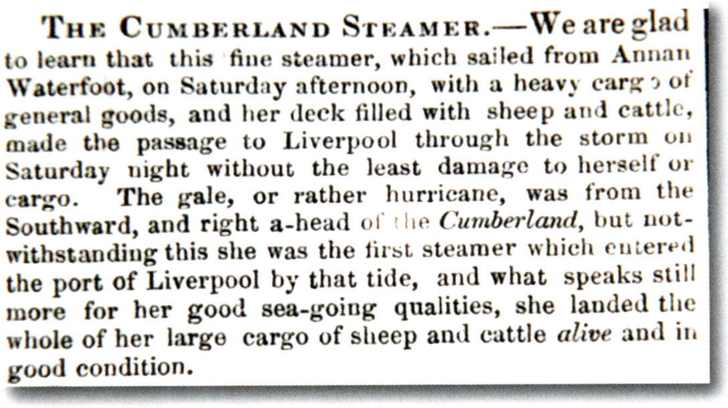

THE CUMBERLAND STEAMER.—We are glad to learn that this fine steamer, which sailed from Annan Waterfoot, on Saturday afternoon, with a heavy cargo of general goods, and her deck filled with sheep and cattle, made the passage to Liverpool through the storm on Saturday night without the least damage to herself or cargo. The gale, or rather hurricane, was from the Southward, and right a-head of the *Cumberland*, but notwithstanding this she was the first steamer which entered the port of Liverpool by that tide, and what speaks still more for her good sea-going qualities, she landed the whole of her large cargo of sheep and cattle *alive* and in good condition.

6. the Lessees to enjoy all the receipts from dues, rents and all privileges the canal company possessed.

After consideration of this offer the canal company eventually turned it down, stating that they could not accept any offer that would produce a return of less than 1% in the first year, 2% in the second. But that was not the end of the debate. Several letters were printed in the papers supporting the proposal which would retain the canal. An editorial in the Carlisle Journal, 30 September l848, summed up the arguments in rather a scathing way :-

"For some time past, we understand, negociations (sic) have been going on between the Carlisle Canal Company, or, rather between the Managing Committee of that body, and certain gentlemen connected with the trade of Carlisle, who are desirous of leasing the canal and trying if they cannot, by a new system of conducting its affairs, rescue it from the Slough of Despond in which it now lies, and in this way give a new impetus to the trade of the city, or, at least, prevent it from slipping away from us. These negociations, we are sorry to hear, have failed - the parties being unable to arrange the terms of transfer. This we think unfortunate. The report which we gave of the proceedings of the last annual general meeting renders it unnecessary, even were it otherwise desirable, to conceal the fact that the canal is an unprofitable undertaking.

Many causes might be assigned to this. In the first place only one half the capital required for its construction was advanced by the company.The other half had to be borrowed, and upon this interest has been paid when the unfortunate shareholders were unable to realize a penny for themselves. Here, then, comes the pinch of the question. Railways have been brought into competition with the canal. From the East, from the West, from the North, and from the South, Carlisle has now the advantage of Railway communication. This is a kind of competition the canal proprietors appear to be unprepared for. While they had only 'slow coaches' and still 'slower waggons' to contend against they felt themselves secure under the 'protection' of high charges. Every penny added to the amount of tonnage charge, they looked upon as a penny added to their exchequer. The golden rule of the calculating tradesman, that two and two do not always make four, does not appear to have formed any part of their studies. The Railways have taken them, as a sailor would say, all 'a back;' and they seem to have formed the idea that by higher charges only can they be compensated for loss of quantity in their carrying account.

The parties proposing to lease the canal have formed a different opinion. They do not undervalue the advantages we derive from the railways; they are fully alive to the importance of quick and certain transit; but they are of the opinion that the trade of Carlisle may be greatly enhanced by the possession of water-carriage power; and that Carlisle ought not to be dependant upon either Annan; Maryport, or Whitehaven for its sea intercommunications - foreign or coastwise. They think, as the tradesmen of Carlisle generally think, that their intercourse with the whole world should be free and independant. We send our ginghams and our cottons to Hamburg, to America, to India and to China, why should we not have direct in return the produce of these several countries? Close the canal which leads direct, and by the shortest cut, to the sea, and the power of securing this is taken out of our hands, and we become the dependants of those who would fain become our rivals. Is this the position at which Carlisle should aim? She may not aim to be the 'first flower of the earth and first gem of the sea,' but if she be anxious to maintain her footing amongst her rivals she must take care not to forego the advantage of that sea communication which she now possesses.

The parties who propose to lease the canal are at direct issue with its present directors. They believe that by a lessening of dues -- by a reduction of fares, --if we may so designate it, --a very large increase of traffic may be secured. In proof of their conviction, of the feasibility of their plan, they have, we understand, offered to guarantee the payment (for three years) of the interest of the borrowed capital of the company, and to secure a certain dividend to the proprietors. One would have thought this an offer too tempting to be rejected. But not so has it been; and it will now remain with the shareholders to say whether such rejection has been conceived in wisdom or adopted in a spirit of absolute folly. Carlisle requires its canal to the sea for the maintenance of its position in the commercial world, and they will have much to answer for who should, by a suicidal policy, such as we have hinted at, deprive it of the power of competition with every sea-port which may set up in rivalry."

The sand bar at the entrance to the docks at Port Carlisle was still a continuing cause for concern. The Canal Minutes of 27 October 1848, ordered —- that Mr Boyd should examine the tongue of sand between the steamer pier and the stone jetty. One week later he was ordered to request tenders for removing the silt to the hard bottom and shortly afterwards Joseph Gardiner was awarded the contract in the sum of £15 - 10s.

It was becoming apparent that the silting up of the harbour was probably due to the

Ravenbank Jetty, recently erected by Lord Lonsdale. So, on 12 January 1849, Mr Nanson wrote, on behalf of the Canal Company Committee, to Lord Lonsdale on this matter.

By June 1849 a new steam tug the *Engineer* had been brought to the Solway from the Tyne. With engines of 40 horse power she was to be used as a tender to the new iron steamer the 'Cumberland' However, when not required for this purpose she was used with other vessels. The Journal reported:-

"Last week she towed a large foreign brig and several other vessels laden with coal and alabaster from Port Carlisle and Annan out to sea, thus enabling them to make a passage when, without such assistance, they must have remained at Annan Water Foot, wind-bound. We understand it is intended to have a pleasure trip with her to Kirkcudbright to afford the inhabitants of Carlisle and Annan a day's excursion by sea and an opportunity of visiting some of the most beautiful and romantic scenery in Scotland. Arrangements will be made to leave Carlisle by the canal boat early in the morning, to embark on board the steam tug at Port Carlisle, and at once proceed on the voyage, which may take about three hours, leaving ample time for a pleasant ramble on the Scottish shore, and to return by the same route in the evening."

In August 1849 another drowning tragedy occurred, this time at the canal basin. Two children, both aged seven, named Anthony Addison and Jane Ingham, were drowned in the dry dock of the canal. They had been playing on the floating logs of timber and had been chased away several times by a Mr. Peter Quin. In the aftemoon their parents, who lived in Caldcoats, started searching for them and, acting upon Mr Quin's information, a search was made under the timber where they were last seen. Their bodies were found near each other. A verdict of accidental death was recorded by the jury with the rider that:- "it appeared to them highly necessary that railing should be erected by the side of the dock, the place being dangerous for children who had unrestricted liberty to go there; and they expressed a hope that the committee would no longer delay so important a protection to the lives of children on their premises."

This was not the first time that playing children had been drowned at the canal basin. In March 1839 a coroner's inquest investigated the death of 17 year old James Donaghue, a 'potter' (generic name given at that time to describe the large group, mainly of Irish origin, scrap metal dealers, rag and bone men, scissor grinders etc. who plied their trade around the streets). The court was told how the youth had been playing with others on planks of wood floating in the timber dock. PC John Kent, famous as the first ever black policeman in the country and known as 'Black Kent', was patrolling the canal basin and came upon the scene. In their hurry to escape ashore they made to jump ashore. Unfortunately Donaghue overbalanced and fell into the water where he remained submerged for some five minutes. Constable Kent and a sailor managed to raise the youth from the bottom of the canal and after a short time

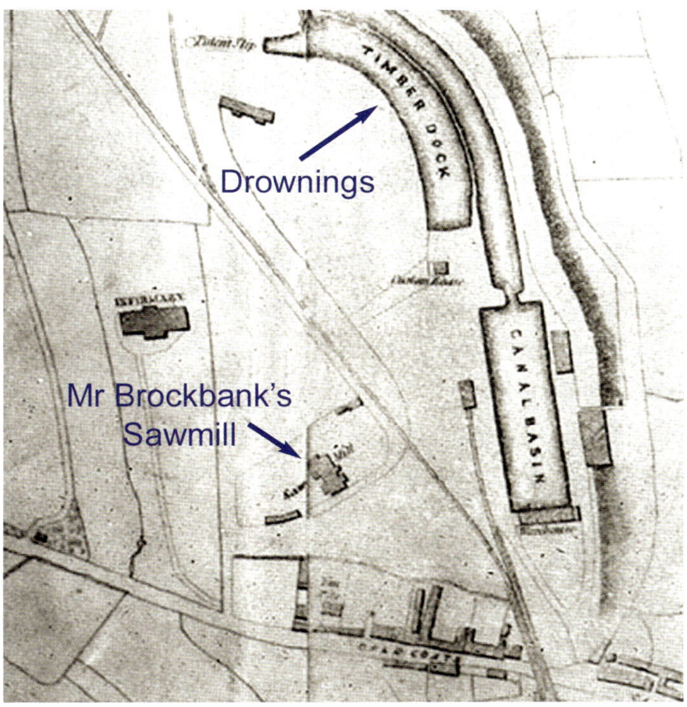

An impression of John Kent, Britain's first black policeman (second from the left),

Taken from an original painting by Mark Custerson hanging at Cumbria Police Headquarters, Carleton Hall, Penrith. The constable on the left is wearing the summer uniform of the city police.

he appeared to be none the worse for his ordeal and was able to talk with them. Three hours later the lad died after suffering violent chest pains and bleeding from the nose and mouth.

The Annual General Meeting of the Victoria Baths, Port Carlisle was held on Thursday 6th February 1850 at which a dividend of 3% was declared (the profits of the last year). The meeting was held in the office of` the Carlisle, Annan and Liverpool Steam Navigation Company. Mr. Jobling was the treasurer and the Mayor (Joseph Rome Esq.) was in the chair. The committee elected for the following year comprised some well known people, namely the Mayor, Mr. R. Cowen, Mr. W. R. Martindale, Mr. Joseph Hope, and Mr. C. Thurnam.

As stated earlier the Carlisle and Liverpool Steamship Company was doing very well at this time having introduced their new 600 ton *Cumberland* steamer in 1847. This was 'not the case with their rival company.

It appears by this time that the *Royal Victoria* steamer, belonging to the Carlisle, Annan and Liverpool Steam Navigation Company, had been sold off. Advertisements of sailings no longer appeared in the local press and on 24 May 1850 it was reported that:-

"This fine steamer arrived in Liverpool on Monday last, from Genoa and Leghorn, calling at Gibraltar, and bringing Her Majesty's mails and twenty cabin passengers from the latter place."

Sure enough the company was to be wound up, as was reported in the Carlisle Journal, 12 July 1850:-

"CARLISLE ANNAN AND LIVERPOOL STEAM NAVIGATION COMPANY, - At a meeting of the shareholders of the Carlisle Annan and Liverpool Steam Navigation Company, held at the Coffee House Hotel, Carlisle, on the 5th inst., R. Cowen, Esq., in the chair, it was resolved to pay a first winding up dividend of £12. 10s. per share on and after, August lst. The outgoing committee were unanimously re-elected, and the thanks of the meeting being voted to the chairman, the meeting broke up."

The canal featured very little in the newspapers during its latter years except when tragedy struck. The winter of 1850 was a hard one and early in January of that year the reservoir on Grinsdale Common was frozen over. Such conditions attracted skaters in large numbers from the city and surrounding villages.

The Carlisle Journal reported as follows:-

"MELANCHOLY CASE OF DROWNING. - On Sunday morning last, a lamentable and fatal accident occurred at the canal reservoir, about two miles from this city (See page 15), which resulted in the death of an active and intelligent youth, named John Tweddle, son of Mr. John Tweddle, warper, of Parham Beck. The reservoir is a large sheet of water, used by the Carlisle Canal Company, for supplying the canal with water in dry weather, and is a favourite resort of our citizens who delight in skating during frosty weather. On Friday and Saturday last a sharp frost set in, and on Sunday morning, crowds of persons proceeded to the reservoir, for the purpose of taking exercise in this favourite amusement. The deceased left home about nine o'clock in the morning, accompanied by some of his companions, and had proceeded direct to the reservoir. His father took a walk in the same direction, and was at the edge of the ice when the accident occurred, between eleven and twelve o'clock. The deceased, along with a number of youths, was running on the ice, and when the portion gave way that led to his death, he was about sixty or seventy yards from the edge of the reservoir, adjoining the Moorhouse road. On the ice giving way, the youth sank into the water- about eight feet deep. Three other boys were close behind him, but were providentially saved. His cap floated on the surface, and his head was seen twice above the ice, previous to his total disappearance; but no one dared to approach to the edge of the broken ice to rescue him. One of the youths on the ice ventured so far towards him as to take his cap out of the water. The alarm was immediately given and a rush was made to the place where the accident had taken place. Among the crowd was the father of the lad who was then under the ice. For a short time all appeared to be struck dumb; the father, assisted by several friends, however, soon succeeded in obtaining a ladder, which was fastened by a rope, and with which he went to the edge of the hole where his son had gone down; the ice again gave way, and had it not been for the secure hold he kept of the ladder, the father would doubtless have also perished. Mr Tweddle retained his position for a considerable time, endeavouring with a long rod to find his son's body; but the severity of the cold compelled him to desist, as he could not remain longer without endangering his own life; and beckoning to be drawn out, he was soon at the side of the reservoir. By this time, the fears of the crowd disappeared, and a large number of persons continued to skate upon the ice while the body of the unfortunate youth was in the water! The sluice which connects the reservoir with the canal was closed, and the father proceeded to Grinsdale, and, on his application, Mr. Edward and Mr. Jas. Nixon readily provided a boat, which they conveyed by horse and cart to the place of the accident, where it arrived about three o'clock. The boat was immediately launched, and the Messrs. Nixon being seated in it, it was pushed on the ice, which soon gave way, and the remainder of the distance had to be 'worked' to break it. The parties in the boat had provided themselves with two long drags, with which they made diligent search for about three quarters of an hour, when the body was found near the place where it had first gone down. It was conveyed home in a gig, and an inquest was held on it on Tuesday last, before Mr. Carrick, coroneer, when a verdict of 'Accidental Death' was returned. The Messrs. Nixon most generously refused to accept any remuneration for the arduous and unpleasant labour they had undertaken; and great praise is due to them for their exertions, and the prompt and handsome manner in which their services were rendered."

In spite of this sad event, which illustrated only too well the dangers of walking on the frozen reservoir, only one week later the Carlisle Journal carried the following item with no mention of the previous tragedy:-

"CRICKET ON THE ICE - A novel and interesting game was played on Wednesday last, on the canal reservoir, in the shape of a match at cricket. The ice being in beautiful condition for the purpose, some of the members of the Carlisle Cricket Club determined to transfer their stumps from the turf to the field of ice for a little practice, on skates, of their favourite amusement, and they accordingly kept up a vigorous contest in this way for three or four hours. The novelty of the scene attracted many spectators."

In May 1851 the Canal Committee were most surprised to learn that they were being charged proportionately more by the Newcastle and Carlisle Railway for coals shipped from the Blenkinsop colliery to the canal basin than that paid by the Carlisle to Maryport

The picture on this page shows the Edenside Cricket Club in 1843 from a painting by Sam Bough. The Canal Buildings and the masts of the ships in the Canal Basin can be seen in the background, as shown in the enlarged section on the left.

This is just another example of how artists who lived before the age of photography have preserved images of our industrial heritage for us to study and enjoy.

Railway. The canal company was being charged ls. 9d. per ton while the Railway Company was being charged ls. 5d. per ton. The proportionate rate for the 21 miles to the canal basin would be ls. 6 $^1/_4$d. per ton. Such practices favouring the railway were obviously affecting the ability of the canal to compete on price. The canal company ordered that a letter be sent to the Newcastle and Carlisle Railway Company to ask why they were being treated in this way.

The detrimental effect of the Ravenbank Jetty on the navigation at Port Carlisle was also exercising their minds at this time and in August 1851 a long letter was sent to Lord Lonsdale on this topic. The canal company brought his Lordship's attention to the report of the Admiralty which stated that the jetty had "not answered the intended purpose for its construction and was positively injuring the navigation. Some of it had already broken off." They offered to remove it at the canal company's expense and place the materials "anywhere convenient for his Lordship's disposal."

It is perhaps surprising that the Canal Committee were prepared to pay for the removal of the jetty as a letter from the Admiralty, dated 18 August 1849, to Lord Lonsdale, clearly stated that the jetty was a nuisance, had been erected without permission and should be removed forthwith.

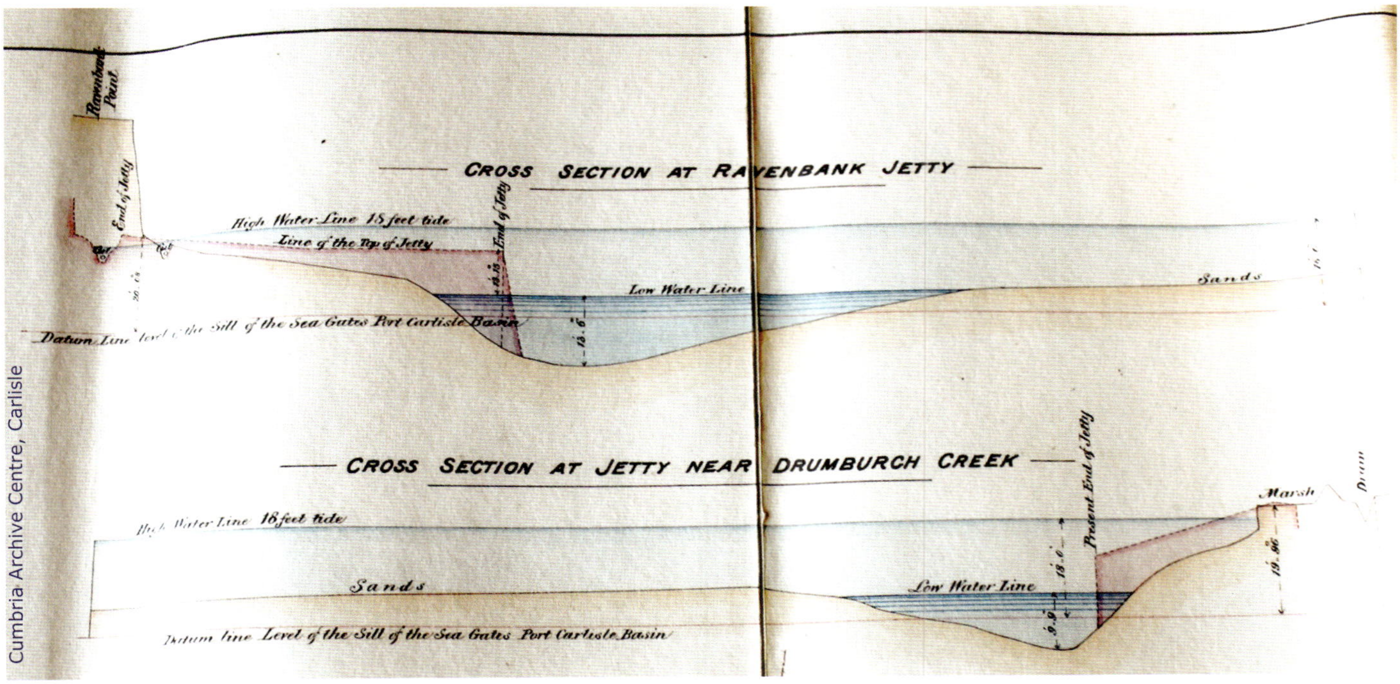

Detail from a plan showing the relationship of the jetty and the tide heights at the canal mouth drawn up during the dispute about the effect the jetty was having on the navigation at Port Carlisle.

Early in August 1851 the Canal Committee had come to some agreement with Lord Lonsdale regarding the removal of the Ravenbank Jetty. They offered £50 towards the cost of` removal and a draft agreement between the two parties was drawn up.

In July 1851 a race meeting was held at Port Carlisle. This was a further example of developing the potential of the port as a recreational centre for the surrounding populace. The Carlisle Journal, 18 July 1851 reported as follows:-

"PORT CARLISLE RACES - Thursday next is to be a 'gala day' among the inhabitants of the Barony of Burgh. The races are to come off as usual on the course near Knock Cross.

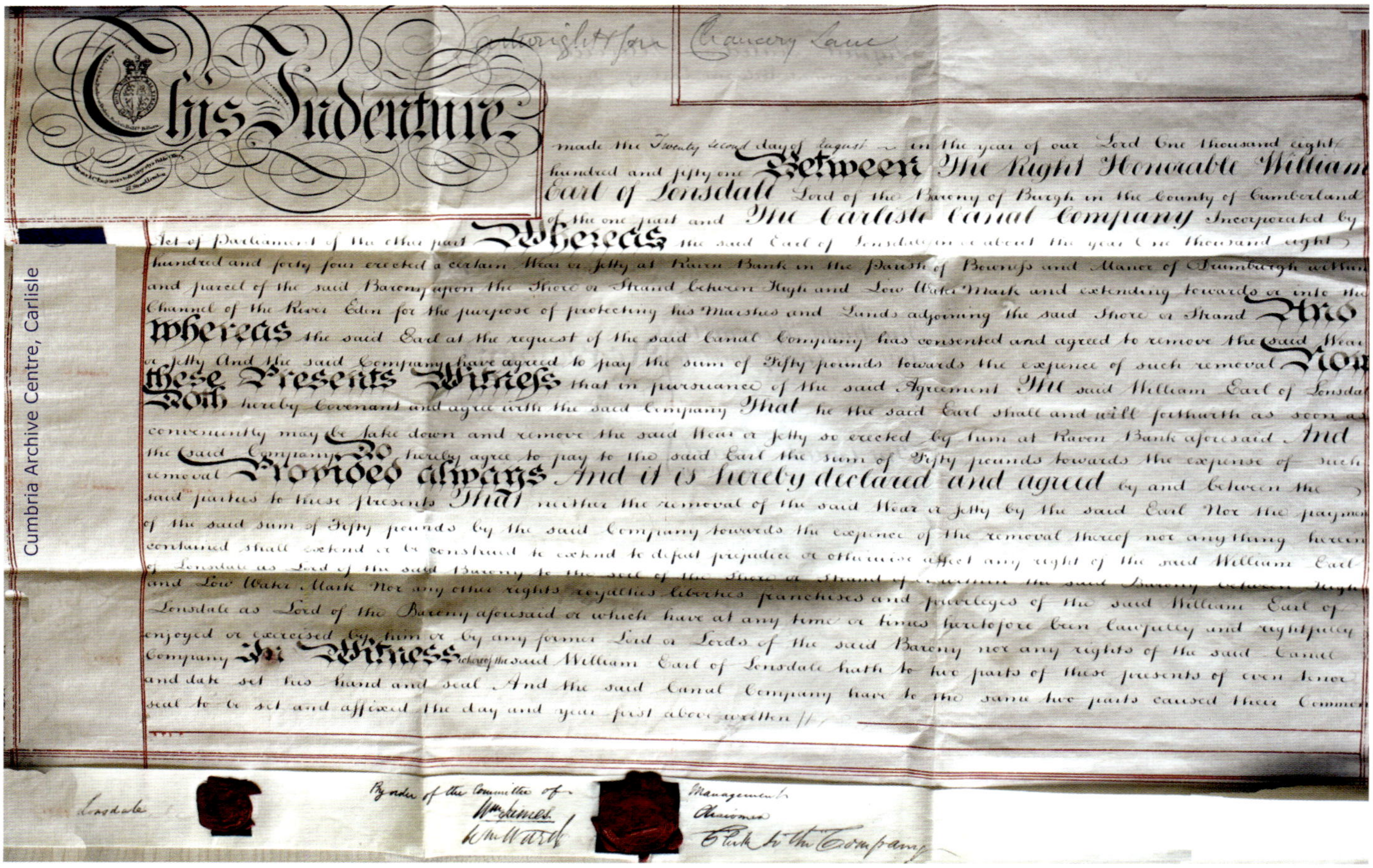

This Indenture made the Twenty second day of August in the year of our Lord One thousand eight hundred and fifty one Between The Right Honourable William Earl of Lonsdale Lord of the Barony of Burgh in the County of Cumberland of the one part and The Carlisle Canal Company Incorporated by Act of Parliament of the other part Whereas the said Earl of Lonsdale in or about the year One thousand eight hundred and forty four erected a certain Wear or Jetty at Raven Bank in the Parish of Bowness and Manor of Drumburgh within and parcel of the said Barony upon the Shore or Strand between High and Low Water Mark and extending towards or into the Channel of the River Eden for the purpose of protecting his Marshes and Lands adjoining the said Shore or Strand And whereas the said Earl at the request of the said Canal Company has consented and agreed to remove the said Wear or Jetty And the said Company have agreed to pay the sum of Fifty pounds towards the expence of such removal Now these Presents Witness that in pursuance of the said Agreement the said William Earl of Lonsdale doth hereby Covenant and agree with the said Company That he the said Earl shall and will forthwith as soon as conveniently may be take down and remove the said Wear or Jetty so erected by him at Raven Bank aforesaid And the said Company do hereby agree to pay to the said Earl the sum of Fifty pounds towards the expense of such removal Provided always And it is hereby declared and agreed by and between the said parties to these presents That neither the removal of the said Wear or Jetty by the said Earl Nor the payment of the said sum of Fifty pounds by the said Company towards the expence of the removal thereof nor any thing herein contained shall extend or be construed to extend to defeat prejudice or otherwise affect any right of the said William Earl of Lonsdale as Lord of the said Barony to the soil of the Shore or Strand of ... the said Barony between High and Low Water Mark Nor any other rights royalties liberties franchises and privileges of the said William Earl of Lonsdale as Lord of the Barony aforesaid or which have at any time or times heretofore been lawfully and rightfully enjoyed or exercised by him or by any former Lord or Lords of the said Barony nor any rights of the said Canal Company In Witness whereof the said William Earl of Lonsdale hath to two parts of these presents of even tenor and date set his hand and seal And the said Canal Company have to the same two parts caused their Common seal to be set and affixed the day and year first above written

The agreement drawn up between the Canal Company and Lord Lonsdale regarding the removal of the Ravenbank Jetty.

The image to the right shows the front cover of the agreement recorded on parchment as was usual at that time.

Dated 22nd Aug 1851

The Right Honorable William Earl of Lonsdale

— and —

The Carlisle Canal Company

Agreement respecting the removal of a Jetty at Raven Bank in the Parish of Bowness Cumberland

Judging from the excellent entries, the able stewardship, with the assistance of that most active of all active 'clerks of the course,' Mr. Daly, it cannot fail to ensure a good day's sport. The Burgh Barony Plate is already causing a good deal of speculation and interest. The sum of seven pounds is this year to be wrestled for, which will no doubt bring together a good field of wrestlers. The *Arrow* canal Boat is engaged to convey the lieges to and from this city, and should the weather prove favourable, doubtless a large number of our sporting citizens will be rushing to the Port. The entry, with the 'names, weights, and colours of the riders' will be found in an advertisement in another column."

Later the same month yet another life was claimed by the canal at Port Carlisle. The details and inquest were reported in the Carlisle Journal, 15 August,l851:-

"A BOY DROWNED -- On Friday last, a boy named Richard Bendle, whose parents reside at Bowness, fell into the canal at Port Carlisle whilst crossing the lock gate, and was drowned. He was seen to fall in by another boy who had been playing with him, and who had not given an alarm for fear of being scolded, though if he had done so the life of the poor little fellow would probably have been saved, as three workman were working within 30 yards of the spot where he fell in. The body was not recovered till 25 minutes after the accident, and all attempts at resuscitation were fruitless. An inquest was held at Mr. Wood's, Solway Hotel, on Saturday, before Mr. Carrick, when a verdict in accordance with the facts was returned, the boy who had neglected to raise an alarm receiving a severe lecture for his carelessness."

Only one week later a worse accident occurred at Port Carlisle. This time it was the Solway that took the lives of four people.

The Carlisle Journal reported as follows:-

"SAD CATASTROPHE ON THE SOLWAY, NEAR ANNAN. -- FOUR LIVES LOST -- The town and vicinity of Annan were on the evening of Saturday last, the 16th inst., thrown into a state of extraordinary excitement, by the report, which proved too true, that the ferry boat of Joseph Brough, formerly of Battle Hill, had been upset on its return from Port Carlisle, about five o' clock, and no fewer than four lives lost in consequence. The boat, which was considered small enough for the company (consisting of Mr. Walter Park, draper in Annan; his late partner, Mr. John Scott; Mrs. Scott, his wife; Mr Anthony Nelson, draper, Port Carlisle; John Beck, farm-servant from the English side, formerly at Talliesfield, by Dornock, and Joseph Brough) had been too late in starting, and having come in contact with the nets between Whinnyrigg and Seafields upset, when Mr. and Mrs. Scott, Mr. Beck, and Mr. Brough, after ineffectual attempts to save themselves, became a prey to the current, which was then very rapid. With great difficulty Messrs. Park and Nelson, by laying hold of the nets, were taken off and saved. Mr. Beck immediately disappeared, while the others for a time endeavoured to cling to the keel of the boat, which, having again, however, been overturned, the remaining three sunk in the waters. Messrs. Byers, Thompson, Faulds, and others exerted themselves well, and were instrumental in saving Messrs. Park and Nelson, but could do nothing for the others. Beck's body was recovered near the scene of the accident; that of Mrs. Scott was not obtained till next afternoon, immediately below the Waterfoot Lighthouse. The body of Mr. Brough was found on Monday morning in the Newby nets; but that of Mr. Scott has not yet been discovered. It is worthy of remark that Brough had crossed the Solway without accident thousands of times, and was ever accounted a safe guide, from his intimate acquaintance with the Firth, for more than half a century. He has left a widow and family to deplore his fate. Mr. and Mrs. Scott, though without offspring, leave aged and respectable parents, with brothers and sisters, and many attached friends; while Beck was the chief support of a frail widowed mother in Annan, to whom he was about to pay a dutiful visit - a few shillings having been found in his waistcoat pocket, they are supposed to have been intended to alleviate her wants. ---."

By November 1851 the Ravenbank Jetty was being removed and the benefits were becoming apparent. A report in the Carlisle Journal, 7 November, 1851 explained:-

"CARLISLE CANAL -- The most rapid and beneficial results have followed the removal of the Raven Bank jetty. Although the work is not yet quite finished, the quantity of sand removed by the operation of the tides amount, by the report of the canal engineer, to upwards of 300,000 cubic yards. The canal committee visited the place last week, and, to their astonishment, found the bank of sand, upon which they had walked six weeks before, and which was then eleven feet high, had disappeared, and, in its place, the whole of the River Eden was flowing in a deep channel towards Port Carlisle, which it is gradually approaching as the sand disappears. The bar at the entrance, which was five feet when the removal of the jetty commenced, has already been reduced to two and a half feet, and it is confidently anticipated that in a short time, the whole will disappear, and thus restore to Port Carlisle its full depth of water."

The remains of the Ravenbank Jetty can still be seen at low tide today.

In December 1851 yet another drowning occurred in the canal near Port Carlisle. As usual the inquest was reported in the Carlisle Journal, 19 December 1851:-

"An inquest was held on Monday last, the 15th inst., before Mr. Carrick, coroner, at Westfield Bridge, near Glasson, on the body of David James, aged sixty years. It appeared from the evidence adduced that the deceased was, on the evening of Saturday, the 13th inst., proceeding along the road by the edge of the Canal, in the direction of Port Carlisle, alone, when he was seen very tipsy by a farm servant at Kirkland, who desired him to stop until he had done the horses and he would set him home, but deceased said, 'Oh, no, I have come up drunker than this.' Witness then warned him to take care of the Canal, and then saw him past their house. Witness subsequently came up the wrong pathway of the Canal, but did not see deceased. The deceased had ultimately reached Westfield Bridge, about six hundred yards distance from Glasson, where he was found on the following morning (Sunday) by Thomas Saunderson, a husbandman, quite dead, lying on his belly, with his face and hand in the water. There were no marks of struggling, but he had apparently grasped the grass with his left hand. His body was on the slope of the bank, which is about four feet from the pathway to the level of the water. The jury returned a verdict of 'accidentally drowned.' "

In April 1852 there was a further report on the removal of the Ravenbank Jetty. The channel had continued working into Port Carlisle such that the sandbar had been reduced to a mere eighteen inches. It was fully expected that the next spring tides would clear it away entirely. The return of the steamer *Newcastle* to Port Carlisle, after an absence of more than three years, was seen as proof of the extent of the improvement to the navigation.

The same month saw the Canal Committee order the engineer, Mr Boyd, to prepare plans for conversion of the canal into a railway. Three months later a special general meeting of the Canal Committee was held at which it was resolved :-

Plans for Conversion of the Canal into a Railway

"that it appears highly desirable and expedient that the Carlisle Canal should be converted into a railway with as little delay as possible."

It was resolved at the same meeting that :-

"Conditional Agreement with Messrs. Losh Wilson and Bell of Newcastle Upon Tyne for the supply of 1700 tons of iron rails to be delivered to the Canal Basin, Carlisle, immediately upon the ACT for converting the Canal into a railway being obtained at the price of £5 - 15s. per ton."

In spite of the re-assurances that continued to be made about the future viability of Port Carlisle as a trading port, the Canal Company left their options open. The Canal Company Minutes of 15 April 1853 contained the following resolution:- "that the Port Carlisle Railway be constructed with a view to the ultimate extension of the railway to Silloth Bay."

In March 1853 the papers carried the death notice of William Bell, shipbuilder of Carlisle, who died at the Canal Cottages on lst March, aged 66. It was perhaps fitting that he died before the canal closed, as his life's work had been spent at the Canal Basin, building ships to sail on the Carlisle canal. This would be the William Bell, shipbuilder of Carlisle, mentioned on the gravestone (see page 40) which records the deaths of his son, William, and his daughter, Dorothy. The death of William Bell was soon to be followed by the death of the canal.

At the end of April 1853 the Canal Bill for converting the canal into a railway was published. The Bill is interesting in that, by summarising the reasons for converting into a railway, it gives an overview of the whole development from start to finish.

The main points are listed below:-

1. that the canal is currently unprofitable and useless but could become a very useful railway.

2. that the canal was built on the understanding that it would be extended eventually to Newcastle Upon Tyne.

3. that in consequence of railways coming into use it was not extended, but instead a single line railway, worked by horse traction was proposed and built. This was then changed to locomotive traction, after the opening of the Liverpool and Manchester Railway.

4. that although the Carlisle Canal was limited in extent, it was of great service to the community, opening out a direct communication with the sea only 11 $^{1}/_{2}$ miles from Carlisle.

5. that the railway system, having now superseded that of canals, the measures recommended in the bill are indispensable.

6. that by the present means of transit, three hours are occupied between Carlisle and Port Carlisle, whence steamers regularly sail, while by railway twenty minutes, or at most half an hour would suffice.

A report on the annual general meeting of the Canal Company, held on Tuesday 4 July

1853, noted that only the company's solicitor, Mr. G. Dixon, and the reporters turned up. The meeting was thus adjourned sine die.

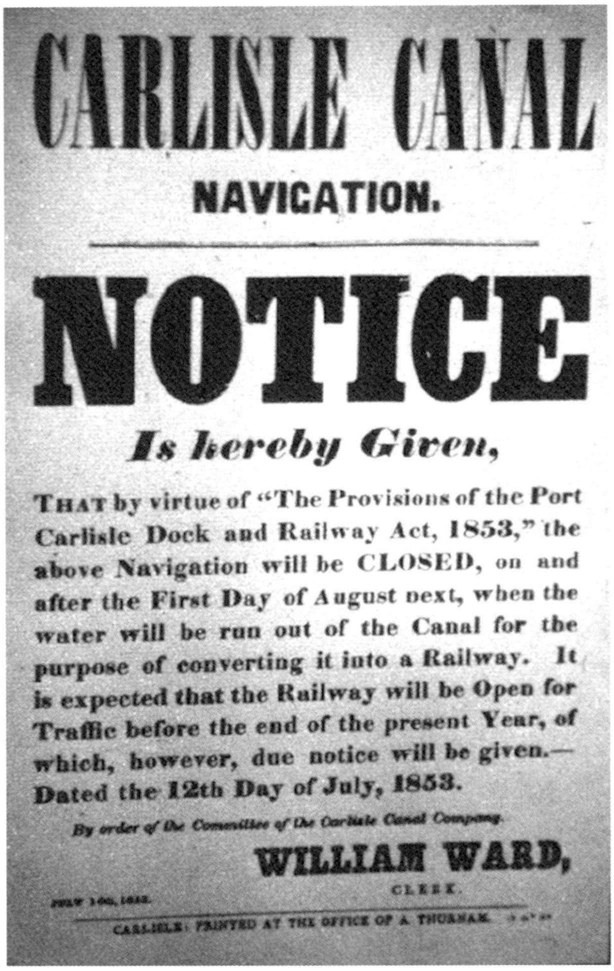

CARLISLE CANAL

NAVIGATION.

NOTICE

Is hereby Given,

THAT by virtue of "The Provisions of the Port Carlisle Dock and Railway Act, 1853," the above Navigation will be CLOSED, on and after the First Day of August next, when the water will be run out of the Canal for the purpose of converting it into a Railway. It is expected that the Railway will be Open for Traffic before the end of the present Year, of which, however, due notice will be given.— Dated the 12th Day of July, 1853.

By order of the Committee of the Carlisle Canal Company.

WILLIAM WARD,

CLERK.

CARLISLE: PRINTED AT THE OFFICE OF A. THURNAM.

On the 12 July 1853 the Canal Committee resolved that :-

"the Canal will be permanently closed on the first day of August next."

At the same meeting it was also resolved that :-

"Mr Asquith be employed to make a survey of the country from the Port Carlisle Railway to Silloth Bay, with a view to making a railway between these points."

Unfortunately, less than a week before the draining of the canal, it was to claim its last victim. An inquest held on 25 July at Glasson enquired into the death by drowning of Hugh Moat, a 26 year old labourer. The Carlisle Journal reported the circumstances:-

"It appeared that deceased, along with others, had been to Port Carlisle with a boat, and having all been the worse for drink, did not leave that place until between twelve and one o'clock in the morning. They had got upwards of three quarters of a mile on the other side of Westfield Bridge, when deceased wished to let them see him swim; they all tried to dissuade him, and held him to prevent his attempting it, he, however, would not be persuaded, and in spite of his companions' efforts to restrain him, succeeded in getting into the water. He swam about a short time, and then sank. Every effort was made by his companions to save him, but they proved fruitless. He was a Cambridge man, and unmarried, and was known by the name of 'Thomas.' Verdict : 'Accidentally drowned'."

After the closure, a horse drawn omnibus service was set up by Mr. John Cowx, cab proprietor, to replace the passage boat between Carlisle and Port Carlisle. Sundays and Thursdays were excursion days to make use of the pleasure facilities at Port Carlisle. On Tuesday, Wednesdays and Fridays the omnibus operated to suit the arrival and departure of the Liverpool steamers. There was no service on Mondays. The coach was called a Dandy (not to be confused with the horse-drawn railway Dandy).

On 5 August, four days after the closure of the canal, the Royal Assent was given to the conversion bill. Work had already started however. The Carlisle Journal, 5 August 1853, reported:-

"Mr Simpson, the contractor for the formation of the railway, has already commenced operations by taking down one of the locks, and from what we know of his skill, experience, and energy in the construction of railways, we have no doubt that the works will be carried out in a substantial and satisfactory manner.

Two weeks later the story was continued :-

"THE CANAL.-- The water of the canal between this city and Port Carlisle has been run off to the extent of about four miles, and Mr. Simpson, the contractor who has undertaken the construction of the railway by which the 'silent highway' is to be superseded, is forthwith about to commence operations. It is several years since railway 'navvies' have been in requisition in this district, and the line to Port Carlisle will afford a field for employment to numbers of loose hands not always in request at the back end of the year."

By October 1853 the works on the line were progressing in a 'very satisfactory manner.' A large number of hands had been employed since the completion of the harvest, and about four hundred were employed. It was fully expected that the line would be in operation by the beginning of the year. This was just as well, as the tradesmen in Carlisle were complaining loudly about the delay in the transit of goods from Liverpool via the west ports.

With the completion of the railway, Port Carlisle was to have a brief revival as a trading port. However in August 1856, only two years after the opening of the railway to Port Carlisle, a branch from Drumburgh to Silloth was opened and Silloth eventually became the new 'Port for Carlisle'. Within a few months the Liverpool steamers moved to Silloth and, due to the consequent reduction in traffic, the railway Dandy coaches were introduced between Drumburgh and Port Carlisle as a replacement to the passenger steam trains.

Port Carlisle struggled on with freight traffic until construction began on the Solway Junction Viaduct Railway to carry West Cumbrian Iron ore direct to Scotland.

The Dandy at Port Carlisle - one of two horse-drawn carriages which replaced the canal between Drumburgh and Port Carlisle after closure. This coach can be seen in York Railway Museum. The other was dismantled and the folding side-seats from it were placed outside the clubhouse of the Port Carlisle Bowling Green. They are still in use today.

The start on the Viaduct in 1865 sounded the death knell for Port Carlisle as a commercial port. On completion it was no longer possible for ships of any size to reach the port. Compensation was paid to remaining users and the port was finally closed to commercial traffic.

However the railway was not a very successful venture as the viaduct suffered from the weather and icebergs (see above) in the late 19th and early 20th centuries caused severe damage. The line was closed in 1921.

All The remains of the viaduct today is a lone set of bridge supports at the end of the stone pier which juts out into the Solway just west of Bowness.

THE END

Remaining evidence of the Carlisle Canal

Over the last 160 years most relics from the time of the canal have unfortunately disappeared but some still remain to this day. Here are a few examples to look out for.

ROAD BRIDGES: two or three of these remain to this day such as the one in the field at Knockupworth (Page 23). The lower stonework is dressed sandstone with curved edges from the old canal bridge with more modern stone pillars spanned by a metal bridge deck on top. This one at Burgh has iron supports to cope with modern traffic.

MILESTONES: milestones, half milestones and other stone artefacts can be found in various places along the line of the canal, not always where they originally stood.

This milestone originally stood at Kirkland caravan park (before it became Hoseasons) marking 1 mile to Port Carlisle and 11 miles to Carlisle. It now stands in the garden of the previous site owner. A similar quarter milepost can be seen at Tullie House Museum in Carlisle.

OTHER STONES: Mooring bollards for the canal can still be found in the grounds of lock houses along the route and the warehouses at Port Carlisle.

A collection of stone artefacts can be seen in the garden of the first bungalow on the right on turning off the coast road to the village of Boustead Hill. One of these bears the inscription CCC. It is not short for Cumbria County Council but was used to mark Carlisle Canal Company property. The resident used to work along the line of the canal and collected them.

__The milestone__ on the left showing 10 miles to Port Carlisle is at the farm at Knockupworth.
__The large sandstone bollard__ lower right is near the dock wall below a canal cottage (previously a warehouse) at Port Carlisle.
__The bollard__ below is in the garden of the same cottage, adjacent to Hadrian's Wall Path.
Below: __the dressed stone wall__ of the first lock into the canal from Port Carlisle Basin, with recesses for the gates and hinges, can still be seen (if you have good wellingtons!).

The Back Drain

The water level in a canal has to be carefully controlled and this can be a problem in times of very wet weather. The Carlisle Canal ran for about four miles across a flat marsh between Burgh and Drumburgh. All of the streams from the higher land to the south could not be allowed to flow directly into the canal and so the Back Drain was constructed on the level section just past the cattle grid west of Boustead Hill.

This worked as a siphon. All of the local streams were diverted to the south bank entrance which dropped down under the canal bed and up again at the other side. When the water reached a certain level above the entrance tunnel it spilled out of the exit tunnel creating a siphon effect. Heavy flap gates at the north side prevented return of the water and protected against high tides.

Entrance to drain on the south side of the canal

Exit from drain on the north side of the canal

Flying along the line of the Carlisle Canal

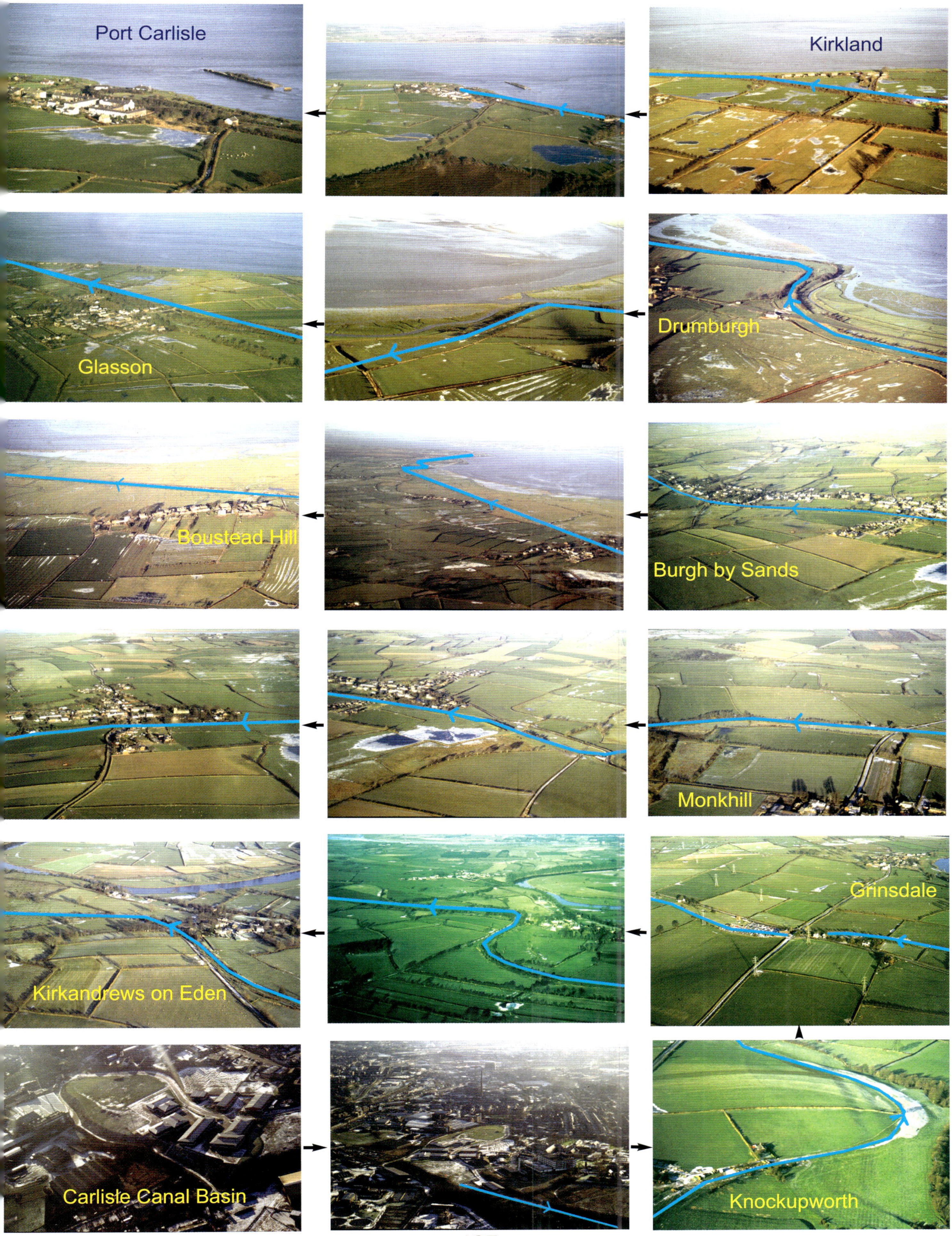

OTHER LOCAL BOOKS AVAILABLE FROM P3 PUBLICATIONS

Title	ISBN	First published
A Century Around Silloth	978-0-9572412-3-7	October 2012
Chanel and the Tweedmaker Weavers of Dreams	978-0-9572412-2-0	September 2012
Watching over Carlisle 140 years of the Carlisle City Police Force 1827- 1967	978-0-9559017-6-8	July 2011
The Cockermouth Floods a photograpic record	978-09559017-3-7	January 2010
The Keswick and Workington Floods a photographic record	978-09559017-4-4	February 2010
Wetheral and Great Corby an illustrated history	978-09559017-2-0	October 2008
The Carlisle Floods a photographic record	978-09547739-1-5	January 2005
Carlisle Breweries and Public Houses 1894-1916	978-09547739-0-X	2004
More Plain People and places on the Cumbrian Solway Plain	978-09548823-2-7	2007
For more books and further details go to **http://www.p3publications.com** Books can be purchased online using Paypal or credit/debit card		